Sustainability and the Fashion Industry

There is widespread rhetorical agreement that the fashion industry must get itself onto a more ethical and sustainable footing. What does this mean in practice, and how can this be achieved in different regions around the world?

This book brings together expert scholars and reflective practitioners via a network of dialogue and exchange to help drive forward an ethical and sustainable future for the fashion industry. With insights from fashion design, management, sociology, philosophy, education, heritage studies and policy, the book asks whether or not fashion can save the world.

Enriched with illuminating case interviews and the perspective of experts, this book will be of interest to researchers and scholars in the fields of sustainable business and the fashion industry, and provides a unique resource for readers seeking to understand more about the need for responsible fashion.

Annick Schramme is Professor and Academic Director of the Master Cultural Management and the Master Responsible Fashion Management at the University of Antwerp/Antwerp Management School, Belgium.

Nathalie Verboven is a Researcher and Teaching Assistant in Cultural Management and the Summer School on Responsible Fashion Management at the University of Antwerp, Belgium.

Responsible Fashion

Editor: Ian King

The fashion industry has in recent years come under increased global scrutiny regarding its practices. Their response reveals a desire to change. But how and what do we record to demonstrate this change? This is our challenge. A reinvention of fashion — away from the frivolous and ephemeral towards one as an enabler of sustainable growth and innovation.

This book series records this change. Working in conjunction with a series of regular live/hybrid international events the series maintains academic standards. Books in the series include authors from different backgrounds to purposefully encourage readers to re-think the potential of fashion and how it needs to evolve in a responsible way henceforth.

Sustainability and the Fashion Industry

Can Fashion Save the World?
Edited by Annick Schramme and Nathalie Verboven

Technology, Sustainability and the Fashion Industry

Can Fashion Save the World?
Edited by Annick Schramme and Nathalie Verboven

For more information about this series, please visit: www.routledge.com/Responsible-Fashion/book-series/RFASH

Sustainability and the Fashion Industry

Can Fashion Save the World?

Edited by Annick Schramme and
Nathalie Verboven

Routledge
Taylor & Francis Group

LONDON AND NEW YORK

First published 2024
by Routledge
4 Park Square, Milton Park, Abingdon, Oxon OX14 4RN

and by Routledge
605 Third Avenue, New York, NY 10158

Routledge is an imprint of the Taylor & Francis Group, an informa business

British Library Cataloguing-in-Publication Data
A catalogue record for this book is available from the British Library

Library of Congress Cataloging-in-Publication Data
Names: Schramme, Annick, 1963– editor. | Verboven, Nathalie, editor.
Title: Sustainability and the fashion industry : can fashion save the world? / edited by Annick Schramme and Nathalie Verboven.
Description: New York, NY : Routledge, 2024. |
Series: Responsible fashion
Identifiers: LCCN 2023057688 (print) | LCCN 2023057689 (ebook) |
ISBN 9781032641102 (hardback) | ISBN 9781032659060 (paperback) |
ISBN 9781032659053 (ebook)
Subjects: LCSH: Clothing trade–Environmental aspects. |
Fashion–Environmental aspects. | Sustainable development.
Classification: LCC HD9940.A2 S88 2024 (print) |
LCC HD9940.A2 (ebook) | DDC 338.4/7687082–dc23/eng/20240116
LC record available at https://lccn.loc.gov/2023057688
LC ebook record available at https://lccn.loc.gov/2023057689

ISBN: 9781032641102 (hbk)
ISBN: 9781032659060 (pbk)
ISBN: 9781032659053 (ebk)

DOI: 10.4324/9781032659053

Typeset in Sabon
by Newgen Publishing UK

Contents

Figures

Tables

Contributors

Margo Barton is a fashion educator at Otago Polytechnic, researcher, organizer of fashion events and a curator of fashion in both traditional and non-traditional senses, most notably through her role as creative director of iD Dunedin Fashion Week and through Citizen Stylist installations.

Silvia Blas Riesgo is a postdoctoral researcher at the University of Zurich, Switzerland, within the Department of Business Administration (IBW). She holds a PhD in Communication (2022) at the University of Navarra (Pamplona, Spain) with a focus on Sustainable Fashion Consumption and Applied Consumer Behavior. During her PhD she was a visiting scholar at Erasmus University Rotterdam (The Netherlands) and at Universita' Della Svizzera Italiana (Switzerland). For the last years of her PhD, she was awarded a scholarship from Banco Sabadell Foundation (2020–2021).

Saartje Boutsen worked as a sustainability manager at Belgian fashion brands JBC & Mayerline and as a sustainable business advisor at the Flemish Chamber of Commerce before starting Studio D.

Naomi Braithwaite is a Senior Lecturer in Fashion Marketing and Branding in the School of Art and Design at Nottingham Trent University (NTU), England. Drawing from an industry career in fashion combined with her academic background in anthropology, Naomi's research uses ethnographic approaches to explore the relationships between fashion, sustainability and identity.

Mónica Codina is a Professor of Communication Ethics at the University of Navarra in Spain. She designed the International Program in Fashion Communication taught at the School of Communication, where she lectures on Communication Ethics and Fashion Communication and Culture.

Karen Cross is Associate Dean for Research and subject lead for Fashion Management in the School of Creative and Cultural Business, Robert Gordon University. Her research interests focus on how fashion and clothing can contribute to the psychosocial well-being of women; the use of immersive technologies within the fashion industry to tell stories of place, provenance, and people; and sustainable practices in fashion and textiles. She has been a co-investigator on several research projects, including Augmented Fashion, Immersive Scotland, Storytagging, CADISHAC and was the principal investigator on the EPSRC-funded Connected Threads project.

David Downes is a Lecturer in the Department of Design and Digital Arts, School of Art and Design, Nottingham Trent University, UK. David's areas of research include X-ray systems, imaging processing and the creative use of technology. David is a member of the Design Research Centre and Imaging Science Group.

Michelle Blair Gabriel is the Graduate Program Director for Sustainable Fashion at Glasgow Caledonian New York College and PhD candidate at the Yunus Centre for Social Business and Health at Glasgow Caledonian University. Michelle speaks widely about the strategies, policies and laws needed to establish widespread sustainable practices in the global fashion industry. Her research investigating how value perceptions in the fashion marketplace are shaped and built through cultural, political and economic systems aims to drive more equitable dynamics across societies.

Yang Jiang is a Professor in Immersive Design, at the School of the Arts, University of Hull, and she is the principal investigator on the AHRC-funded Augmented Fashion project (www.augmentedfashion.co.uk). Her research specialisms include 3D visualizations and character animations, real-time motion capture, immersive technologies, computer gaming and user-centred design in human-computer interactions.

Jake Kaner is Professor of User Centred Furniture Design at the Nottingham School of Art and Design, Nottingham Trent University, UK. He has a background in furniture conservation specializing in 20th-century objects, including the Mackintosh furniture for 78 Derngate, Northampton. He is vice chair of the Plastics Heritage European Association.

Ian King was, until recently, a full research Professor at the University of the Arts, London. He is currently visiting professor at three universities in Belgium, the UK and the USA. His background originates in the theater and the music business. His PhD was titled 'Strategic Decision-Making in the Popular Theatre'. Ian has published widely both in journals and books in the fields of art, philosophy, organization studies and fashion. He originally started the Fashion colloquium series with four institutions associated with the big four fashion capitals: London College of Fashion, IFM (Paris), Domus Academy (Milan) and Parsons (New York). The success and interest that this series generated led to further colloquium events in The Netherlands, Belgium, Italy, Ghana, Brazil, China and Vietnam.

Aino Korhonen is a doctoral researcher in the Department of Design at Aalto University, Finland, and part of Fashion/Textile Futures research group. Her research examines the emergence, development and character of so-called 'regenerative fashion' in the fashion industry.

Louise Laroque graduated from Institut d'Études Politiques d'Aix-en-Provence and pursued her studies at Institut Français de la Mode in the MS Management de la Mode et du Luxe program. She also participated in the Fashion Sustainability Certificate conducted by Kering and IFM, which trains a cohort of students to global sustainability and CSR strategies in the fashion and luxury industry. After starting her professional path at Saint Laurent in product development, she now works at Elsa Schiaparelli as a collection fabrics developer and buyer.

Mariangela Lavanga is Associate Professor of Cultural Economics and Entrepreneurship at the Erasmus University Rotterdam. She is the Academic Lead on Fashion Sustainability Transition at the Design Impact Transition (DIT) platform, part of the Erasmus University Rotterdam 'Strategy 2024'. Mariangela is also the Academic Coordinator of the Master in Cultural Economics and Entrepreneurship as well as co-founder and coordinator of the Minor Fashion Industry. Mariangela researches and teaches on cultural and creative industries and sustainable urban development with active stakeholders' engagement. In particular, she focuses on the transition to a more sustainable fashion and textile industry.

Andrée-Anne Lemieux has a PhD in Industrial Engineering and has devoted her thesis to transformation and innovation through lean management and agility in the fashion and luxury sector. After 15 years of experience in the fashion and luxury industry along the value chain, she now devotes herself to higher education and research in sustainability at Institut Français de la Mode as Director of Sustainability IFM-Kering Chair.

Nadica Maksimova, PhD, is an independent researcher working at the intersection between Fashion Studies, Media Studies and Sociology of Culture and Communication. Her research interest is centered on the relationship between fashion and sustainability, with particular attention to the symbolic production of sustainability-related fashion media discourses. She is also interested in the contemporary Made in Italy dynamics, focusing on socially and environmentally responsible practices. She is teaching Textile Culture and Fashion Publishing at Accademia Italiana, Florence, and is Adjunct professor at University of Bologna. She is a fellow member of the International Research Center Culture Fashion Communication at the University of Bologna.

Jane Malthus is a dress historian, honorary curator for dress at Otago Museum, New Zealand. She researches material culture and social history with a New Zealand focus. She writes, curates and presents on topics such as dressmakers in 19th-century New Zealand, waterproof clothing, the lace collection and the Eden Hore Dress collection.

Rose Marroncelli graduated from Nottingham Trent University with a BA in Fashion Management, MA in Culture, Style and Fashion and recently completed her PhD. Her PhD examined the workings of the fashion trend system in the context of sustainability, and established new perspectives on the manifestations of trends and their impact on sustainability and consumers. Rose is currently a lecturer in the Fashion Department at NTU.

Kirsi Niinimäki is an Associate Professor in Design, especially in Fashion research in the Department of Design at Aalto University, Finland. Her research has focused on holistic understanding of sustainable fashion and textile fields and connections between design, manufacturing, business models and consumption. Her research group, the Fashion/Textile Futures, http://ftfutures.aalto.fi, is involved in several significant research projects.

Annick Schramme leads the master in Cultural Management and the competence center Cultural Management & Policy (Faculty of Business & Economics) at the University of Antwerp. She is also the Academic Director Creative Industries at the Antwerp Management School. In 2018 she started a new international Master's program in Fashion Management and the Flemish-Dutch leadership program in Culture (LinC LL). She is publishing and teaching on topics such as cultural policy, cultural entrepreneurship and cultural governance. She is also active on various boards of directors and European expert groups and the Flemish Unesco commission. Since 2020, she was appointed by the Flemish government as the chair of the SARC (Strategic Advisory Council for Culture in Flanders).

Josie Steed is Associate Dean for Research at Gray's School of Art, Robert Gordon University. She studied Constructed Textiles, specialising in Fashion Knitwear at the University of Middlesex and has an MSc in Textile Technology from Huddersfield University. Her research explores the role and relevance of traditional hand skills in contemporary textiles and the value and status of craft process. She has produced several peer-reviewed papers within smart textiles, digital craft textiles, and textile manufacturing for international academic and industrial conferences. She was the principal investigator on the RSE-funded Immersive Scotland project, co-investigator on the Augmented Fashion project, and principal investigator for a 2-year knowledge exchange project with Harris Tweed Hebrides.

Leanne Tonkin is a Research Fellow in Sustainable Fashion and Textile and Conservation Practice and Lecturer, Nottingham Trent University, UK. She has a PhD in fashion conservation, with over 25 years professional experience in textiles and fashion manufacture and conservation. She is currently Co-Vice Chair of the Textile Society, UK.

Katherine Townsend is Professor of Fashion and Textile Practice, Nottingham Trent University, UK. Her research into clothing design and use in contemporary, historical, and artisanal contexts is informed by participatory methodologies that positively impact social, cultural and environmental sustainability.

Lisa Trencher is a Senior Lecturer in Fashion Business at Manchester Fashion Institute, Manchester Metropolitan University (MMU), England. With a strong fashion industry background, her research focuses on responsible business practice and the development of employability skills. Working on the premise that knowledge and attitudes toward responsible business practice are a key employability skill she is currently working on developing student-led research through extra-curricular activities to develop curriculum resource linking the two areas together.

Amy Twigger Holroyd is Associate Professor of Fashion and Sustainability at Nottingham Trent University in the UK. Her Fashion Fictions project is supported by a Research Development and Engagement Fellowship, funded by the Arts and Humanities Research Council.

Charlotte Vandierendonck previously worked as an international sales and wholesale manager for fashion brand CKS and as a senior consultant at Capgemini Consulting.

Nathalie Verboven is a PhD researcher in the Department of Management at the University of Antwerp. She obtained a Master degree in History and a Master degree in Cultural Management. Since 2018 she has been involved in various studies of competence center Cultural Management & Cultural Policy and supports the Summer School on Responsible Fashion Management at the University of Antwerp. In 2023 she started her PhD on the impact of organizational turbulence on organizational effectiveness and the mediating role of workforce diversity.

Moira White is Humanities Curator at Tūhura Otago Museum and writes, curates and presents on dress and textiles, ceramics, the Antarctic collections, material culture and its collectors and museum history. She is secretary of the Costume and Textile Association of New Zealand.

Introduction

Annick Schramme and Nathalie Verboven

Covid-19 proved to be a crisis that was nothing like anything we have ever faced before. In planning for the 2021 edition for the Responsible Fashion Series to be held in Antwerp, we were reminded of our Antwerp experience from the beginning of the 1980s and 1990s. Back then, we were facing in Europe important societal changes, increasing globalization, an escalation in migration and the breakthrough of populist parties all over Europe. Antwerp became in 1993 the cultural capital of Europe and ran with the 'tagline': 'Can the arts save the world?'

What Antwerp 93 wanted to stimulate was a reflection and debate about the societal role that Arts and Culture (including fashion) could play and thereby offering innovative approaches through arts and culture as a utopic remedy. We felt that in the midst of the Covid-19 crisis, we might need something similar. Thus, accordingly, we updated our thinking and asked: 'Can fashion save the world?' Of course this is mentioned to challenge the thinking within the fashion sector to look different at their role and responsibilities in the world. Rather than framing its role negatively, we would like to look forward and see how fashion can provide solutions for the challenges of today, like the climate and energy crisis, and how the whole supply chain that needs to be rethought. We would also like to look at technological innovations and how fashion can be also a leverage for a more inclusive society.

With the Responsible Fashion Series Antwerp, we claimed that no other field of study and practice embraces change like fashion. We also want to look at the role of fashion education in this process. The Antwerp fashion designers—also known as the Antwerp Six—have for a long time been known for their creativity and disruptive imagination. Therefore, we also ask: 'Might creatives play a greater role in a changing world?'.

Back in the 1980s creativity was mostly understood as being based on the individual genius and/or practice of certain skills (craftsmanship). Today, some 40 years later, it might be more accurate to appreciate that creativity no longer resembles this guise but rather now has evolved into something that is no longer seen as exclusively individual, but rather something that draws for its inspiration from new sources: sometimes from other disciplines, from other cultures or in terms of re-evaluating our heritage, etc.

Thus, we are witnessing a new birth and guise for creativity: perhaps one that is an interdisciplinary response? In these circumstances, we need to think differently and provide more support for creativity than we offered 40 years ago, for example: new ways of working including forms of collaboration, new technologies and processes? Perhaps what these observations lead to is a further question: do we need to break a few things down before we can rebuild a more responsible, creative and innovative fashion system? Examining which business models are necessary in order to survive and prosper in a sustainable way?

Our call for contributions seemed to capture people's attention. We received for the 2021 edition of the Responsible Fashion Series edition more than 200 abstracts from more than 35 countries. Ultimately, 97 proposals were selected (following an exhaustive double-blind review by the scientific committee).

The result was a plethora of rich and high-level contributions from people (not all academics!), leading us to decide to publish two publications, the first with a focus on sustainability and the second on fashion and technology, fashion education, fashion heritage and the role fashion can play for more diversity and an inclusive society.

In this first book we bring together insights from academics as well as practitioners from different disciplines, including: fashion design, management, sociology, philosophy, education and policy. They reflect on the question whether or not fashion can save the world from different perspectives. Enriched with illuminating case interviews and the perspective of experts, this publication provides an interesting contribution to those who want to know more about fashion needs to become more responsible—in terms of sustainability, ethics, supporting local communities etc. The call for a more sustainable fashion industry has never been so urgent, not only in terms of resources and design but also the way of producing, distributing (retail) and consuming. The need for a circular approach in order to be effective is high. The different chapters in both of these two books reflect actual concerns and often provide solutions for the complex problem of sustainability.

Aino Korhonen and Kirsi Niinimäki discuss the term 'regenerative fashion' in the first chapter of the book. In the context of fashion, the term is often associated with regenerative agriculture: a way of growing natural raw materials that claims to go beyond traditional sustainability. Thus, the current regenerative approach often aims to go further than merely reducing harm. It claims to help mitigate climate change by increasing soil carbon capture during raw material production. However, social movements and industry actors now use the term 'regenerative fashion' in a variety of ways and there is no consensus regarding its definition. Their chapter looks at two rather distinct regenerative approach narratives that are forming the fashion industry. One is a fashion practice that is a quantitative, market-based approach to regeneration; the other argues that fashion sustainability suffers from a serious equity deficit and takes a more qualitative, context-related and structural approach. The analysis draws from regenerative sustainability, design justice literature and environmental discourse analysis. Placing regenerative fashion within this theoretical framework illuminates the need for a series of questions concerning regenerative interventions in the fashion industry.

In Chapter 2, Amy Twigger Holroyd analyzes 120 short fictional outlines of alternative fashion cultures and systems that were contributed to the Fashion Fictions project she conducted between January 2020 and August 2021. The analysis identifies common themes arising within the fictions and considers the imaginaries that the fictions draw upon. It thereby reveals the range and scope of contributors' imagined alternatives—the fashion systems they are, collectively, wishing for—and the multiple dimensions of society, economy and ecology with which their ideas intersect.

For Chapter 3, Jane Malthus, Moira White and Margo Barton discuss how they worked together on the curation of *Fashion FWD: Disruption through Design* at Tūhura Otago Museum (*Fashion FWD*). Disruption to fashion-as-usual was part of their ethos for the exhibition, as was showing that fashion designers have long thought about social, cultural and environmental issues in their work. The exhibition included the work of emerging designers from around the world who had been finalists in the Dunedin-based iD International Emerging Designer Awards—over its past 17 years, museum artifacts and one piece each from a group of Dunedin fashion practitioners who have been very supportive of the Awards and emerging designers. Chapter 3, which is highly illustrated with beautiful imagery, reflects on several themes that were central to this exhibition.

Karen Cross' chapter is also a reflection of a larger project running from 2020 to 2021. The project brought together creative industries' SMEs in Scotland, impacted by the Covid-19 pandemic. Twenty SMEs participated, discussing their experiences and issues encountered during lockdown. Three Scottish sustainable fashion and textile SMEs and a circular economy expert were also brought together in a set of workshops to discuss their sustainability stories, successes and aspirations. The chapter argues that there are two types of fashion practitioners. The reactive practitioner is willing to adapt and uses upskilling as a form of innovation, with digital upskilling identified as a significant need. The reflective practitioner prefers to wait for shifts to settle before committing to significant change, remaining focused on their sustainability ethos and practices despite the challenges of Covid-19 and uncertainty around how consumption will evolve post-pandemic. The importance of storytelling emerges as a key finding, with stories important to different audiences; stories for communicating with consumers and stories for sharing among SMEs. For communicating with consumers, the importance of digital storytelling in enhancing accessibility and overcoming distance is acknowledged.

In Chapter 5, Leanne Tonkin identifies 'designer intent' as a way of evaluating authenticity in the conservation of fashion artifacts incorporating postmodern, transient materials and technologies. The term designer intent, in the context of this research, refers to the wearer experience the designer intends to create. This new approach to conservation supports the idea of a dress object's 'continual identity', a notion that connects different archival stakeholders to sustain the cultural value of postmodern fashion. Establishing the authenticity of a postmodern fashion artifact, from a curatorial perspective, is to represent the creative output of a designer at a given point in time, as accurately as possible. Within this research, Material Engagement Theory (MET) by Malafouris is employed as a conceptual framework for artifact examination, defined as the 'in-between' space of the mind and the maker. In addition, the author undertook the thematic analysis of a series of interviews with professionals in the field of fashion collection care and conceptual fashion designers to accrue examples of current practice.

In Chapter 6 Michelle Blair Gabriel focuses on the issue of overconsumption related to sustainability. Overconsumption undergirds the myriad problems the fashion industry faces today as the scale and scope of the industry is a major factor in issues such as water use, carbon emissions and waste. Overconsumption makes growth possible in an already saturated fashion market. A discussion about the role of the consumer in relation to the issues of the global fashion industry has grown louder over the last few years. Despite the emergence and growth of the 'Slow Fashion' movement of the last two decades, there are very few conversations seeking to unpack the complicated and nuanced relationship consumers have to fashion companies, the role and use of power in that relationship and the role desire plays in consumer's ability to effect change in their consumption habits and thus participate meaningfully in dynamics related to overconsumption within the fashion industry. Michelle Blair Gabriel's research examines consumer narratives through the lens of Foucault and Barthes to understand the intersection of power and desire and their employment through the shared language of fashion. Reflecting on 100 informal and impromptu street interviews with fashion consumers in busy New York City shopping areas conducted in Spring 2019, she investigates the relationship fashion consumers have with fashion companies and how the power dynamics present in that relationship affect the ability of fashion consumers to examine their relationship to overconsumption.

Through an in-depth content analysis of the *Vogue Italia* archive, in this case, centered but not limited to the contents of the supplements *Vogue*

Talents, Nadica Maksimova aims at shedding light on the evolution of the sustainability-related discourse in the context of one of the most influential fashion magazines in Chapter 7. The discussion reads the findings in the light of the very needed holistic approach to fashion, highlighting the Earth Logic values and landscapes, investigating the concepts of de-growth, re-centering and scaling, in relation to the ways in which fashion, as a cultural, industrial and social dimension, is understood, practiced and recounted. In this light, the study provides critical insight regarding the engagement of the fashion media giants regarding sustainability, opening for a reflection on whether fashion can save the world. What is certain is that fashion, in a systematic effort, can show the path toward a more responsible, inclusive and respectful society, opened for the multiverse of unexplored pluralities.

Chapter 8, written by Naomi Braithwaite and Lisa Trencher, presents the pedagogical approaches taken by two fashion educators based within different UK Higher Education institutions. Breaking away from more traditional teaching methods, the authors have encouraged their fashion business students to take the lead in generating sustainable knowledge that informs the curriculum, supporting academic development and future employability. The chapter presents the design and implementation of the two different approaches that were developed with different cohorts and, drawing from the students' reflections, assesses their value in supporting a future generation of sustainable citizens. Both pedagogical approaches enable students to actively contribute sustainable knowledge, supporting the further development of their curriculum and creating platforms which facilitate knowledge exchange. While tackling different aspects of fashion and sustainability, these teaching methods blur the boundaries between the academic, professional and personal student, paving the way for a holistic approach toward sustainable education and a generation of graduates who will trailblaze the way to a more responsible fashion industry.

Chapter 9 comes from PhD researcher Rose Marroncelli. She states that the fast fashion business model seems to question the longevity of style. However, using research drawn from a high street garment archive housed in Nottingham Trent University's (NTU) School of Art and Design, her chapter provides insights into how the fast fashion trend cycle has evolved and evidences that trends do re-emerge frequently. This unique archive is called FashionMap and spans the period 2000–2018. The archive contains over 2,000 garments and accessories, which have been sourced from the central shopping area in Nottingham, by fashion students at NTU.

Silvia Blas Riesgo, Mariangela Lavanga and Mónica Codina also reflect on consumer behavior when it comes to sustainable fashion in Chapter 10. While there is an increasing demand for sustainable fashion, consumers fail to translate their interest for or intention to buy sustainable fashion into purchasing behavior, they state. To this date, consumer attitudes, values, drivers and barriers regarding sustainable fashion remain relatively under-researched.

Therefore, the purpose of this chapter is to identify the enabling and disabling factors that influence consumer behavior and to identify and profile the sustainable consumers, contrasting their behavior with the average consumers.

In Chapter 11, Louise Laroque and Andrée-Anne Lemieux ask the question if we need to develop new types of contributors to the fashion world? How can we improve and find innovative and sustainable business models and new collaborative forms? The goal of their research is to analyze how firsthand actors invest in the secondhand market and how their initiatives can be categorized, leading to the need for new business models and data-oriented services. It aims at identifying trends and specificities that are emerging in this new ecosystem, while integrating in the framework two current subjects in the fashion industry: sustainability on one hand and data mining on the other hand.

Chapter 12 concludes this first book in the series with a response to the question whether 'Can fashion save the world?' coming from practice. Saartje Boutsen and Charlotte Vandierendonck (co-founders of Studio D in Belgium) ask the question if sustainable fashion can be affordable if you take true pricing into account. More and more fashion retailers who offer clothing in the lower price segment are also launching sustainable collections today. In their chapter, Boutsen and Vandierendonck want to find out to what extent true pricing in fashion production can also be economically reconciled with consumer prices that are affordable for all layers of the population.

These 12 chapters provide a rich and comprehensive set of important insights. We want to thank all the authors for contributing to the book, for their patience during the long process of bringing this together.

We also want to stress the importance of the Responsible Fashion Series as a series of events in the current climate where dialogue about sustainability, circularity and technology is ever more important and the level of attention to these topics needs to be maintained. As a result of hosting the series, at University of Antwerp, we have also reshifted the focus of our already existing Summer School on Fashion Management to the Summer School on Responsible Fashion Management, where we invite speakers from the network as well as teachers and practitioners who share the same values.

We hope you enjoy and find the experience of reading these chapters very valuable, for your academic research as well as for practice and policy making.

Chapter 1

Framing Regenerative Fashion

Aino Korhonen and Kirsi Niinimäki

1.1 Introduction

Global supply chains are the backbone of the fashion industry and are deeply problematic by design. These supply networks are largely based on extractive practices with colonialist legacies that pay little attention to the well-being of local bioregions and their inhabitants, resulting in severe environmental damage and social inequality (e.g., Arslan, 2019; Luna, 2019). For instance, the industry is responsible for eight to ten per cent of global CO_2 emissions (Niinimäki et al., 2020) and is estimated to employ over 60 million workers globally, many in exploitative working conditions (Nolan, 2022; Mezzadri, 2008).

Over the last years, various stakeholders in the fashion industry have framed these critical concerns into concrete attempts to define an appropriate agenda for action. This has prompted several calls for sustainability transitions, addressing, for example, low-carbon fashion (United Nations Climate Change. Global Climate Action, 2018), increased producer responsibility (e.g., structuring policy tools for extended producer responsibility in the European Union) and radical reconstruction of the industry based on principles of degrowth (as proposed in the *Earth Logic Fashion Action Research Plan* by Fletcher and Tham, 2019). In other words, the fashion industry seems to agree that the fashion system is flawed and that significant changes are needed. But what exactly these changes are remains unresolved.

As a counterforce to the existing fashion system, the notion of 'regenerative fashion' is garnering greater interest. It is seen as imperative that the industry moves from the mindset of harm reduction to a regenerative mindset of *doing more good*. The term *regenerative* (Cambridge Dictionary, 2022), relating to the improvement of a place or system, seems to speak to a wide range of actors in the fashion industry, from companies to social movements. Some discourses use it to describe raw material production that increases soil carbon capture, while others see that the term should first and foremost concentrate on structural issues such as problematic power relations within the industry. As a term, 'regenerative' acknowledges the problematic

DOI: 10.4324/9781032659053-1

status quo of the fashion industry, yet its interpretation leaves room for different ways of defining regeneration. This is both a strength and a weakness. Political scientist Maarten Hajer has stated that the political conflict of environmental discourse is hidden in the question of how the problem should be defined, which aspects should be included and which should be left undiscussed (Hajer, 1995). Hence, the definitions and implications of regenerative fashion need clarification and wider discussion.

In essence, a regenerative process for extended, regenerative sustainability should contrast with the current predominant sustainability narrative in the industry. The present sustainability narrative emphasises environmental constraints and the reduction of damage over a net-positive, regenerative approach that is rooted in procedural sustainability (Robinson & Cole, 2015). According to Robinson and Cole (2015), procedural sustainability acknowledges that sustainability cannot be defined in absolute terms and emphasises its normative and political nature and the need to integrate different perspectives and recognise that sustainability is a process, not an end-state.

Regenerative fashion has many approaches, but the interventions and increased responsibility in the early tiers of the supply chain have received significant attention. Often the approaches concern natural raw material production, enhancing the link between fashion and agriculture. These two issues are deeply intertwined through natural fibre and dye supply chains in fashion (e.g., Burgess, 2020; Textile Exchange, 2022). For example, currently large clothing companies often focus their regenerative practices on a way of producing natural fibre for their raw material needs through 'regenerative agriculture'. Many narratives on regenerative fashion use a regenerative agriculture framework interlinked with regenerative fashion for defining appropriate practices.

As in the case of regenerative fashion, there is presently no consensus on the official definition of regenerative agriculture (e.g., in contrast to the term *agroecology*). In the article 'What Is Regenerative Agriculture? A Review of Scholar and Practitioner Definitions Based on Processes and Outcomes', Newton et al. (2020) review the processes and outcomes that are included in descriptions of regenerative agriculture. Common processes were, for example, reduced tillage, livestock integration and the use of cover crops (Newton et al., 2020). Recurrent outcomes included improving soil health, increasing carbon sequestration and improving biodiversity. These same processes and outcomes reoccur in many—if not most—narratives on regenerative fashion. Taking soil as a pivot point, the use of regenerative agriculture can be seen as a potential point of entry into more sustainable and just methods of production in the fashion industry (Burgess, 2020).

The research questions of this study are as follows: How are discourses framed within regenerative fashion? What are the ideas, concepts and categories through which meaning is currently given to it, and in what kind of contexts are these produced and received? We take a broad look at the discourses surrounding regenerative fashion, including social movements, fashion practices and the regenerative movement in general, in agriculture, for example. The hypothesis in this research is that these emerging discourses on regenerative interventions in the fashion industry could potentially set new aspirations and maybe even initiate a systems change in the industry. Yet, there are concerns that this phenomenon is equally in danger of becoming just another marketing gimmick for the fashion industry.

1.2 Background: regenerative narratives in fashion sustainability

The meaning of sustainability is often contested and continues to be debated in several ways in almost every industry. More than 30 years ago, the Brundtland Commission's report developed guiding principles for sustainable development as it is understood today. It highlighted the role of preventive actions and defined sustainable development as development that meets today's needs without endangering the ability of future generations to meet their needs (UNWCED, 1987).

Over the last decade, the concept of regeneration has received growing attention. It advocates systems change through a net-positive approach, indicative of growing responsibility. It aims to enable social and ecological systems to maintain a healthy state and evolve through positive feedback loops (Brown et al., 2018; Cole, 2012). It speaks for a more hopeful predominant narrative and questions the 'mechanistic worldview' linked to technological innovations. Regenerative sustainability focuses on adaptation, resilience and regeneration, as well as on a holistic 'ecological worldview' (Cole, 2015, pp.3,6). This worldview is expressed in the application of nature-based solutions, designs and planning that consider humans an integral part of nature (ibid.). It specifically considers the regional and cultural attributes of 'place' and respects the specific socio-ecological interactions between people and place when addressing the root causes of unsustainability (Haselsteiner et al., 2021; Cole, 2011; Gibbons, 2020).

Regenerative sustainability requires different, complementary approaches to discussing 'success' to those currently deployed and is rooted in an understanding that reality (including concepts such as 'sustainability' and 'regenerative') is contested and socially constructed (Gerhards & Greenwood, 2021; Cole, 2011). This view sees sustainability in procedural terms: as the emergent property of conversations about desired futures that is informed by some understanding of the ecological, social and economic consequences of different courses of action (e.g., Mang & Haggard, 2016; Robinson & Cole, 2015).[1]

Much used and discussed in the context of the built environment, the terminology of regeneration has spread to agriculture, design and, most recently, fashion. In the context of regenerative sustainability, fashion must seek just frameworks to use the design process to both dismantle structures that exploit nature and human experience through systems of domination and to sustain, heal and empower communities towards more sustainable futures (Costanza-Chock, 2020).[2]

The link between regenerative fashion and agriculture weaves the discourses of these two fields together. The conversations on justice in agricultural systems are years ahead of the fashion system and have served to jumpstart core systemic questions regarding regenerative fashion. The agrarian political economy discourses on ownership, democratic processes and the distribution of wealth are now increasingly expanding the narratives of sustainability in fashion. This connection was accelerated by the interest in structural injustices in food and fashion supply chains being amplified by Covid-19 and by social movements' protests receiving more visibility during the early years of the global pandemic in 2020.[3]

When it comes to fashion's complex and global supply chain structure, we lean on the ideas of its conceptualisation introduced by cultural studies scholar Susan B. Kaiser. Fashion, like culture, is both a social process and a material practice—it involves becoming collective with others (Kaiser, 2012). In our reading of Kaiser's text and in the context of fashion and regeneration, this means that a single piece of clothing alone can never be described as 'regenerative'. Being or becoming regenerative concerns how the act of creating clothing—starting from the early tiers of the supply chain—can be a catalyst for positive change and add value to the unique 'place' in which it is situated. In other words, regenerative practices cannot be layered on top of existing, unsustainable operations. They require changes on a structural level and must account for the full supply chain. Ideally, regenerative practice weaves together both social processes and material practice in order to sustain, heal and empower the collectives involved in production and design processes.

1.3 Research process

Linking fashion to regenerative agriculture has worked as a catalyst and introduced and connected fashion to several existing discourses on sustainability, agricultural practices and climate justice. This has resulted in questions about the roles, responsibilities and shortcomings of the different actors in the fashion supply chain. However, the efforts to frame regenerative fashion tend to be made within distinct disciplinary narratives, reflecting the underlying values that shape the way in which the stakeholders view and interpret the world.

In this context, we are interested in exploring how regenerative approaches in the fashion industry are framed and studying the synergies and tensions between the different framings. Problem definition is a key component of design processes and influences the range of possible solutions (Costanza-Chock,

2020, pp.120–121). We study this by reviewing the narratives on the regenerative practices in fashion and using critical discourse analysis to examine how the 'problem' is framed in different discourses (Flick, 2018; Hajer, 1995; Hamilton et al., 2015) and from the design justice perspective (Costanza-Chock, 2020). We map what is considered 'under threat' and how/by whom the problem is fixed and the priorities of action according to different interpretations under the umbrella of regenerative fashion. We also look at how these narratives have gained influence, who tries to control them and from which social positions (Hajer, 1995, p.264). We do not claim that one narrative is superior to any other, but we encourage reflexive debate on the definitions of regenerative fashion. Reflexive debate could clarify options and costs, calling for a more explicit political description of and reflection on the desired developments (ibid., p.283).

Scoping and framing design problems produces a particular set of conversations and measures related to solutions, contexts and outcomes (Costanza-Chock, 2020, p.123). By identifying current discourses and narratives and focusing on the meanings from the point of view of power and empowerment (Costanza-Chock, 2020; Flick, 2018; Hamilton et al., 2015), we aim to draft some preliminary ideas that shape our thinking on regenerative fashion and to initiate a discussion on its possible definition. The data that we reviewed consisted of academic articles on design, agriculture and regenerative sustainability; book chapters; media sources such as blog posts, social media posts; and news articles on regenerative fashion, regenerative agriculture and the regenerative movement. Industry examples were drawn from this material. This study therefore built its analysis by linking this material to regenerative sustainability and design justice literature and a critical reading of environmental discourses.

Our research identified two stereotypical framings—the qualitative narrative and the quantitative narrative. Although these two types of narrative have significant connections, tensions also exist between them. As we discuss later in the chapter, to capture the issue of regenerative fashion in an encompassing manner, we cannot rely on monoframing. Therefore, for the purpose of the chapter, it became important to identify and compare multiple framings of the problems and definitions of regenerative fashion. We acknowledge that these narratives are simplifications of complex issues but hope that by reviewing them we can inform and encourage the discussion on the subject of regenerative fashion. In the following text, we describe our findings and separate them into qualitative and quantitative narratives. We also connect these narratives to real-life cases.

1.4 Qualitative narratives

The audiences of critical fashion system analysts such as the Slow Factory Foundation, Fibershed, Remake, Fashion Revolution and the Garment

Worker Center grew rapidly in 2020 after the pandemic revealed the structural weaknesses of the fashion system to the wider public. Notably, it is women who lead these critical conversations: Remake is led by Ayesha Barenblat, Slow Factory by Céline Semaan, Fibershed by Rebecca Burgess, Fashion Revolution was founded by Carry Somers and Orsola de Castro and the Garment Worker Center is directed by Marissa Nuncio. Along with a plethora of other actors interested in fashion system justice, they focus on exposing the blind spots and collectively unlearning the prevailing historical memory[4] of the power relations in the current mainstream sustainability discourses in the fashion industry. They discuss 'sustainability' as a form of cultural criticism and share knowledge, often free-of-charge, via social media and open education online. The sphere of conversation is global, but these organisations are based in North America or Europe. Discussions are mainly held in English and in a Western context.

The concepts of regenerative fashion and extended sustainability are widely discussed and used in this narrative. In an open education event by the Slow Factory Foundation, regenerative textile systems were defined as follows:

> an approach that transforms current systems by centering indigenous, geographically specific practices that enhance and preserve ecological bioregions. This results in climate change mitigation, maintenance of healthy soil and natural waterways and thus—an alternative regional social ecology and economy
>
> (Adisa-Farrar, 2021)

Other regenerative attributes according to Adisa-Farrar's definition include using seeds and other raw materials that are native to the region, not using pesticides or other chemicals in the process and production on a limited scale (ibid.).

Like social science scholar Damien F. White, the qualitative narrative sees that a focus on quantitative issues in an environmental debate (such as regenerative fashion) may overlook several environmental problems that may emerge from capitalism as the system is driven to reduce and simplify human labour and resource ecologies to exploit them more effectively (White et al., 2017). Their historical narrative does not bypass the hundreds of years of Western imperialism and colonialism on which today's fashion industry is predicated and acknowledges the scale of structural change needed.

The capture of decision-making bodies by elite interests is one visible theme in this narrative. For example, policies and initiatives, such as the UN Alliance for Sustainable Fashion, launched in 2019 to address the damage caused by fast fashion, have been accused of over-valuing the mainstream, Western business perspective in their events and reports (see, e.g., Bates Kassatly & Baumann-Pauly, 2021). The way in which large corporations capture systems (e.g., control seed supply for fibre production) and the private sector being considered the only solution to the climate crisis (Budryk, 2021) is seen as a threat to sustainability. Building regenerative practices that support the community and the region in which the products are created is seen as a better alternative (Adisa-Farrar, 2021).

1.4.1 Examples of qualitative narrative in industry

Story mfg. is a UK-based small brand that names and uses regenerative agriculture in its processes. It produces handcrafted clothing from seed-to-stitch in India and Thailand. Founded in 2013, the brand is inspired by vintage outdoor gear, combined with embroidery and hand printed details on clothing made from natural fibres and dyes. In India, it works with the Oshadi Collective, headed by Nishanth Chopra. Touching on themes of sustainability, capitalism and green-neo-colonialism, Story mfg. owner Saeed Al-Rubeyi writes on the brand's website:

> Story mfg. is a brand that cares deeply about sustainability, craft practices, people, politics and doing the right thing [...] Sustainability is seen through a Western lens—we fixate on Western issues and make it a global focus [...] The West seems to believe it's leading the charge on the subject of sustainability—which is a powerful irony considering the mess we are in is largely a result of Western capitalism, overconsumption and race-to-the-bottom pricing. Sustainability on a global level will only be achieved if we radically change our approach and break away from Western-centric problem-solving mindset.
>
> (Al-Rubeyi, 2020a)

Oshadi is an artisan collective in Tamil Nadu, born from a cooperation between Chopra and Fibershed's Rebecca Burgess (Oshadi also works with, e.g., American brand Christy Dawn).

Launched in 2015, the Oshadi Collective has received a great deal of media space in the mainstream fashion media that discusses regenerative fashion. It appears to be one of the rare examples amplified in the media that has succeeded in constructing a robust, short and local supply chain with holistic aims in both environmental and social aspects. Chopra works with South Indian artisan communities to reinvent traditional practices with modern designs and 'sustainably innovative' materials. He describes the community as 'self-sufficient and self-sustainable, that doesn't have to rely on external factors' (Al-Rubeyi, 2020b). The community includes hand weavers, natural dyers and a block print studio. Chopra has also hired farmers so the collective can grow and harvest their own cotton and dye plants, describing his work as 're-ruralisation work' (ibid.).

Farmers working for Oshadi have dual incomes: one from farming cotton and the other from spinning, weaving and dyeing the yarn (Al-Rubeyi, 2020b). It is hard to estimate the real changes in wealth distribution as not all the details are available, but the collective claims that the wages are negotiated with the artisans and farmers to account for a 'true living wage'. For example, their cotton prices are not based on the cotton commodity price; they depend on the cultivation year and the availability of crops, reducing the season-dependent risk of the lowest supply chain levels (vs industrial cotton that has a standard market rate, protecting companies from price shifts and thus risking farmers' incomes) (ibid.).

Alongside Al-Rubeyi, Chopra is keen to change the narratives of power in fashion. About fashion systems outside the Global North, he states

> When Raf Simons collaborates with an artist in Paris, no one says he's 'supporting a starving artist' or 'saving a heritage craft' [...] But when you hear about designers working with artisans in India, it's always about charity, or doing it to 'support' them... The story is never about how they do this absolutely incredible work. [...] We're working together—we're collaborators, we're partners. If everyone had that perspective, it could change things for the better [...] There is so much wisdom and heritage in India that I always felt was undervalued and now it's starting to be recognised.
>
> (Farra, 2020)

1.5 Quantitative narratives

Rebecca Burgess, founder and director of an influential non-profit organisation for regional fibre systems, 'Fibershed' (and the author of a book by the same name), has extensively researched regenerative agriculture practices and *soil-to-soil* clothing concepts (Burgess, 2020, p.107). The 'Climate Beneficial' process, which she has developed, describes and verifies that by growing the materials (fibre plants and animals) carbon farming plans are implemented (Burgess, 2020, pp.80,99). As a prolific figure in the discourses on regenerative fashion, she is one of the few people recognised for and cited in both the narratives presented here. Burgess is behind pioneering industrial fashion projects that could be called regenerative. She has worked to produce 'The Backyard Hoodie' and 'The Cali Wool Collection' with The North Face (US-based company owned by textile conglomerate VF Corporation) to create bioregional garments by a large-scale brand (Burgess, 2020, p.76).

Recent years have seen several large-scale companies invest in 'regenerative practices' with accelerating speed. One example of large-scale sourcing in regenerative agriculture is the cooperation between the Savory Institute and French luxury group Kering, connected via Savory's 'Land to Market' programme which advocates verified regenerative sourcing and aims to expand the regenerative agriculture framework in fashion's global supply chains (Kering, 2018; Savory Institute, 2018). Through the same programme, Savory has partnered with womenswear brand and sustainability avant-garde Eileen Fisher (Savory Institute, 2019). Other large brands, such as Patagonia, have developed more comprehensive approaches. Patagonia launched a 'Regenerative Organic Certified Pilot Cotton' clothing collection and is also part of the team behind a new certification for food, textiles and personal care ingredients using regenerative agriculture, Regenerative Organic Certified (Horn, 2020). As these examples show, the current waves of most visible industrial regenerative practices in fashion are largely made by brands based in the US.

Carbon capture through raw material production is a central theme in regenerative fashion. It is an important issue for both narratives but appears to be more pronounced in the quantitative narrative. Many fashion companies have been quick to adopt this upbeat form of regenerative narrative: it gives the much-criticised industry an opportunity to say they are actually doing something good for the earth. Hence, the danger of green-washing and exaggerated claims could be even greater here than in the previous sustainability narrative, which emphasised reducing impact.

Even if their goal is to regenerate solely via carbon farming practices, the companies do not yet have reliable statistics to prove their products' positive impact on the earth. Measuring captured soil carbon per grown piece of clothing is complicated and lacks comparable standards, although effort to fill this gap is growing (Davide, 2021; Oldfield et al., 2022). In addition, the regenerative practices often form only a small part of the supply chain or are merely a capsule collection with no integrated plan to scale up. However, the increasing investment and interest on this side of regenerative fashion can be seen as an accomplishment of the quantitative narrative. Veritable tracing and measuring technologies for soil carbon capture are much needed in the industry to back up the claims of carbon sequestration.

1.5.1 Example of quantitative narrative in industry

American luxury label CO launched their regenerative capsule collection made of entirely natural fibres and wool sourced from ranches practising regenerative agriculture in the autumn of 2021. In one interview, they explained how the collection began:

> We had been bumping into a lot of walls […] With all the information out there between packaging, shipping and materials, our concern was what would actually be meaningful […] We're in such a grave place right now, it didn't feel like enough to 'contribute' by just buying deadstock fabrics or using leftovers from last season.
>
> (Farra, 2021)

The company describes regenerative fashion as 'fashion that [...] actively helps heal the earth, in ways that are measurable, verifiable and transparent' (CO, 2021).

The brand credits entrepreneur and environmentalist Paul Hawken and Rebecca Burgess from Fibershed for the background work on its collection and offers detailed figures on the sequestered carbon (7,109 metric tons per year) of the two ranches on which they source the wool (ibid.). Vintage environmental classics, like the first edition of Rachel Carson's book *Silent Spring*, are sold alongside the Natural World collection of off-white blouses and wool sweaters. They also share an open-source directory of the growers and manufacturers that have made the wool garments of the collection, from ranch to yarn spinning and knitting facilities, in order to support the budding infrastructure of local production. These places are described in such detail that they can be easily traced or even visited by anyone interested, thus offering a high level of transparency. Nevertheless, no similar details are available for the rest of the CO collection; even the country of origin is not always stated on the website.

1.6 Framing regenerative fashion

This study investigated the boundaries between different interpretations of regenerative fashion using critical discourse analysis. It showed how one framing of fashion systems' unsustainability makes certain elements appear fixed and other elements appear problematic. Deconstructing the discourse around regenerative fashion allows us to examine how key actors uphold the status quo in the fashion system.

Table 1.1 summarises the main findings of this study. Once again, it is important to emphasise that the debate on regenerative fashion cannot be reduced to these two seemingly competing narratives. Many interpretations of regenerative fashion operate in several grey zones weaved around these definitions. Paying attention to larger social constructs could be more fruitful. As Maarten Hajer suggests, the new environmental conflict 'is to be seen as a complex and continuous struggle over the definition and the meaning of the environmental problem itself' (Hajer, 1995, pp.14–15).

What is most notable is that the shared core of the two illustrated narratives includes a cluster of key issues that alone challenge the status quo of the fashion system. Both narratives agree that we need to take the reality of the environmental crisis seriously and act urgently. They see the dynamics and trajectories of the current fashion system as needing repair and are ready to actively seek solutions. Fashion's problematic dependency on fossil fuels is recognised, and the will is strong to explore alternative solutions that extend the sustainability responsibilities of stakeholders and create long-term positive feedback loops needed for regenerative sustainability as suggested by Cole (2015).

Table 1.1 Ways of Framing Regenerative Fashion

Quantitative approach	Shared core	Qualitative approach
Fashion system is failing because of its impact on the environment	Fashion system is failing	Fashion system is failing because of its inability to sustain, heal and empower along its supply chains
Natural resources under threat	The insufficient sustainability narrative	Social justice under threat
Fashion system is fixed by low-carbon approaches, technological innovation, market-led approach	Fashion industry must divest from fossil fuel fibres	Fashion system is fixed by democratic processes and collective measures
Priorities: measured, certified approach to reducing the carbon footprint. Raw materials that increase carbon capture	Soil can work as a pivot point for systems change	Priorities: workers' rights, decentralisation, historical memory work, rethinking the distribution of wealth
New policy discourse needed to encourage technological innovation, e.g., regenerative start-ups		New policy discourse needed because structural change is required; corporations need stricter regulation
Depoliticised discourse		Politicised discourse

Environmental discourse classification table drafted according to Hajer's division of discursive space for ecological modernisation (254: 1995), Béné et al.'s narratives about food system failures (118:2019) and White et al.'s dimensions of environmental debate (85:2017)

Yet, the practical ways in which these main narratives seek to challenge the constructs of current fashion systems differ. The quantitative position on regeneration stays on the technology-level in its analysis, whereas the qualitative narrative encourages wider analysis of the structures on which the current fashion system is built.

The assessment of regeneration on the technology-level tends to focus on things that can (or could in the future) be calculated, such as sequestered carbon. These aspects are important, but a complete assessment of regeneration requires also assessing environmental and social impacts as well as social and political contexts. Measurement systems for calculating, for example, carbon sequestration, are increasingly needed but should be carefully and transparently developed to distinguish the differences between regenerative projects. Business-led definitions of problems and solutions are already recognised as a major sustainability barrier in the field of fashion and are a concern to researchers (Fletcher et al., 2019).

The qualitative narrative is by no means a silver bullet or a coherent approach to regeneration by itself, but it could be argued that it offers a broader look at the systemic issues around fashion. It views the non-politicised approach to fashion sustainability as the enemy of transformative change, standing in the way of democratic processes and collective change. Thus, the qualitative narrative sees a need for tighter mandates over self-regulation by companies.

The qualitative narrative argues that the quantitative approach to regenerative fashion is fragmented in its claims of extended sustainability when concentrating on carbon capture. It sees that the quantitative way of thinking accentuates the contradictory standards for measuring the impact, of which fashion is often accused (e.g., in the case of material indexes on sustainability). Regenerative practices need holistic, flexible and context-sensitive ways of measuring sustainability (Gerhard & Greenwood, 2021, p.3).

The role of justice and equity perspectives is increasing in the quantitative narrative, but commerce and entrepreneurship are seen as the transformative actors of regeneration. 'Sustainability' is viewed as improved materials for companies' and customers' needs, but this view lacks a deeper interest in pre-existing, community-based design practices and generally ignores the greater historical power injustices of global supply chains.

On the other hand—as the qualitative approach argues—there are very visible ways to measure context-sensitive regeneration in the global communities, which make up the majority of the production process stakeholders. It suggests starting from basic labour rights in the form of a 'real living wage' with overtime compensation, for more equal distribution of the wealth created and the rethinking of ownership models. This view sees regenerative agriculture practices as being less about measuring carbon capture and more about unlearning current industrial practices, relearning indigenous land stewardship and reconsidering current land rights. It sees that the real analysts of the fashion system and its (dys)functions are not the CEOs of fashion companies but the many people working in its global supply chains who are now treated as passive witnesses: a diverse cohort of people from farm workers to garment workers.

The qualitative side sees that the singular focus on soil carbon capture in material processes could possibly evolve into new types of green washing. Although improving materials is an important pursuit, concentrating on only this neglects the other structural problems and allows the reproduction of designed inequality to continue in the fashion system. In this narrative, actions to support transitions to regenerative practices focus on the single markets of the Global North and see sustainability as an issue that can be linked to one geographical area at the expense of other countries. Seeing sustainability as 'a growing social trend' and a 'lifestyle' instead of a necessity and a demand places stakeholders in the global textile supply chains in very different positions and systematically reproduces discrimination outside the borders of Western countries.

This poses the threat of an 'economy of repair'—the logic that unsustainable use 'here' can be repaired by sustainable practices 'there' (Fairhead et al., 2013, p.6). By focusing relatively little on the system, an economy of repair mostly captures the quantitative features of the problem and the qualitative aspects of the environmental problems are lost (e.g., Agyeman, 2013; Fairhead et al., 2013). Framing the issue of regeneration around carbon capture could be seen as a way of avoiding the more difficult core issues related to sustainability in fashion.

The theory and processes of this 'economy of repair' narrative are often cited for influential American environmentalists with an uplifting green business narrative and carefully chosen mainly US-based production locations. The qualitative narrative argues that these 'jewelbox farms' do not represent the realities of the majority of small farmers and fibre producers. Hence, the definition of regenerative agriculture—a prominent feature of regenerative fashion—is mainly linked to its opportunities for measured carbon capture and new certifications and is introduced as a new fix to end the climate crisis. Although presented as apolitical, this narrative's analysis of the problems and the required actions is tightly inside the current framework of market mechanisms, emphasising the role of Western thought leaders and visionary companies.

1.7 Discussion and conclusions

This chapter has looked at the ways in which an ensemble of ideas, concepts and categories are used in different ways to give meaning to regenerative fashion. The way in which regenerative fashion frames sustainability and the failures of the fashion system can have profound implications not only on a practical level but also for policy implementation and for the theoretical discourses surrounding it. Therefore, its definitions urgently need broader discussion. This chapter has highlighted that any single framing fails to understand regenerative processes in an encompassing manner but that the narratives share some core understanding of the measures needed for extended sustainability in fashion.

Regenerative fashion has the potential to develop shifts in social material cultures, but we should remain critical. When asking 'what is new?', we also need to ask 'what is the same?' (Fairhead et al., 2013, p.11). Creating evaluation systems and measuring the impact on environmental as well as social issues in regenerative fashion are important and need to be further developed to be more context sensitive, flexible and holistic. Although increasingly complex quantitative measurements of regeneration, especially soil carbon sequestration, are useful, they can also have high development costs and a high threshold for stakeholder participation. This poses a problem, as they should not remain in private ownership or be exclusively used by experts and corporations without transparent access. They should be open to the public domain and to public scrutiny.

Using a narrow description of sustainability as a selling point for techno-cratic, market-centred orientation is challenging for regenerative fashion. Thus, it would become a part of the dominant discourse on environ-mental problems in Western countries: a discourse that extracts issues of power, difference, justice and inequality from environmental issues (White et al., 2017).

Current regenerative practices that frame development as technological advances do not address the earlier pressure points in the supply chain, where more purposeful systemic changes towards environmental—and social—impact could be created. Structural change through collective action and ambitious policies alongside public sector investment could transform supply chains and reduce dependence on the private sector as the 'innovator'.

The present way in which the fashion industry frames unsustainability problems often depoliticises design processes by decoupling them from the structure, history and considerations of systemic forms of oppression in the said system. The narratives illustrate how regenerative fashion holds a great deal of potential for systemic change by framing sustainability in procedural terms: as the emergent property of conversations about desired futures which is informed by some understanding of both the environmental and socio-economic aspects of different courses of production.

Now is the time to start developing and adopting appropriate practices and policies for regenerative fashion research, development and market rollout. To be able to create regenerative sustainability, fashion research needs to focus more clearly on the politics behind fashion supply chains. In this way, generative fashion can provide a new, more extended understanding of sus-tainable fashion. If the discourse on regenerative fashion is only funnelled towards carbon sequestration and soil health, destructive patterns are likely to be repeated. We suggest further research on regenerative fashion, focusing on defining the concept and further exploring the narratives and political consequences in different discourses.

Drawing from a critical reading of environmental discourses within fashion, future research could be used as a lens to analyse how the design of products and supply chains could be transformed to create regenerative sustainability. By engaging in this discourse, fashion research could help ensure that regenerative fashion plays a positive role in the development of extended sustainability that respects the unique socio-ecological interac-tions between people and place, while also addressing the root causes of unsustainability.

Acknowledgements

This research was funded by Academy of Finland's Strategic Research Council's Grant no 327299 Sustainable textile systems: Co-creating resource-wise business for Finland in global textile networks/FINIX consortium.

Notes

1 For more in-depth analysis of the differences between regenerative design and regenerative sustainability, see Robinson and Cole (2015).
2 As a parallel reading to Costanza-Chock's book, see also 'Design Justice Issue 3—Design Justice in Action', Design Justice Network.
3 'PayUp' campaign for garment worker rights is one example of structural intervention in the fashion industry, centring the most vulnerable stakeholders in the supply chain. PayUp was formed in March 2020 after the fashion industry's decision to refuse payment for clothing orders. PayUp centres workers' rights in fashion sustainability and made way for the groundbreaking SB62, the Garment Worker Protection Act that passed in September 2021 in California.
4 'Historical memory' refers to the politics of collective memory and to the ways in which nations, groups, collectivities or others construct and identify with particular narratives on historical periods or events.

References

Adisa-Farrar, T. (2021) Regenerative design: textile systems. *Slow Factory*. https://slowfactory.earth/courses/regenerative-design/

Agyeman, J. (2013). *Introducing just sustainabilities: Policy, planning, and practice.* Zed Books Ltd.

Al-Rubeyi, S. (18 June 2020a) Evidence of the hand: Thoughts on the cost of the craft, the cost of sustainability, the cost of everything. *Story mfg.* www.storymfg.com/blogs/essays/evidence-of-the-hand-thoughts-on-the-cost-of-craft-the-cost-of-sustainability-the-cost-of-everything

Al-Rubeyi, S. (Host). (28 October 2020b) With Nishanth Chopra of Oshadi (No. 1) (Audio podcast episode). *Story Worlds Podcast.* www.storymfg.com/blogs/essays/podcast-with-nishanth-chopra-of-oshadi

Arslan, M. (2019). Mechanisms of labour exploitation: The case of Pakistan. *International Journal of Law and Management*, 62(1), 1–21. https://doi.org/10.1108/IJLMA-07-2018-0145

Bates Kassatly, V., & Baumann-Pauly, D. (2021). The great green washing machine part 1: Back to the roots of sustainability. *Geneva Center for Business & Human Rights*. https://gcbhr.org/insights/2021/09/the-great-greenwashing-machine

Béné, C., Oosterveer, P., Lamotte, L., Brouwer, I. D., de Haan, S., Prager, S. D., ... & Khoury, C. K. (2019). When food systems meet sustainability–Current narratives and implications for actions. *World Development*, *113*, 116–130.

Brown, M. M., Haselsteiner, E., Apró, D., Kopeva, D., Luca, E., Pulkkinen, K. L., & Vula Rizvanolli, B. (2018). Sustainability, Restorative to Regenerative. COST Action CA16114 RESTORE, Working Group One Report: Restorative Sustainability.

Budryk, Z. (26 March 2021). Kerry: 'No government is going to solve' climate change. *The Hill*. https://thehill.com/policy/energy-environment/545125-kerry-no-governm ent-is-going-to-solve-climate-change/

Burgess, R. (2020). Feedback on EU Strategy for Sustainable Textiles. 2020. Accessed 11.5.2020 https://ec.europa.eu/info/law/better-regulation/have-your-say/initiatives/ 12511-Environmental-performance-of-products-&-businesses-substantiating-cla ims/F547438_en [accessed 1.7.2021]

Burgess, R., & White, C. (2019). *Fibershed: Growing a movement of farmers, fashion activists, and makers for a new textile economy*. Chelsea Green Publishing.

Cambridge Dictionary. (2022). https://dictionary.cambridge.org

CO Collection (October 2021). Natural World. CO. https://co-collections.com/pages/ natural-world

Cole, C. (2011). A theory of information need for information retrieval that connects information to knowledge. *Journal of the American Society for Information Science and Technology*, 62, 1216–1231. http://dx.doi.org/10.1002/asi.21541

Cole, R. J. (2012). Regenerative design and development: Current theory and practice. *Building Research & Information*, 40(1), 1–6.

Cole, R. J. (2015). Net-zero and net-positive design: A question of value. *Building Research & Information*, 43(1), 1–6.

Costanza-Chock, S. (2020). *Design justice: Community-led practices to build the worlds we need*. The MIT Press.

Davide, M. (2021). Technical Guidance Handbook – Setting up and implementing result-based carbon farming mechanisms in the EU, Ecologic Institute US. Germany. https://policycommons.net/artifacts/2036251/technical-guidance-handb ook/2788694/ on 05 Feb 2024. CID: 20.500.12592/f2jkcg

Fairhead, J., Leach, M., & Scoones, I. (2013). *Green Grabbing: A new appropriation of nature* (Vol. 1, No. 25, pp.1–25). Routledge in association with GSE Research.

Farra, E. (27 October 2020). This Design Collective Is Helping Fashion Embrace Regenerative Agriculture. *Vogue*. www.vogue.com/article/oshadi-studio-regenerat ive-agriculture-ethical-sustainable-fashion

Farra, E. (1 September 2021). Regenerative Agriculture Comes to the Luxury Market with Co's California-Grown, American-made Capsule, Natural World. *Vogue*. www.vogue.com/article/co-natural-world-launch-regenerative-agriculture

Fletcher, K., Grose, L., Rissanen, T., & Tham, M. (18 February 2019). Manifesto. *Union of Concerned Researchers in Fashion*. https://concernedresearchers.org/our-manifesto/

Fletcher, K. & Tham, M. (2019). EARTH LOGIC Fashion Action Research Plan. Research commissioned by JJ Charitable Trust.

Flick, U. (2018). *An introduction to qualitative research*. Sage.

Gerhards, J., & Greenwood, D. (2021). One planet living and the legitimacy of sustainability governance: From standardised information to regenerative systems. *Journal of Cleaner Production*, 313, 127895.

Gibbons, L. V. (2020). Regenerative—The new sustainable? *Sustainability*, 12(13), 5483.

Hajer, M. A. (1995). *The politics of environmental discourse: Ecological modernization and the policy process*. Clarendon Press.

Hajer, M. A. (2006). Doing discourse analysis: Coalitions, practices, meaning. *Netherlands Geographical Studies* (ISSN 0169-4839), *344*, 65–74.

Hamilton, H. E., Tannen, D., & Schiffrin, D. (2015). *The handbook of discourse analysis*. John Wiley & Sons.

Haselsteiner, E., Rizvanolli, B. V., Villoria Sáez, P., & Kontovourkis, O. (2021). Drivers and Barriers leading to a successful paradigm shift toward Regenerative neighborhoods. *Sustainability*, *13*(9), 5179.

Horn, R. G. (2020). The great cotton experiment. *Patagonia Stories*. www.patagonia.com.au/blogs/roaring-journals/the-great-cotton-experiment

Kaiser, S. B. (2012). Fashion and Cultural: Cultural Studies, Fashion Studies. *Fashion and cultural studies (1st ed.)*. Berg Publisher.

Kering. (6 December 2018). Kering and Savory Institute collaborate for first verified regenerative sourcing in fashion. *Kering*. www.kering.com/en/news/savory-institute-collaborate-first-verified-regenerative-sourcing-in-fashion

Luna, J. K. (2019). The chain of exploitation: Intersectional inequalities, capital accumulation, and resistance in Burkina Faso's cotton sector. *The Journal of Peasant Studies*, *46*(7), 1413–1434.

Mang, P., & Haggard, B. (2016). *Regenerative development and design: A framework for evolving sustainability*. Wiley.

Mezzadri, A. (2008). The rise of neo-liberal globalisation and the 'new old' social regulation of labour: The case of Delhi garment sector. *The Indian Journal of Labour Economics*, *51*(4), 603–618.

Morrow, D. R., Thompson, M. S., Anderson, A., Batres, M., Buck, H. J., Dooley, K. & Wilcox, J. (2020). Principles for thinking about carbon dioxide removal in just climate policy. *One Earth*, *3*(2), 150–153.

Newton, P., Civita, N., Frankel-Goldwater, L., Bartel, K., & Johns, C. (2020). What is regenerative agriculture? A review of scholar and practitioner definitions based on processes and outcomes. *Frontiers in Sustainable Food Systems*, *4*, 577723. doi: 10.3389/fsufs.2020.577723

Niinimäki, K., Peters, G., Dahlbo, H., Perry, P., Rissanen, T., & Gwilt, A. (2020). The environmental price of fast fashion. *Nature Reviews Earth & Environment*, *1*(4), 189–200.

Nolan, J. (2022). Chasing the next shiny thing: Can human rights due diligence effectively address labour exploitation in global fashion supply chains? *International Journal for Crime, Justice and Social Democracy*, *11*(2), 1–14.

Oldfield, E. E., Eagle, A. J., Rubin, R. L., Rudek, J., Sanderman, J., & Gordon, D. R. (2022). Crediting agricultural soil carbon sequestration. *Science*, *375*(6586), 1222–1225.

Raven, P. H., & Wagner, D. L. (2021). Agricultural intensification and climate change are rapidly decreasing insect biodiversity. *Proceedings of the National Academy of Sciences*, *118*(2), e2002548117.

Robinson, J., & Cole, R. J. (2015). Theoretical underpinnings of regenerative sustainability. *Building Research & Information*, *43*(2), 133–143.

Savory Institute (18 December 2018). Kering focuses efforts on reducing environmental impact of its fashion empire. *Savory*. https://savory.global/kering-focuses-efforts-on-reducing-environmental-impact-of-its-fashion-empire/

Savory Institute (20 September 2019). Eileen Fisher and Savory Institute partner on verified regenerative sourcing solution for fashion. *Savory*. https://savory.global/eil een-fisher-and-savory-institute-partner-on-verified-regenerative-sourcing-solution-for-fashion/

Textile Exchange (January 2022). Regenerative agriculture landscape analysis. *Textile Exchange*. https://textileexchange.org/app/uploads/2023/07/Regen-Ag-Framew ork-Overview.pdf

United Nations Climate Change. Global Climate Action. (2018). Fashion Industry Charter for Climate Action. Internet document, source: https://unfccc.int/sites/defa ult/files/resource/Fashion%20Industry%20Carter%20for%20Climate%20Acti on_2021.pdf

White, D., Rudy, A., & Gareau, B. (2017). *Environments, natures and social theory: Towards a critical hybridity*. Bloomsbury Publishing.

World Commission on Environment and Development. (1987). Our common future. Report of the World Commission on Environment and Development.

Chapter 2

Writing Sustainable Fashion Worlds

Amy Twigger Holroyd

2.1 Introduction

The globalised fashion and textile industry is deeply implicated in the devastation of Earth's life-supporting systems, with negative environmental and social impacts generated at every stage of a garment's lifecycle (Fletcher, 2014). As understanding of these issues has developed in the last two decades—driven by academic research and rising public concern—an array of industry-led sustainability initiatives has emerged, typically focusing on production-related issues such as material choice, traceability and recycling. Yet any positive gains delivered by these initiatives are overshadowed by a dramatic growth in clothing production and consumption: the number of garments sold worldwide doubled from 2000 to 2015 (Ellen MacArthur Foundation, 2017). With the IPCC (2018) calling for 'rapid, far-reaching and unprecedented changes in all aspects of society' in order to limit climate change to 1.5°C above pre-industrial levels, the need to pursue a profoundly different approach could not be more urgent.

'Earth Logic Fashion Action Research Plan', a recent publication by fashion and sustainability pioneers Kate Fletcher and Mathilda Tham, provides a compelling framework for radical academic work in the fashion and sustainability field. Fletcher and Tham's argument is simple: sustainability cannot be achieved within the 'growth logic' that drives the fashion sector and other capitalist business, and thus, a new paradigm of 'Earth logic'—working within the Earth's capacity to support life—must be created. As they explain, this paradigm requires an uncompromising reduction in resources used in the global North, of between 75% and 95% (Fletcher and Tham, 2019). To achieve this, we must look beyond specific strategies for design, manufacture and disposal—which remain the focus of much public, professional and academic attention—to reimagine the entire fashion system.

A participatory research project that I founded in 2020, Fashion Fictions, responds to the need for radical change by bringing people together to generate, experience and reflect on engaging fictional visions of alternative fashion cultures and systems. Fashion Fictions uses speculation to imagine

DOI: 10.4324/9781032659053-2

radically different fashion systems, rather than—as is the typical approach—attempting to build solutions within the inherently unsustainable contemporary system. Various thinkers, from science fiction writer Ursula K. Le Guin to Transition movement founder Rob Hopkins, have highlighted the crucial role of imagination in social change and climate justice. As David Fleming (2016, p.209) states, 'If the mature market economy is to have a sequel ... it will be the work, substantially, of imagination'.

This chapter presents and analyses the 120 short fictional outlines of alternative fashion cultures and systems that were contributed to the Fashion Fictions project between January 2020 and August 2021. The analysis identifies common themes arising within the fictions and considers the imaginaries that the fictions draw upon. It thereby reveals the range and scope of contributors' imagined alternatives—the fashion systems they are, collectively, wishing for—and the multiple dimensions of society, economy and ecology with which their ideas intersect. The analysis has been used within the Fashion Fictions project, informing the choice of fictions for development in subsequent prototyping and enactment activities. By highlighting both concrete ideas for action and contentious issues for debate, it can also act as a resource for fashion activists, researchers and educators seeking new pathways for transformative change.

2.2 Generating fictional worlds

Fashion Fictions' participatory process for collective speculation has a three-stage structure, with Stage 1 inviting people to submit 100-word written outlines of worlds in which invented historical junctures have led to familiar-yet-strange sustainable cultures and systems. In Stage 2's prototyping workshops, diverse groups of participants add complexity to these fictions, while in Stage 3's 'everyday dress' projects, participants performatively enact the prototyped cultures and systems. Alongside insights into the material and social practices that arise in the fictional worlds, the research aims to identify historical or contemporary real-world examples with potential relevance to the fictional systems. The overall ambition of the project is to help reshape academic, professional and public understandings of the possibilities for sustainable fashion, from incremental changes to the design and manufacture of clothes to radically different ways of fashioning our identities.

The scope for the imagined worlds outlined in Stage 1 is broad: they could be inspired by personal daydreams as much as academic research or accounts of historical dress practices, leading to scenarios in which, for example, wartime clothes rationing continues to the present day; learning to sew is a teenage rite of passage; or Cuba has become a postcapitalist fashion centre. These outlandish—though physically possible—fictions enable the exploration of diverse approaches to sustainability in fashion, conceptually liberated from the constraints of the status quo.

I wrote the outlines of the first five fictional worlds, drawing on my experience, since 2003, of practising and researching in the field of fashion and sustainability. Recognising the value of diverse perspectives to the project, I then opened an invitation for others to contribute their own worlds. I published details of how to contribute on the project website[1] and publicised the call to my networks via Twitter and Instagram. To catalyse the development of submissions, between November 2020 and June 2021, I ran six 2-hour online interactive workshops which guided people through the process of imagining and writing a world. The first workshop was promoted via a festival promoting public engagement with academic research and via Eventbrite; the sixth was run as part of the public events programme of a higher education institution (not my own). The others were promoted via my social media accounts and by email to those who had expressed interest in taking part in the project. Various higher education institutions around the world ran their own Fashion Fictions activities with their students— from short workshops to extended projects—which generated around a quarter of the contributions.

When the call was launched, I provided some initial guidance for contributors, advising that fictions should (a) imagine contemporary realities in parallel worlds, rather than futures in our own world; (b) explore positive and enticing worlds, in terms of individual satisfaction, social justice and sustainability; (c) focus attention on use and associated practices, rather than design and production of garments; (d) be physically possible, and yet think beyond what feels plausible, from the contributor's perspective. As I ran the workshops, I iteratively developed this guidance into a flexible step-by-step process for writing a fiction. Integrated into this process is an interactive fiction generator which can be used either to illustrate the 'building blocks' of a fiction or to kickstart ideas. I published the process on the project website,[2] along with advice for anyone wishing to run their own world-writing workshop, in early 2021.

The process encourages contributors to start by targeting an issue that they find particularly frustrating within the real-world fashion system. A small selection of frustrations, as recorded on the fiction submission form, provides an insight into the varied nature of these starting points: 'extractive neo-colonialism'; 'the cult of newness'; 'international human and labour justice'; 'overloaded closets'; 'lack of inclusivity in the fashion industry'; 'increased consumption'; 'retail apocalypse'. The frustration is then reversed to create a positive idea. For example, a frustration with homogenous fashion culture might be flipped to create an idea based on localised fashion cultures; a frustration with clothes becoming quickly outmoded might inspire a fiction based on the dominance of classic styles or even uniforms. The next step is to consider and integrate the context for the fiction, for example specifying whether the fashion culture being described is mainstream or underground, and whether it spans the world or is located in a particular region.

A backstory is then added to explain how the fictional world developed differently to our own, including a critical juncture at which the paths of history split from one another. Finally, contributors are invited to concisely outline what everyday fashion life is like in the fictional world.

Completed 100-word fictions, along with optional responses to three supplementary prompts (relating to the core 'what if', real-world frustration or issue addressed, and inspiration), are submitted to the project via an online form.[3] In keeping with ethical research practices, full participant information is provided; the form documents the contributor's informed consent, anonymisation preference and agreement to apply a Creative Commons licence to their creative submission. This licence allows the use or adaptation of the fiction in the subsequent stages of the project. Each submission is then minimally edited (to integrate a unique world number to the fiction and to correct any obvious typographical errors) and published as a unique page on the project website. I write a short summary of around 8–12 words to describe each fiction on a page displaying an overview of the full collection of worlds.[4]

2.3 Analysis process

This chapter presents an analysis of the first 120 worlds submitted to Stage 1 of the Fashion Fictions project. The majority of the fictions are written by individuals, with some group submissions. I do not ask contributors to describe the nature of their interest or expertise on the submission form but am familiar with those who are within my personal network and have met others at the world-writing workshops. From these contacts I am aware that the contributors include people with professional or academic fashion experience and knowledge, as well as people whose motivation to participate is driven solely by personal interest. In terms of geographical location, over half (64) of the 120 worlds are written by contributors based in the UK, including 9 which I have written; 7 worlds are from the rest of Europe; 23 are from Asia; 15 are from Australasia; 9 are from the US and Canada and 3 are from Latin America.

My analysis focused only on the 100-word world descriptions, rather than the supporting information provided by the contributor—unless this information clarified an otherwise ambiguous element of the fiction. Furthermore, I did not analyse parts of the fiction that described the historical juncture or how the world developed, looking only at descriptions of the contemporary situation in the fictional world.

I conducted a content analysis, defined by Krippendorff (2013, p.24) as 'a research technique for making replicable and valid inferences from texts (or other meaningful matter) to the contexts of their use'. More specifically, I used what Drisko and Maschi (2015) describe as an interpretive approach to content analysis, which involves 'narratively describing the meaning of communications, in specific contexts'. They explain that interpretive content analysis requires consideration of both manifest content (that which is literally present in the text) and latent content (that which is 'implicit or implied by a communication, often across several sentences or paragraphs') (Drisko and Maschi, 2015). While the process used for the analysis will vary from project to project, 'good content analysis must be systematic, methodologically based, and transparently reported' (Drisko and Maschi, 2015).

In this case, the content analysis was documented on an Excel spreadsheet, with one world entered per row and topics added in the columns as I identified them in the data. '1' entered in the relevant column indicated that a topic was mentioned in a specific world, enabling automatic tallies per topic and therefore the incorporation of some basic quantitative elements within the primarily qualitative approach. The initial coding generated 215 topics, with some inadvertent duplication. To aid navigation I then reorganised these topics into rough categories and sub-categories, which I term *groups* and *dimensions*, prompting refinement of the topic list. After some time away from the process, I worked through the full set of worlds again, adding detail to the coding. The generation and sorting of the interim topic list helped to highlight where I had omitted potential coding, particularly on the first worlds I had coded, and many more topics were added.

During this phase I also identified between one and three topics that I considered to be the central ideas that underpinned the fiction, indicated by a coloured box on the spreadsheet. In identifying these central topics, I gave consideration to the notion of the 'imaginary', used by Lockton and Candy (2018, p.3) to refer to a variety of ideas that influence our conceptions of the present and the future, including 'societal-level conceptions [and] shared conceptions of issues such as climate change'; 'myths and beliefs which can motivate collaboration'; 'sociotechnical narratives'; and 'individual or small-scale notions … such as mental models … metaphors … and so on'.

I chose to prioritise brevity when settling on the names for the groups and dimensions, aiming for simplicity where possible. For the topics I tried to stay close to the wording used by the participants in their fictions, including terms that would distinguish each topic from others within the same dimension. The group and dimension names are intended as a means of exploring the data rather than a fully considered taxonomy of aspects of a fashion system; there is scope for further discussion and refinement. Where individual topics are referred to in this chapter, I identify the dimension and group (in the format *Group > Dimension > Topic*) and use the same approach for dimensions (*Group > Dimension*).

The final analysis comprises 632 topics, with a notable 'long tail' distribution: 63% of the topics are only mentioned once; 32% are mentioned two to five times; 4% are mentioned six to ten times and less than 1% are mentioned more than ten times. These topics are organised into 67 dimensions, which in turn are organised into 15 groups. Both dimensions and groups vary in size: there are between 2 and 27 topics per dimension and between one and ten dimensions per group. While the full spreadsheet is available in the Fashion Fictions data archive (see data availability statement), key extracts are presented in this chapter in table form. The groups and dimensions are shown in Table 2.1; this summary highlights the broad span of the fictions, from areas that are clearly closely relevant to fashion systems, relating to the clothes worn, trends and self-expression, to those that are much broader, from gender and time to relationships with nature and geopolitics.

While I endeavoured to conduct this analysis as rigorously as possible, the subjectivities involved in the process must be acknowledged. As explained above, interpretive content analysis involves inferring the implicit meanings within a text—and I may have inferred different meanings to those that the author intended, especially considering that many contributors will have different cultural references to me and that some have written in English as a second language. Furthermore, while I tried to adopt a consistent approach to coding—coding to an existing topic where the meaning was the same or very similar, and generating a new topic where the meaning was different—at some times this decision was less clear-cut than others. Decisions over the placement of topics within the dimensions, and dimensions within groups, similarly presented dilemmas. To share just one example: the *Natural dyes* topic, which I have located within the *Clothes > Colour* dimension, could equally have been placed within *Nature > Processes and approaches*. Another researcher would have made different decisions and generated a different coding and categorisation.

I will also acknowledge the limitations of this data. Considering the comparatively modest number of contributions and given that many of the contributors are drawn from my existing professional and academic networks, we cannot treat the fictions as representing a cross-section of the general population, or even of those with interests in fashion and sustainability. Moreover, it is likely that the shared affinities that have shaped the development of my networks, which include domestic making and repair, will be reflected to some extent in the data. There would certainly be value in seeking Stage 1 fictions from a more diverse group of contributors and this is an ongoing objective for the project. Despite the limitations, I am confident that the analysis provided below can offer valuable insights into the variety and complexity of ideas generated by the people who have generously chosen to participate.

2.4 Digging into the data

First, I will explore the data in terms of the frequency with which the topics within particular groups and dimensions were mentioned. Table 2.1 lists the 15 groups (with the component dimensions shown for information); it also

Table 2.1 Groups; their component dimensions; and frequency with which topics within each group are mentioned or central

Group	Dimensions	Number of worlds in which topics within group are mentioned	Number of worlds in which topics within group are central
Clothes	No material clothes; materials; types; standardisation; personalisation; characteristics; design strategies; colour; design elements; markings	75	12
Manufacture	Contexts; configurations; processes; workers; transparency; controls, limits	52	14
Consumption	Wearer perspectives; restrictions; cost; wardrobes; sharing	44	15
Reuse	Secondhand; repair, alteration	56	14
End of life	Disposal; beyond disposal	19	4
Washing	Washing	6	3
Spaces	Local-global; locations; places; events; media	71	21
People	Wearer demographic; stakeholders; organisations	60	7
Skills, knowledge	Learning contexts; extent; domains	42	10
Embodiment	Bodies; inclusivity; senses; health, well-being	21	10
Cultures	Distinctiveness, heritage; patterns; interconnection; groups; gender; time; real-world specifics	80	29
Fashion	Themes; communication; expression; trends; dress codes; diversity; value; connections; visual culture; marketing	76	16
Nature	Processes, approaches; relationships	23	8
Economics, law	Finance strategies; alternative economies; capitalism, degrowth; legal strategies	42	3
Global issues	Climate action; geopolitics; technology	25	7

Table 2.2 Most and least frequently mentioned dimensions, sorted by number of worlds in which the world is mentioned

Dimension	Group	Number of worlds in which topics within dimension are mentioned	Number of worlds in which topics within dimension are central
Repair, alteration	Reuse	47	11
Stakeholders	People	41	2
Places	Spaces	36	2
Value	Fashion	33	1
Secondhand	Reuse	30	4
Organisations	People	30	4
Learning contexts	Skills, knowledge	30	7
Contexts	Manufacture	29	3
Patterns	Cultures	29	9
Legal strategies	Economics, law	29	0
Standardisation	Clothes	6	1
Cost	Consumption	6	0
Washing	Washing	6	3
Capitalism, degrowth	Economics, law	5	1
Senses	Embodiment	4	1
Technology	Global issues	4	1
Marketing	Fashion	3	1
Health, well-being	Embodiment	3	1

provides figures on how many of the 120 worlds mention the topics within each group, and on how many worlds the topics within the group are central. These totals show that topics within the *Fashion, Clothes* and *Spaces* groups are mentioned in the highest numbers of worlds, and that topics within the *Washing* group are mentioned in the smallest number of worlds. Tables 2.2 and 2.3 provide more detail on the dimensions and topics that are mentioned frequently and rarely. Table 2.2 shows the most and least frequently mentioned dimensions (with group shown for context), sorted by the number of worlds that mention a topic within that dimension. Table 2.3 shifts to the granular level, showing topics that are mentioned in eight or more worlds, plus those that are mentioned fewer times but are central in at least three worlds.

The tables also provide insights into the groups and dimensions that the analysis identified as being more or less significant, via the figures showing the number of worlds in which they are central. Some dimensions and groups are mentioned frequently but are central in relatively few worlds, suggesting that these areas are included within the fictions for context rather than being the crux of the story. For example, while 75 of the worlds mention topics in the *Clothes* group, which describe physical aspects of the clothes worn

Table 2.3 Most frequently mentioned topics (those mentioned in eight or more worlds), and topics which are most frequently central (in three or more worlds)

Topic	Dimension	Group	Number of worlds in which topic is mentioned	Number of worlds in which topic is central
Repair, mending	Repair, alteration	Reuse	27	4
Laws, bans, regulations	Legal strategies	Economics, law	21	0
Upcycling, repurposing	Repair, alteration	Reuse	19	3
Domestic making, homemade, DIY	Contexts	Manufacture	17	1
Creativity, imagination, play, fun	Patterns	Cultures	12	1
Celebrities, influencers	Stakeholders	People	10	2
Durability, longevity	Characteristics	Clothes	10	1
Valuing, respecting garments	Value	Fashion	10	0
Swapping/trading/exchanging clothes	Secondhand	Reuse	9	1
Spaces for sewing/mending/washing	Places	Spaces	9	0
Craft/making skill	Domains	Skills, knowledge	9	0
Cultural heritage/identity	Distinctiveness, heritage	Cultures	9	0
Circular system, closed loop	Beyond disposal	End of life	8	2
Secondhand, reuse	Secondhand	Reuse	8	1
Using plants	Processes, approaches	Nature	8	1
Schools	Places	Spaces	8	0
Local production	Local-global	Spaces	7	3
Transparency, labelling, metrics	Transparency	Manufacture	6	4
Androgyny, unisex	Gender	Cultures	6	3
Local fibre production	Local-global	Spaces	5	3
Subcultures, counter-culture, periphery	Groups	Cultures	5	3
Clothes library	Wardrobes	Consumption	4	3

Traditional dyeing knowledge

Environmental impacts of textiles

Understanding of plants, agricultural practices

Understanding of body flora

How to produce textiles from plants   Theatre, ecology, mindfulness

Waste management, impacts of textile waste

Clothes-growing techniques

Craft / making skill

Garment production skills

Knowledge of charity shops

How to reimagine our clothes

Understanding of textile / garment production

Material understanding   Fashion knowledge

Garment vocabulary, literacy, knowledge

Well-fitting garments, long-lasting garments

Figure 2.1 Topics within the *Skills, knowledge* > *Domains* dimension, with text size reflecting topic frequency.

in the fictional world, topics in the group are central in only 12 worlds. In contrast, the *Spaces* > *Local-global* dimension is central in more than half of the worlds in which it is mentioned, suggesting that when this aspect of a fashion system is incorporated within a fiction it often acts as an underpinning imaginary.

An important aspect of the content analysis not revealed by the tables is the range of ideas about a particular dimension that have been generated by the project contributors. As an example, Figure 2.1 presents the topics within the *Skill, knowledge* > *Domains* dimension. This crowdsourced list of knowledge and skills that could be relevant to a sustainable fashion system makes fascinating reading, ranging from the practical to the cultural and stepping into fields such as body flora, agricultural practices and theatre. This variety of topics demonstrates that fashion is not a siloed domain: it is deeply connected to many other aspects of life. Fashion educators considering this list of topics may be challenged to extend the skills and expertise that they support their students to develop, beyond material choices and environmental impacts to less conventional areas of knowledge.

Consideration of both frequency and variety can bring to light less obvious aspects of the data. For example, a quarter of the worlds mention topics within the *People* > *Organisations* dimension, which identify the organisations that are involved in the fictional worlds' fashion systems. Examination of the topics that are frequently mentioned within this dimension (each appearing in five or more worlds) reveals contrasting ideas about the central players in the fictional fashion worlds: from the private sector (*high street/fashion brands*) to the community (*community-led)* and the state (*local authority as coordinator; state as coordinator*). In the real world, sustainable fashion initiatives are largely driven by industry, rather than the state; grassroots community-led initiatives are plentiful but limited by a lack of funding and infrastructure. It is interesting, therefore, to see contributors imagining worlds in which the hierarchical relationships between these stakeholders are dramatically reconfigured. Fictions coded to these topics could be productively used to inform a debate about economic systems and the appropriate balance of power between the private sector, public sector and communities. In more practical terms, contributors' creative ideas for ways in which in the state could support and shape sustainable fashion initiatives could suggest new avenues for exploration and development.

Further contrasts can be identified in the data; a clear example would be the tension between the seven worlds that mention trends or fashions and the four that describe a lack of trends. Reflection on the implications of the ideas being proposed, and particularly on the imaginaries that the ideas evoke, point to deeper tensions. A proportion of the worlds align with what Payne (2019) describes as a 'Promethean' or 'techno-optimist' mindset, which 'propose[s] a future in which cleaner technologies can lead to the gradual evolution of a better industry', while others align, whether explicitly or implicitly, with a 'Soterian' approach, which 'seek[s] to unbind fashion from the unsustainable growth imperative of capitalism itself' (Payne, 2019, p.6). As Payne (2019, p.18) explains, these two positions 'represent not only different perspectives on sustainable fashion, but also two (of many) different perspectives on the way forward for the human enterprise in the Anthropocene'.

2.5 Resonances with the wider field

Another way of exploring this data is to consider how the topics discussed correspond with activity within the wider field of fashion and sustainability. With this in mind, I will first examine ideas that are readily apparent both in the fiction data and in contemporary activity.

Reuse > Repair, alteration is the most frequently mentioned dimension. *Repair, mending,* a topic within this dimension, is the most frequently mentioned topic overall, with other topics in the dimension also frequently mentioned. These mentions of repair activities tally with a rise of interest in textile mending in recent years, as evidenced by a slew of new books on the subject (e.g. Rodabaugh, 2018; Sekules, 2020; Lewis-Fitzgerald, 2021). Evidence of interest in respect for garments, which connects with this emphasis on repair, comes through in the *Clothes > Characteristics > Durability, longevity* topic and the *Fashion > Value* dimension. Longevity and durability are major themes in the sustainable fashion discourse, from WRAP's 'Love Your Clothes' campaign launched in 2014 (Love Your Clothes, n.d.) to Vollebak's

100-year Hoodie, designed 'to combat every element on Earth ... to last for the rest of your life' (Vollebak, 2021).

Further ideas within the data clearly connect with the wider fashion and sustainability field. The dataset reveals solid interest in the *Reuse > Secondhand* dimension. *Swapping/trading/exchanging clothes* and the more general *Secondhand, reuse* are the most mentioned topics in this dimension. This interest corresponds with a recent increase in the social acceptability of secondhand: research in the US in 2019 found that 70% of women were prepared to buy secondhand clothes, compared with 45% in 2015 (Butler 2021). Turning to localism, 24 worlds mention the *Spaces > Local-global* dimension, which articulates various connections between local systems and the global context, with the majority describing restricted movement of materials and/or waste. The most frequently mentioned topic in this dimension is *Local production*, mentioned in seven worlds. This focus on localism resonates with the growing Fibershed movement, which works to develop regional 'soil-to-skin' textile economies (Fibershed, 2021). These examples demonstrate that Fashion Fictions contributors are adept at shifting practices and ideas from real-world discussions to the speculative frame, typically amplifying the scale of activity in the process.

I will now turn to ideas that are dominant in the fashion and sustainability field but, perhaps surprisingly, do not come through strongly in the fiction data. Organic materials, which have an enduring presence in the sustainable fashion discourse, are explicitly mentioned in only one world. Although transparency is commonly discussed as a priority for sustainable fashion, highlighted by Fashion Revolution's Fashion Transparency Index (Fashion Revolution, 2021) and technology-enabled initiatives to share full details of production (Arthur, 2017), only seven worlds mention topics within the *Manufacture > Transparency* dimension. Considering the points made about repair and secondhand above, the evidence would suggest that these ideas, while dominant in commercial sustainable fashion discourse, are not highly valued by contributors. Similarly, despite excitement about the possibilities of digital fashion to address problems of sustainability (Pitcher, 2021), only three worlds mention the *Clothes > No material clothes > Digital clothing, avatars* topic. It seems that the media hype surrounding the metaverse is not shared by project contributors—at least in terms of its potential for a better fashion system.

Some areas are arguably underexplored in both the wider field and the fictions —most notably the theme of washing clothes. As Rigby (2016, p.131) explains, laundry is a resource-intensive and highly polluting practice, yet 'in the field of fashion and textiles design research, [it] remains a largely underexplored area'. It is also underexplored in the wider sustainable fashion field, with discussion—in my experience—limited to campaigns to promote lower washing temperatures and concern over microfibres. There is little discussion that explores 'the nuanced details of human behaviour and the reasons why laundry routines evolve in environmentally significant directions' (Rigby, 2016, p.137). This absence is reflected in the fictions, with just six of the worlds mentioning topics within the *Washing* group. This gap suggests that even when trying to imagine freely, contributions reflect longstanding blind spots in the wider discourse. Consideration of these blind spots and the creative development of strategies to address them are crucial as we seek to create sustainable fashion systems.

Looking beyond the fashion sphere, there are some aspects of contemporary culture that are surprisingly underrepresented in the fictions. For example, despite a notable increase in interest in mental health and well-being in recent years, just three worlds mention topics in the *Embodiment > Health, well-being* dimension. Decolonisation is a further area of societal debate which, while appearing in four worlds via topics within the *Global issues > Geopolitics* dimension, is underrepresented in relation to its contemporary profile. These collective oversights may be due, at least to some extent, to the way in which the project is framed. Although I have tried to encourage contributors to think openly about their frustrations with the fashion system and in terms of personal satisfaction and social justice as well as issues that are more typically associated with sustainability, it is likely that preconceptions of the project have shaped the contributions. In any case, there is great potential for speculation in these underexplored realms.

Perhaps the most exciting use of the data is to look for ideas that are less dominant within the fashion and sustainability field, or that push into different conceptual spaces and thereby tap into different imaginaries. The dataset, for example, demonstrates a surprisingly strong interest in domestic making. *Manufacture > Contexts > Domestic making, homemade, DIY* is the fourth most mentioned topic overall. Tallying with this, *Skills, knowledge > Domains > Craft/making skill* is the most frequently mentioned topic in its group. Interestingly, the fictions show a particular desire for user-led making—and clothing maintenance practices—taking place in shared spaces outside the home: the most frequently mentioned topic in the *Spaces > Places* dimension is *Spaces for sewing/mending/washing*. Other popular topics in this dimension are *Salons, studios, making-based shops*, reflecting a desire for small-scale production and personal service and *Schools*, reflecting an emphasis on learning. While all these ideas are present in the wider fashion and sustainability discourse, in my experience they are not as prominent as they are within the fiction data. By exploring the fictions that include these topics, activists and researchers would discover an array of ideas for infrastructure to support DIY activity that could be adapted for real-world settings.[5]

Given that the project invites people to think openly, imagining worlds beyond the constraints of the status quo, it is pleasing to see radical suggestions being explored—from fictions in which people wear no clothes at all (five worlds) to fictions in which standardised garments such as uniforms are the norm (six worlds). The dataset reveals a notable interest in economic and legal strategies, particularly via the *Economics, law > Legal strategies > Laws, bans, regulations* topic. While a legal imperative is a convenient fictional device to explain a rapid shift in fashion culture (and indeed a device that I mention within the world-writing guidance as a possible juncture), the prevalence of such regulations within the fictions suggests a genuine appetite for stronger governance in the fashion system. As Fletcher and Tham (2019, p.65) point out, 'While fashion industry representatives and policy makers have been alert to environmental and social challenges since the early 1990s, attention to governance structures and decision-making processes, a fundament for achieving change, has been missing'.

Some of the most unexpected ideas explored in the fictions are those in the *Cultures* group. Within this group are dimensions relating to various cultural aspects that are not specific to fashion, including *Distinctiveness, heritage*; *Patterns* (comprising topics about common characteristics of diverse cultures); *Interconnection* (describing various ways in which people connect to one another); *Groups* (detailing types of cultural group, such as *Subcultures* and specific interests that people cluster around, such as *Veganism*); *Gender*; and *Time*. This is an important group in the dataset: two-thirds of all worlds mention topics in the group, and topics in the group are central in 29 worlds. Thus, the analysis provides evidence that people are yearning for ways of living with their clothes that prioritise notions of culture and community.

Patterns is the most frequently mentioned dimension in the *Cultures* group. The most frequently mentioned topics in this dimension are *Creativity, imagination, play, fun* and *Storytelling, stories*—which, interestingly, mirror the core elements of the Fashion Fictions project itself. This focus on imagination and stories—not the aspirational storytelling of branding and fashion communication, but rather stories rooted in personal experience and material relationships—indicates a desire for ways of pursuing sustainability in fashion that operate on a different register to the dominant debates around metrics and material impacts. Other topics in the *Cultures > Patterns* dimension provide intriguing and unconventional ideas that are ripe for exploration: *Rite of passage, coming of age*; *Ritual*; *Spirituality, religion*; *Common belief*; *Superstition*; *Taboos*; *Rebellion*; *Commoning*; *Sharing food, tools*; *Conviviality*; *Ethics—do no harm*. If we were to develop initiatives based on these ideas, we would expand the range of imaginaries shaping the field of fashion and sustainability. An expanded range of imaginaries would, in turn, enable those working for change to draw on more diverse ways of being and knowing and, it is hoped, generate more inclusive, engaging and transformative movements.

2.6 Conclusion

In this chapter I have presented an interpretive content analysis of 120 fictional parallel worlds, written by contributors around the world to portray a diverse array of alternative fashion cultures and systems. The analysis has considered both how frequently topics are mentioned and the variety of ideas present within the fictions. Contrasting ideas are evident in the data, from specific aspects of fashion systems to underlying paradigms. By comparing the ideas found within the fictions with the wider field of fashion and sustainability, I have highlighted aspects that are surprisingly underexplored in the fictions along with those which are notably prevalent, radical or varied. The content analysis process has helped to draw out the more unconventional concepts embedded within the collection of fictions, such as those connected to cultural patterns. The analysis thus provides novel insights into the desires and daydreams of those who have contributed to Stage 1 of Fashion Fictions.

These insights could be used by sustainable fashion activists, educators and researchers wishing to explore fresh territory; many productive yet underexplored ideas can be identified in this data. The analysis has already informed the next phase of the Fashion Fictions project, guiding the selection of Stage 1 fictions to be explored in greater depth through the creation of visual and material prototypes at Stage 2 workshops. For this selection I particularly focused on the ideas that I identified as being central to each fiction and the imaginaries that these ideas invoke; I endeavoured to choose worlds for further investigation that represent a variety of perspectives, while keeping in mind the project's aim of contributing to Fletcher and Tham's (2019) 'Earth logic' scholarship and activism.

The positive response that this project has received to date provides evidence of a latent desire for imagination, speculation and playfulness in the sphere of fashion and sustainability. Certainly, we can see that contributors' dreams of a better fashion system are bolder, broader and far more diverse than the industry-led initiatives that dominate the field. This collaboratively created body of work—nurtured via the simple but transgressive question, 'what if?'—is offered to all as a rich resource of ideas and of hope.

Acknowledgements

I would like to thank all those who contributed Worlds 1–120 to the Fashion Fictions project. Thanks are also due to those who facilitated the workshops and student projects that helped to generate these fictions, including Matilda Aspinall, Martin Bonney, Rebecca Collins, Sally Cooke, Kate Harper, Lizzie Harrison, Zoe John, Noorin Khamisani and Georgia McCorkill. Fashion Fictions is funded by an Arts and Humanities Research Council Research, Development and Engagement Fellowship (reference AH/V01286X/1).

Data availability statement

The original fictions that have been analysed for this chapter are openly available on the Fashion Fictions website: http://fashionfictions.org/the-worlds. They are also archived, along with the full analysis spreadsheet, in Zenodo at http://doi.org/10.5281/zenodo.6991840.

Notes

1 https://fashionfictions.org
2 https://fashionfictions.org/contribute-a-world/
3 https://fashionfictions.org/contribute-a-world/#submit
4 https://fashionfictions.org/the-worlds/
5 The analysis spreadsheet can be used to identify the specific fictions that have been coded to a particular topic, dimension or group.

References

Arthur, R. (2017). "From Farm to Finished Garment: Blockchain Is Aiding This Fashion Collection with Transparency," *Forbes* (10 May 2017). Available from www.forbes.com/sites/rachelarthur/2017/05/10/garment-blockchain-fashion-transparency/ [accessed 18 April 2021].

Butler, S. (2021). "'Pre-loved' Fashion Moves from Niche to Mainstream as Retailers Join the Fray," *The Guardian* (1 May 2021). Available from www.theguardian.com/fashion/2021/may/01/pre-loved-fashion-moves-from-niche-to-mainstream-as-retailers-join-the-fray [accessed 25 July 2021].

Drisko, J.W. and Maschi, T. (2015). *Content Analysis* [eBook]. New York: Oxford University Press. Accessed via Oxford Scholarship Online.

Ellen MacArthur Foundation (2017). A New Textiles Economy: Redesigning fashion's future. Available from https://ellenmacarthurfoundation.org/a-new-textiles-economy [accessed 25 September 2021].

Fashion Revolution (2021). Fashion Transparency Index 2021. Available from www.fashionrevolution.org/about/transparency/ [accessed 25 September 2021].

Fibershed (2021). Regional Textile Economies. Available from https://fibershed.org/programs/regional-textile-economies/ [accessed 23 September 2021].

Fleming, D. (2016). *Lean Logic: A Dictionary for the Future and How to Survive It.* White River Junction, VT: Chelsea Green Publishing.

Fletcher, K. (2014). *Sustainable Fashion and Textiles: Design Journeys.* Abingdon: Routledge.

Fletcher, K. and Tham, M. (2019). *Earth Logic Fashion Action Research Plan.* London: The JJ Charitable Trust.

IPCC (2018). 'Summary for Policymakers of IPCC Special Report on Global Warming of 1.5°C Approved by Governments', news release, 8 October 2018. Available from www.ipcc.ch/site/assets/uploads/2018/11/pr_181008_P48_spm_en.pdf/ [accessed 25 September 2021].

Krippendorff, K. (2013). *Content Analysis: An Introduction to Its Methodology* (3rd ed.). Thousand Oaks, CA: Sage.

Lewis-Fitzgerald, E. (2021). *Modern Mending: How to Minimize Waste and Maximise Style*. Tunbridge Wells: Search Press.

Lockton, D. and Candy, S. (2018). 'A vocabulary for visions in designing for transitions' in Proceedings of Design Research Society Conference (pp.908–926). Limerick: University of Limerick.

Love Your Clothes (n.d.). Available from www.loveyourclothes.org.uk [accessed 25 September 2021].

Payne, A. (2019). 'Fashion Futuring in the Anthropocene: Sustainable Fashion as "Taming" and "Rewilding",' *Fashion Theory*, 23:1, 5–23, DOI: 10.1080/1362704X.2017.1374097

Pitcher, L. (2021). 'Is Digital Design the Answer to Fashion's Waste Problem?', *Atmos*, 10 June 2021. Available from https://atmos.earth/is-digital-fashion-design-good-for-the-planet/ [accessed 23 September 2021].

Rigby, E.D. (2016). 'Mundane matters: laundry, design and sustainability' in Proceedings of Circular Transitions: A Mistra Future Fashion Conference on Textile Design and the Circular Economy (pp. 131–140). London: University of the Arts London.

Rodabaugh, K. (2018). *Mending Matters: Stitch, Patch, and Repair Your Favorite Denim and More*. New York: Abrams.

Sekules, K. (2020). *Mend! A Refashioning Manual and Manifesto*. London: Penguin.

Vollebak (2021). 100 Year Hoodie. Available from www.vollebak.com/product/100-year-hoodie/ [accessed 23 September 2021].

Chapter 3

Disrupting Fashion-as-Usual in the Southern Hemisphere

Jane Malthus, Moira White and Margo Barton

3.1 Introduction

We, three New Zealand authors, are a dress historian and retired academic, an anthropology-trained humanities collection curator and a fashion educator, practitioner and fashion event organiser who all also curate exhibitions (Malthus, White and Barton, 2021). From 2019 we worked together on the curation of *Fashion FWD: Disruption through Design* at Tūhura Otago Museum (*Fashion FWD*), which opened in late March 2021. Disruption to fashion-as-usual was part of our ethos for the exhibition, as was showing that fashion designers have long thought about social, cultural and environmental issues in their work. The exhibition included the work of emerging designers from around the world who had been finalists in the Dunedin-based iD International Emerging Designer Awards—over its past 17 years, museum artefacts and one piece each from a group of Dunedin fashion practitioners who have been very supportive of the Awards and emerging designers.

Dunedin, Otago, New Zealand may seem an odd and peripheral place to host such an Awards and exhibition, but it has a reputation for nurturing businesses and activities that break moulds and rules. It has been called the Antwerp of the South for punching above its weight in fashion design as well as for its 'grumbling weather'.[1] Dunedin's physical surroundings (ocean, harbour and mountains) and tangential physical position in the fashion world have contributed to the edginess and risk taking exhibited in its fashion design, something that was elucidated and celebrated in *A Darker Eden: Fashion from Dunedin*, an exhibition held in Auckland, New Zealand's largest city (population: 1.6 million) in 2015 (Malthus et al., 2015). Dunedin's history and heritage includes Māori, Scottish, Irish, Chinese and Lebanese settlement, all of which have added texture to landscapes, built environment and people and can affect textile and colour choices, garment shapes and forms (Malthus et al., 2015). Living so far from the perceived centres of fashion in Europe can allow freer exploration, play and adventurousness in the creation of stimulating and intriguing fashion.

DOI: 10.4324/9781032659053-3

A strong textile production and clothing manufacturing history in the province of Otago, a rich home-crafting legacy and the presence of clothing, textile and fashion tertiary education, has engendered a rich vein of independent fashion designers (Koch, 2019). Margi Robertson of NOM*d, Sara Munro of Company of Strangers, Charmaine Reveley, Tanya Carlson of Carlson and Donna Tulloch of Mild Red produce unique and collectable fashion designs from Dunedin that are popular throughout New Zealand and further afield. They are also well known for their nurture, support and mentoring of young designers and fashion students, particularly those who study at Otago Polytechnic in the city. For this reason, in *Fashion FWD* we called them 'the godmothers'. They 'are steeped in the city's physical surroundings and have imbibed and interpreted the auras' of their place to produce conceptually driven fashion that translates 'abstract ideas from their many and various stimuli into appealing clothes and accessories that embody those concepts and allow wearers to feel different and special' (Malthus et al., 2015, p.1401). Margarita Robertson, in particular, has been likened to Rei Kawakubo of Comme des Garcons and Martin Margiela, conceptual designers par excellence (Drichel, 2011). Her NOM*d designs involve

> self-consciousness and reflexivity; constructivism as a principle of ornamentation; reappropriation and recycling of vintage garments; the creation of multiple-possibility garments; techniques of bricolage; the borrowing and repositioning of streetwear conventions; the promotion of an androgynous bulky body; and the paradoxical pursuit of an anti-consumer aesthetic in a consumer environment.
>
> (Smith and Radner, 2011, p.19)

While our 'godmothers' operate as part of the fashion industry in New Zealand, they have selected their own pathways, such as most choosing to remain based in Dunedin when much of the industry is based in Auckland at the other end (almost) of the country (Figure 3.1).

3.2 Fashion-as-usual in New Zealand

The fashion and apparel industry in New Zealand has operated like most others around the world on a commercial business model of competition and continued growth. However, competition with overseas production was mediated until the late 1980s by tariffs being imposed on imported products. With phased removal of tariffs, influxes of fashion brands produced offshore and local fashion companies moving their manufacturing to cheaper locations in order to survive, New Zealand joined the globalised fashion supply chain (McEwan, 2017). Current exports of textiles, clothing and footwear are approximately 1.3 billion NZ dollars, while imports of textiles, clothing and footwear amount to 3 billion NZ dollars.

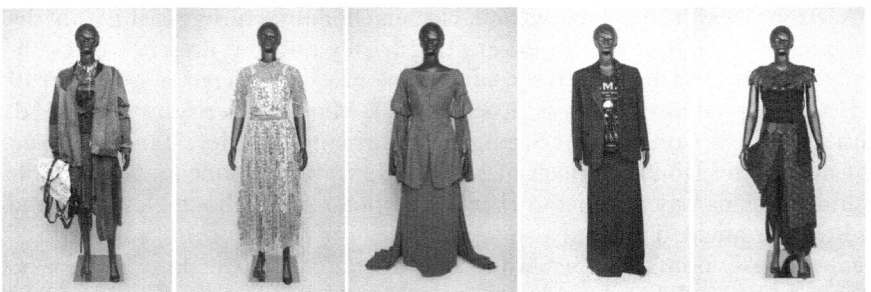

Figure 3.1 The Godmothers section, *Fashion FWD >> Disruption through Design,* Otago Museum, Dunedin, New Zealand, 2021.

Although fashion design and production is a highly competitive industry, it is still perceived to be economically lucrative (if also exploitative) (Barry, 2021), so in New Zealand as in other parts of the world young people want to study it (Tilson-Scoble, 2017). This, coupled with New Zealand's geography as a long thin country of two main islands, with high costs of travelling from one end to the other, results in numbers of vocational and academic fashion education programmes. There are at least nine tertiary providers of fashion design education spread throughout the two main islands. Otago Polytechnic in Dunedin, which offers certificate, diploma, undergraduate and postgraduate fashion design programmes, is a major sponsor and supporter of the iD Dunedin International Emerging Designer Awards.

Independent fashion designers have operated successfully in New Zealand since at least the 1940s and some have been successful outside the country (Hammonds, Lloyd Jenkins and Regnault, 2010; Lassig, 2010; Malthus, 2007). Auckland-based Kevin Berkahn, for example, had a studio and shop in Australia for a time from 1973 and took a show of New Zealand fashion on tour to Australia, the USA and England in the early 1970s (Malthus, 2007).

Rosaria Hall started a hippie boutique in 1971 and grew a business operating multiple stores throughout the country and supplying shops in Australia before retiring in 2003 (Malthus, 2020). In 1999, NOM*d, Zambesi and Karen Walker showed at London Fashion Week and have since supplied markets in a number of countries (Hammonds, Lloyd Jenkins and Regnault, 2010). In the 21st century the New Zealand fashion scene has been dominated by female designer-led companies such as Zambesi, World, NOM*d, Helen Cherry, Kate Sylvester, Karen Walker and Trelise Cooper, with Maaike, 27 names and Kowtow more recent additions.[2] Many of these designers attempt to straddle the commercial imperatives of the industry and operate with social, cultural and environmental consciences.

3.3 Disruption in New Zealand fashion

Some fashion practices in New Zealand have long disrupted colonial, cultural and environmental processes of the fashion industry (Barry, 2021). While Māori adopted European garments after colonisation but were sometimes derided for wearing them in their own fashion, modern Māori fashion cultures hark back to the visible activism of Whetu Tirikatene-Sullivan, of Ngai Tahu and Ngāti Kahungunu and Member of Parliament for Southern Māori (Te Tai Tonga) 1967–1996, wearing Māori-inspired fashion in Parliament from the late 1960s onwards. The Pacific Sisters collective work in showcasing Māori and Pasifika design and materials and stands like that of MP Rawiri Waititi wearing a taonga (treasure) instead of a tie in Parliament have continued the resistance to the supremacy of colonial fashion.[3] Miromoda, established in 2008, champions and launches Māori and Pasifika fashion designers and prioritises the values of te ao Māori (the Māori world-view), aspects of which include working collectively and in harmony with the natural world (Richards, 2021). Amber Bridgman, (Ngai Tahu, Kati Mamoe, Waitaha, Rabuvai and Aborigine) a Dunedin fashion designer and traditional Māori arts practitioner, showed her label Kahuwai, which combines Māori and western materials and designs, at London's Pacific Fashion week in September 2022 using her sons as models (Day, 2022).

Other local fashion designers and educators have also begun questioning the traditional take, make, waste model and trying more sustainable alternatives. For example, Holly McQuillan specialises in zero-waste fashion design and practice, designing zero-waste patterns and garments and facilitating exhibitions to communicate her ideas to others (McQuillan et al., 2018; McQuillan, 2019). A recently published study about renting rather than buying fashion located ten firms in New Zealand operating such businesses (Gyde and McNeill, 2021). We are aware of younger designers in New Zealand engaging in artisanal practices, being active makers, producing slow fashion, working sustainably in terms of materials and practices. We hear too of consumers who shop local and seek out the slow and lasting, handcrafted, unique, reworked vintage or second-hand fashion rather than the mass produced and fast fashion. Being able to reach consumers directly via online platforms helps break the traditional fashion business mould, but as Ella Martin and Lisa McEwan point out, uneven access and a lack of helpful regulations don't make it easy to obtain accurate information about environmental impacts of fashion production (Beckett, 2022).

As part of *Fashion FWD: Disruption through Design*, Otago Museum organised a 'Fashion Fridays' public programme, with weekly events that included a panel discussion about the fashion industry involving all 'godmothers' and individual interviews with each of them. In talking about the way they worked, their design influences and the practicalities of running businesses, it was clear that one way they break moulds and disrupt competitive business models is by being very collegial despite competing in a relatively small market: they share information about suppliers, manufacturers, photographers and more and recently one even hosted a pop-up of another's clothes in her shop.[4]

The combining of emerging designers' clothes with historical artefacts in *Fashion FWD* was made possible in part because Dunedin (population 114,000) is home to iD Dunedin Fashion. Managed by a dedicated voluntary committee, iD Dunedin Fashion organises an annual fashion show featuring the above-mentioned designers and others and since 2005 has coordinated the iD International Emerging Designer Awards (iD Awards). There are no restrictions on what kind of garments designers can enter in the Awards, from swimwear to lingerie to high fashion and there is no age limit; the only criterion is that the designer must be in their final year or within five years of their graduation from a recognised fashion degree (Barton, 2021). 'Design entries show diverse, yet also similar, fashion ideas, themes and trends, which are explored and expressed from an array of cultural standpoints' (Barton, 2021). The entrants come to Dunedin, to meet each other and interact with other designers, judges and local students and staff, among others. International judges have included Zandra Rhodes (2010), Akira Isogawa (2011), Lutz Huelle (2012), Stephen Jones (2013), Martin Grant (2014), Doris Raymond (2015), Emilia Wickstead (2016) and Paulo Melim Andersson (2017) (Barton, 2021). However, the Covid-19 pandemic disrupted the 2020 and 2021 Awards shows, which were forced to become virtual[5] and also disrupted our exhibition planned to highlight the history of the iD Awards and show their expanding relevance. Instead of the planned May 2020 opening, *Fashion FWD >> Disruption through Design* opened at Otago Museum, Dunedin, New Zealand, on 27 March 2021.

3.4 Fashion FWD: Disruption through design: Themes

To begin the curation process of *Fashion FWD*, we asked all finalists who still had their collections, to submit one of their looks with a statement about the ideas on which it was based. From the 400-plus former finalists, 24 finalists' garments were selected for the exhibition from countries as far flung from New Zealand as Malaysia, Croatia, England, Iceland, the USA and Bangladesh.

It became clear that certain themes resonated for all designers. The shared design concepts and drivers we chose to highlight were escapism, gender, illusion, re-interpretation, sculpture, transformation and wellbeing. The emerging designers' garments beautifully illustrated how fashion breaks moulds and rules. Their clothes express how fashion plays a disruptive role in reshaping and camouflaging bodies, questioning and blurring gender stereotypes, creating, mutating and metamorphosing materials, reviving and reinterpreting past styles, commenting on the physical, psychological and environmental state of the planet and imagining a better world (Barry, 2021).

We also wanted to disrupt presentist design thinking by showing that these themes had historical resonance: designers and makers had thought about these issues in the past as well as now. So, we chose historical dress and accessories from Otago Museum's collection as examples for each theme. The dress collection at Otago Museum is significant in its breadth and depth in a New Zealand context: it includes about 6,000 items of women, men and children's wear from the early 19th century onwards, most of which have a New Zealand provenance (Malthus and White, 2021). Touch screens in the exhibition and a catalogue added text and images, providing visitors with the emerging designers' conceptual visions and the curators' thoughts about the themes (Malthus, White and Barton, 2021).[6] Below we briefly examine how our choices of emerging designer and historical examples within each theme disrupt and challenge ideas, shapes or processes used in fashion creation.

3.5 Escapism: Disruption to life-as-usual

Metaphorical and real escapes, including dreaming of a less repressed life, freedom from control, absconding or taking flight, becoming equal, going back to the innocence of childhood, were all sewn into the clothes in Escapism (Figure 3.2). Carla van Lunn's 2005 iD Awards first-place winning entry encouraged escape from concrete jungles by parachuting into a country idyll for a picnic, perhaps on the shores of a babbling brook. The imagined life of a childhood pet parrot, Ruby, became the focus of Rebecca Carrington's entry. Scaled-up toys formed the shapes of her garments and inspired the prints, embellishments, masks, keyrings and soft toys that accompanied them. Rebecca won first place in 2019 for her whole collection. Chin Hau Tay created genderless, sexless attire for men, avoiding the paradigms of traditional forms and allowing for an escape from the myriad expectations

Figure 3.2 Escapism section of *Fashion FWD >> Disruption through Design*, Otago Museum, Dunedin, New Zealand, 2021.

societies place on men. The three-piece suit in *Fashion FWD*, shown at iD Awards 2014, consists of a tartan and fake fur jumpsuit or onesie, an organza cape with a large padded neck support and an enormous cape-coat with fake fur and padded collar. Travelling to new places to see the world formed the inspiration for Rakel Blomsterberg's colourful digital prints and garments, which cleverly incorporated rug hooking techniques. This collection took first place in iD Awards 2013.

In the past many women dreamed of escaping their mundane lives, even temporarily. Boudoir caps were a 1920s fashion, worn in the privacy of the home, over newly bobbed hair. Lace, embroidery, crochet, ribbon-work embellished these confections offering the wearer a feeling of a grander life, perhaps.

Driving coats worn in early cars protected women from dust, drafts, weather and noise, to some extent, as they were exploring places they had not been before, under their own power. Summer coats like the one in *Fashion FWD*, called dusters, were accompanied by wide-brimmed hats and veils.

A going away outfit represented a large change of status in a woman's life, escaping possible spinsterhood for married life, moving away from parents to living with a husband. The bride would change into travelling clothes or a new dress and set off for a few days break before real married life began. The wool gabardine suit of 1922 was chosen by New Zealander Dr. Dorothy Smith to wear after her wedding in Edinburgh, where she had studied medicine. She and her new husband went by train to Glasgow for their honeymoon.

The promise of an escape to a tropical island is evoked in the printed fabric of a 1950s sundress. Coconut palms and other hot climate vegetation and swimsuit-clad musicians in gold and white on a red cotton fabric are stitched into a demure sundress. For Māori in the 20th century, joining a kapa haka group helped them escape western culture for immersion in Māori time, space and language. Pari (bodices) were first worn by wāhine (women) in that context after Christian missionaries imposed their ideas of modest dress on Māori. The detail on the modern pari in *Fashion FWD* is patterned on traditional tāniko, but cross-stitched in the design of the Araiteuru Club, Dunedin.

3.6 Gender: Disruption of stereotypes

Fashion can reflect traditional ideas of gender and sex or provide a platform for designers and wearers to challenge those ideas, dispute gender roles, explore gender fluidity and expand the spectrum of what we can wear. Dylan McCutcheon-Peat chose to blur binary gender boundaries by combining underwear and outerwear, in the forms of worsted pinstripe and women's lingerie in clothes designed for men (iD Awards, 2018).

Exploring his homosexuality, choice to study fashion design and complicated relationship with his traditional southern Italian father, Alessandro

Figure 3.3 Gender section of *Fashion FWD >> Disruption through Design*, Otago Museum, Dunedin, New Zealand, 2021.

Trincone used feminine fabrics such as chiffon, silk satin and tulle to make clothes for men. His bridal suit with many bows has a ruffled front instead of a bridal train and a veil-like headpiece (iD Awards, 2017).

Ruth Bucknell's (iD Awards, 2009) designs commented on the many and varied roles women have today, questioning the sustainability of these expectations. Work, motherhood, home economics, health, fitness, education, friendships, family support and many other roles have to be juggled daily. Her all-white muslin garments featured many different textile techniques from tailoring to smocking to netting to signal the difficulties of combining all these tasks.

For comparison, we contrasted these emerging designer creations with some traditionally gendered garments from the museum collection. A man's tailcoat suit from the 1930s and a silk marquisette gingham dress from the late 1950s emphasised western cultures' broad-shouldered conservative masculinity and the desired but sophisticated femininity in the 20th century. A 1940s women's utility-styled suit in a serviceable dark pinstripe fabric offers a slightly different reading, with its business-like serious squared padded shoulders and straight skirt and a group of aprons telling a longer story about women's domestic roles (Figure 3.3).

3.7 Illusion: Obvious disruption to bodies

Fashion often idealises the human body, smoothing, camouflaging, streamlining, distorting or extending to create desire and beauty. Such illusion was traditionally and cleverly hidden in the cut and shaping of garments, but now such artifice is called out by designers by making it obvious (Figure 3.4).

Fiona Ralph (iD Awards, 2007) protested the fashion industry's obsession with very thin models, so introduced padding in her collection to create curvy bodies in a palette of red, white, pink and blue. Influenced by what designers such as Vivienne Westwood and Rei Kawakubo were creating, her garment forms pre-empted what celebrities such as Kim Kardashian did to their actual bodies.

Figure 3.4 Illusion section of *Fashion FWD: Disruption through Design* exhibition, Otago Museum, Dunedin, New Zealand, 2021.

Sharn Blackwell took a slightly different approach, celebrating the rarer forms that human bodies can develop naturally. Kyphosis (an abnormally curved spine), clubfoot, adipose deposits and conjoined twins affect some people and have in the past been exploited for entertainment. Her collection drew attention to our varied sizes and shapes using pre-loved fabrics (iD Awards, 2008). Her conjoined twins design was part of *Fashion FWD: Disruption through Design*.

Black and white stripes were used by Alexandra Walker to distort, mislead and overwhelm the wearer and viewer in her collection called 'Between the Lines' (iD Awards, 2010). Layers of pieces, some with padding and different sizes and angles of stripes, created visual deception.

Tailors have always been masters of illusion, creating their bespoke suits to subtly enhance the wearer's figure. The cutting, stitching and padding streamlines the outer fabric to hide pigeon chests, narrow shoulders or even corpulence. In *Fashion FWD* a frock coat made in Cork, Ireland, in 1906, is displayed inside out to show sections of 'corrective' padding and quilting in the side chest area.

Also from the Otago Museum collection, a 19th-century top hat and ca. 1960 stiletto-heeled shoes illustrate ways men and women's bodies have been extended by accessories. The top hat was a symbol of social status and power and the shoes also give the illusion of symmetrical feet! A 1948 New Look wool suit by Robert Piguet demonstrated the illusions of rounded shoulders, nipped-in sloping waist, padded hips and slim skirted silhouette first shown by Christian Dior the previous year. This suit was purchased from Piguet's show by the New Zealand Wool Board to inspire women in our country to make more stylish use of wool fabrics.

3.8 Reinterpretation: Disruption to traditional designs

Reviving styles, reworking past designs, recreating textures or patterns, or freshening the dress of others were all part of the Reinterpretation theme. Kate Anderson (iD Awards, 2007) grew up on a farm and worked at an abattoir in her student holidays. She was inspired by her colleagues' attempts to style and personalise their uniforms. Her sheepskin coat with lambskin collar and overalls reinterpret the sights and materials she experienced. Meg Gallagher looked to the distant past for inspiration as she grappled with the roles of women today. That some Egyptian women could rule and have the same rights as men spurred her bifurcated designs and printed gold textures (iD Awards, 2009). Gazing not quite so far back was Steve Hall who reinterpreted Japanese samurai and ninja clothing and armour by using soft materials and altering proportions. The colours, shapes and patterns in contemporary safety clothing most often worn by men motivated Tess Norquay to use those elements in her feminist commentary on patriarchal power in fashion (iD Awards, 2017). By including her own textile designs, she drew attention to her agenda.

Fashion has always reinterpreted historical style details, as exemplified in a late 19th-century two-piece dress made in a Dunedin shop. It has Elizabethan-style slashing on its sleeves and ruff at the neck. Another late 19th-century garment adopted military styling. A jacket made by French dressmakers Clotilde and Alice; it looks like it has a contrasting waistcoat and is decorated with braid and buttons (some of which have subsequently been removed).

An English man's linen smock with panels of honeycomb work was a utilitarian garment for working men from the 18th century until the late 19th century, when smocking was transposed to women and girls' clothes, thanks to artistic dress and Kate Greenaway-inspired children's smocks (Topliss, 2021). A dress originally worn by Whetu Tirikatene-Sullivan, New Zealand's first Māori woman cabinet minister, reworks ngutu kaka or kaka beak plant designs from kōwhaiwhai—whare nui (meeting house) rafter patterns—in eye-catching embroidery. Tirikatene-Sullivan incorporated many elements of traditional patterns and colour into her clothing and commissioned a large number of garments incorporating Māori motifs by contemporary artists. A fun, possibly even silly re-interpretation of men's sleeping attire, was a green paisley nightshirt and nightcap from the hippie 1970s (Figure 3.5).

Figure 3.5 Interpretation section detail, *Fashion FWD >> Disruption through Design*, Otago Museum, Dunedin, New Zealand, 2021.

Figure 3.6 Sculpture section of *Fashion FWD >> Disruption through Design*, Otago Museum, Dunedin, New Zealand, 2021.

3.9 Sculpture: Disruption of silhouettes

Form superseded function in *Fashion FWD*'s sculptural section. Improbable silhouettes have been fashionable at various times and emerging designers have taken inspiration from those, but also from architecture and modern art (Figure 3.6).

Creating a moving sculpture from many layers of fabric shapes stitched onto a base undergarment allowed Roxanna Zamani to explore her own blending of culture and lifestyle (iD Awards, 2010). She cut her shapes to represent architectural silhouettes from European and Middle Eastern buildings she knew in her past, finding the expression of opposites that occurred such as straight, curved; masculine, feminine; soft, hard; concealing, revealing, served as useful metaphors.

Sohong Lim was inspired by American artist Romare Bearden, who mixed collage, cubism and abstract expressionism in his works. Sohong recycled old military bags and vintage fabrics, deconstructing, patchworking, collaging and sculpting them into very wearable garments (iD Awards, 2013).

Artist Lucio Fontana provided Vedrana Mastela with the impetus to experiment with perforating fabrics for her collection (iD Awards, 2012). In doing so, she created new textures, visual and tactile sensations and new creative meanings in her resultant garments.

Yvonne Lin was keen to make clothes that moved away from the traditional shapes western fashion usually works with. Stimulated by Michael Hansmeyer's ornamented columns, she transformed pleather into sculptural forms to adorn the human body.

Examples of sculptural fashion from Otago Museum's collection included an 1820s dress with gigot sleeves and wide hem circumference that help emphasise a narrow waist, a 1950s petticoat with a blow-up tube to create skirt volume, a sensational bubble-skirted cocktail dress by London design house Frank Usher in which cut and drape are assisted by wire at the hem and a 1953 Susan Small five gore skirt with sculpted surface design achieved thanks to heat setting technology.

3.10 Transformation: Disruption through clever reuse

Found or repurposed materials have been metamorphosed by past and present designers, giving new life and fresh perspectives to unwanted or utilitarian objects, fabric samples and animal skins, for example (Figure 3.7).

Justine Tindley transformed second-hand garments into new forms of fashion (iD Awards, 2014). A 1980s leather jacket combined with a 1950s man's suit became a coat; knitwear became leggings and a jumper. Sustainability as well as honouring the former wearers of these clothes motivates her creativity.

Global nomadism inspired Cassandra Casas Rojas to create clothing that transforms into life necessities such as a backpack, tent or sleeping bag (iD Awards, 2019). Her oversized dress in *Fashion FWD* came complete with tent pegs and ropes so it can be pitched for shelter.

Seeing the waste that is dead stock in the apparel industry stimulated Paul Castro Alvarez to design 'Amassment', a collection that combined multiples into compelling garments (iD Awards, 2017). The example in *Fashion FWD* cleverly mutated men's long-sleeved white shirts into high fashion.

Red deer were introduced to New Zealand in the 19th century and quickly became a destructive nuisance, killing off native flora and destroying bird

Figure 3.7 Transformation section of *Fashion FWD >> Disruption through Design*, Otago Museum, Dunedin, New Zealand, 2021.

habitats. Culls were organised in the 1930s. A coat in Otago Museum's collection was made from the skins of the very young fawns from such a cull in 1939. While we abhor cruelty to animals and question farming animals just for their pelts, it does make sense to use such skins rather than just destroy them from a sustainability standpoint.

A 1970s belted reversible coat offered a different kind of transformation. Red and black poplin were precisely constructed into both a red coat with black edging and a black coat with red edging by Gus Fisher's El Jay label in Auckland, New Zealand.

Hei tiki have become iconic emblems of both the Māori people and New Zealand. They are almost always carved from pounamu, New Zealand nephrite (sometimes known as greenstone), and are prized Māori ornaments, passed down through generations as family taonga (treasures). The production of fake hei tiki in various materials, by non-Māori, has a long history. Mass-produced plastic imitations became part of the souvenir trade in the 20th century. In the 1960s and 1970s, green plastic hei tiki were given to passengers on New Zealand's national airline. However, contemporary Māori artists such as Rangi Kipa (Te Ātiawa, Taranaki, Ngāti Tama ki te Tauihu)[7] and Joseph Te Wharau Moore McEnteer (Ngati Maru, Ngaati Whanaunga, Ngati Tamatera and Scottish) are rearticulating the conversation while working with traditional symbolic connotations. Joe Te Wharau is passionate about exploring future tech, indigenous art forms and unique expressions. His hei tiki are 3D printed from nylon polyamide and have embedded microchips that allow the wearer to save whakapapa (lineage, family history) and other aspects of their lives digitally.

Imaginatively recycling fabric samples and sewing notions provided further examples of transformation in *Fashion FWD: Disruption through Design*. Hexagonal patches of many different fabrics were beautifully hand pieced by Frances Eames in the 1940s–1950s to create a dressing gown, one of many she made, and textile artist Vita Cochran transformed op-shop finds of zippers and gloves and fashion designer offcuts into quirky and desirable handbags.

3.11 Wellbeing: Disruption to improve lives

The 'Wellbeing' section of *Fashion FWD: Disruption through Design* was dedicated to those exploring issues affecting people and the planet. Emerging fashion designers created collections that gave voice to concerns about emotional health and mental wellbeing, imprisonment and physical constraint; to hopes for multiculturalism, social harmony and tolerance for the beliefs of others; and concern for the environment; while examples from the Museum collection demonstrated decades of concern with the physical health of communities. According to various researchers, there is a lack of conceptual clarity about what wellbeing is and how it works (Baldwin, Sinclair and Simons, 2021) and it is a clear example of a complex social phenomenon (Maggino and Alaimo, 2021). The Wellbeing Institute at the University of Cambridge defines wellbeing as 'positive and sustainable characteristics which enable individuals and organisations to thrive and flourish',[8] while others argue that because it is a social and cultural construct, it is difficult to quantify and categorise.[9] Many peoples see it as holistic, 'encompassing everything in and around the person including family and kin, environment, land, sea and waterways, as well as spirituality and culture' (Sutherland and Adams, 2019, p.49). Despite these issues of definition, we realised that some designers, both now and in the past, have had definite ideas about how clothes could improve physical health and aid people to feel good about themselves and others and our planet. The process of designing for others can also enhance the designer's wellbeing by stimulating emotions such as 'interest, joy, contentment and pride' (de Wet and Tselepis, 2020, p.352). We included pieces from three emerging designer's collections and five pieces from Otago Museum collections in the Wellbeing section (Figure 3.8).

George Clarke's streetwear collection 'Freedom of Expression' was shown at the 2019 iD International Emerging Designer show, winning the Blunt Umbrella Design Award. For him, inspiration came from uniforms and clothes found in institutions that deny people freedom, such as prisons or mental hospitals. His young son's free and expressive drawing was turned into a print on some textiles. He continues to design sustainable streetwear, upcycling and reworking existing items to create new, unique silhouettes, prints and textures.

Figure 3.8 Wellbeing section of *Fashion FWD >> Disruption through Design* exhibition, Otago Museum, Dunedin, New Zealand, 2021.

A four piece from Ilham Ismail's 'Universal Fingerprints' collection of 2016 celebrated multiculturalism and peaceful co-existence and offers to assist spiritual wellbeing. Her prints alluded to colours and designs found in the architecture of both mosques and Christian churches and the garments are highly fashionable while also being modest. A University of Technology Sydney graduate, Ilham Ismail, has since started an eponymous brand targeting the emerging market of Muslim women living in western countries who want to keep up with contemporary trends and textile innovation while maintaining adherence to a modest dress code. As her website says, the label creates high-end-street-style fashion with a focus on fabric embellishment and innovative textiles which makes it appealing for anyone who loves fashion.

Concern for nature, the environment and poverty gave Rokaiya Ahmed Purna the impetus to combine ideas, textiles and garment forms from indigenous communities in her country, Bangladesh. In 'Urban Tribal', handspun and woven khadi fabrics coloured with natural dyes, mixed with denim, silk and wool accents. Responsible, sustainable, eco-friendly slow fashion won her an Entrepreneurial Prize at the iD Awards in 2018. She continues to produce fashion fusing traditional Bangladeshi textile culture with the country's creative economic and sustainability goals, while working to empower women and girls.

From Otago Museum's collections a baby gown recalled the efforts of Sir Frederic Truby King to improve mother and infant's health and decrease infant mortality in the early 20th century. He established the Society for the Promotion of the Health of Women and Children in 1907, which became known as the Plunket Society, still operating today. A network of

Karitane hospitals and nurses that focused on care of babies was established throughout New Zealand and helped significantly reduce infant deaths. The pattern for this baby gown was supplied to expectant mothers and others by Karitane nurses, so many of New Zealand's 20th-century babies were clothed in these warm, then easy-care, but non-restrictive garments.

Physical exercise and freedom from restrictive lifestyles are symbolised in a wool gabardine-divided skirt from the early 20th century. Women were starting to ride horses astride and bicycles in public, despite often being ridiculed by men and boys. While we do not know the name of the maker of this skirt, dressmakers and tailors could make skirts like this: culottes with skirt flaps that fasten closed in front and back so decorum is maintained when dismounted.

Another kind of freedom from restriction is portrayed by the boxer shorts in *Fashion Forward*. There was a popular theory in the 20th century that such underpants were beneficial for men's sperm counts as the loose fit allowed air to circulate around the genitals. Scientific testing has resolved that whether men wear tight or loose underpants makes little difference to overall fertility, but for men with low sperm counts boxer shorts may help a little. We choose pairs featuring the Phantom just for fun!

Finally we included a recently identified tea-gown from the collection, made from a woollen tapestry weave paisley shawl. Tea-gowns allowed an hour or so of respite from the restrictive corset, time to sit and breathe normally before donning evening or dinner dress. Not many such tea-gowns exist in museum collections in New Zealand as far as we know, since they were semi-private dress worn within the home. The social pages in local newspapers mention them from the late 1870s onwards and ladies' columns include drawings in the 1890s when this one was made. Otago Museum has a few dresses that may have functioned as tea-gowns, reflecting the fact that Dunedin was New Zealand's biggest, richest, most industrialised city at the time, with vigorous businesses, a university and a mix of settlers. There were a significant number of large houses where tea-gown wearing may have occurred.

3.12 In conclusion: Emerging designers as responsible fashion makers and disruptors

Many designers, past and present, work within systems and constraints of their times that may prevent them from straying too far from norms, but the stories the emerging designers sent us and those from the godmothers told of their desires to use their fashion practice to create change and break moulds and rules. The iD Awards finalists included in *Fashion FWD: Disruption through Design* are breaking the mould in their career choices, using their personal cultural capital to change what they do, how and why they do it and even the vocabulary they use to discuss it. All are conscious of the harm the fashion industry has done to people and the planet and choose to operate in more mindful ways. They are aware that sustainable strategies need to be embedded in the design and production process from its conception. They know that they cannot change the fashion world on their own, but by working in a more sustainable way and helping to enable consumer choices for such values, they can contribute. Many are not interested in working in large-scale fashion manufacturing, or developing fashion empires, but are adopting different microscale business models, designing and making their own fashion, individually or collaboratively, following a more sustainable slow fashion pathway.

Using multiple channels such as Instagram and online marketplaces, they can reach and even educate diverse markets. Some are targeting groups that have been marginalised by mainstream fashion (Barry, 2021). For example, one is producing modest fashion aimed at Islamic women and at least two make fashion for queer and trans people. Others use preloved materials in their production of children's wear or streetwear and one is working with her local textile communities to empower them by designing fashion from their fabrics. Choosing a slow, sustainable and environmentally friendly approach to their fashion almost inevitably means they need to be agile, supplementing this creativity with other fashion roles such as consulting, photography, writing or working for others in production or retail and some have chosen other jobs outside fashion. A few have become fashion or materials teachers, inspiring others to become sustainable creators and some work for established fashion companies encouraging change from the inside.

While we don't yet know what 'a holistic, flourishing, responsible fashion and textiles system for the 21st century might look like' (Whitty, 2021), we do know that fashion can refigure itself to become part of 'a utopic remedy',[10] as long as there is the will to do this. These contributors to *Fashion FWD: Disruption through Design* have shown that will and flexibility by adopting slow-fashion methods and business models, upcycling materials, working locally and sustainably to protect their own mental and physical health as well as that of their colleagues and environments. They are well aware of the multiple consequences of the global fashion industry and are keen to adapt, knowing that all small steps towards saving the world are worth doing. By helping to empower and educate consumers of fashion, they reinforce the ability of wearers to drive change. Will the consequences of the Covid-19 pandemic and the impacts of climate change, hate crimes and new wars provide further impetus for them and the whole fashion system to reconfigure to benefit rather than harm cultures, environments and human health in ways that still allow business and economies to flourish?

Notes

1   blacklognz.blogspot.com/2011/10/whats-undone-in-dunedin.html.
2   See www.moneyhub.co.nz/top-new-zealand-fashion-designers.html and https://nzfashionmuseum.org.nz/entrepreneurial-women-in-new-zealand-fashion/   for more examples and information.

3 www.nytimes.com/2021/02/10/world/asia/new-zealand-rawiri-waititi-tie.html
4 shop@charmainereveley.co.nz email, 9/11/21.
5 2020 iD Awards https://youtu.be/VDdZ-RaYl2w and 2021 iD Awards https://youtu.be/BXnOXhutV-o
6 The exhibition can be viewed online at https://my.matterport.com/show/?m=BAHWQ82aszM.
7 www.maoriart.org.nz/rangi-kipa.html
8 www.wellbeing.group.cam.ac.uk/
9 www.healthknowledge.org.uk
10 www.uantwerpen.be/en/conferences/responsible-fashion/

References

Baldwin, D., Sinclair, J., & Simons, G. (2021). What is mental wellbeing? *British Journal of Psychiatry Open, 7*(S1), S236–S236. doi: 10.1192/bjo.2021.631

Barry, B. (2021). Fashion in a state of emergency. In *Fashion FWD: Disruption through Design Exhibition Publication* (pp.14–16). Dunedin: Otago Museum.

Barton, M. (2021). iD emerging designer awards. In *Fashion FWD: Disruption through Design Exhibition Publication*, (pp.24–27). Dunedin: Otago Museum.

Barton, M., Malthus, J., & White, M. (2021). *Texts throughout Fashion FWD: Disruption through Design Exhibition Publication*. Dunedin: Otago Museum.

Beckett, T. (2022). Two fashion sustainability educators on whether you can be eco-friendly and still shop fast fashion. www.stuff.co.nz/life-style/style/300629485/two-fashion-sustainability-educators-on-whether-you-can-be-ecofriendly-and-still-shop-fast-fashion

Cambridge University Wellbeing Group (s.d.). Wellbeing. www.wellbeing.group.cam.ac.uk/

Day, K. (2022). London beckons Dunedin designer. *Otago Daily Times*, 15 June. www.odt.co.nz/lifestyle/london-beckons-city-designer

de Wet, A. J. C., & Tselepis, T. J. (2020). Towards enterprising design: A creativity framework supporting the fluency, flexibility and flow of student fashion designers. *International Journal of Fashion Design, Technology and Education, 13*(3), 352–363.

Drichel, S. (2011). Unpacking my wardrobe. In Smith N., and H. Radner (Eds.), *NOM*d: The art of fashion* (pp.45–49). Dunedin: University of Otago; Centre for Research on National Identity.

Gyde, C., & McNeill, L. S. (2021). Fashion rental: Smart business or ethical folly? *Sustainability 13*, 8888. https://doi.org/10.3390/su13168888

Hammonds, L., Lloyd Jenkins, D., & Regnault, C. (2010) *The Dress Circle: New Zealand Fashion Design since 1940*. Auckland: Godwit.

Health Knowledge. (s.d.). Concepts of health, wellbeing and illness, and the aetiology of illness: Section 3. Concepts of health and wellbeing. www.healthknowledge.org.uk

iD Dunedin. (s.d.). iD Dunedin Fashion. www.idfashion.co.nz

Koch, K., (2019). Clothing upcycling, Textile waste and the ethics of the global fashion industry. *ZoneModa Journal 9*(2), 173–184.

Lassig, A. (2010) *New Zealand Fashion Design*. Wellington: Te Papa Press.

Maggino, F., & Alaimo, L. S. (2021). Complexity and wellbeing: Measurement and analysis. In Bruni, L., A. Smerilli, and D. de Rosa (Eds.), *A Modern Guide to the Economics of Happiness* (Ch.7, pp. 113–128). Cheltenham: Edward Elgar Publishing. DOI:https://doi.org/10.4337/9781788978767.00016

Malthus, J. (2007) One man's fantasy: The Eden Hore collection of high and exotic fashion garments. In Labrum, B., F. McKergow, & S. Gibson (Eds.), *Looking Flash: Clothing in Aotearoa New Zealand* (pp. 206–241, 270–272). Auckland: Auckland University Press.

Malthus, J. (2015). A Darker Eden. In New Zealand Fashion Museum with Otago Polytechnic School of Design (2015) *A Darker Eden: Fashion from Dunedin* (p. 7). Auckland.

Malthus, J. (2020). Rosaria Hall. Unpublished manuscript delivered as a talk in The Luck of The Irish series, Toitū Otago Settlers Museum.

Malthus, J., McCaw, C., Glen, L., & Barton, M., (2015). Interplay and inter-place: A collaborative exhibition addressing place-based identity in fashion design. In Popovic, V., A. Blackler, D-B. Luh, N. Nimkulrat, B. Kraal, and Y Nagai, (Eds.), *IASDR 2015 Interplay Proceedings* (pp. 1396–1414). ISBN -978-0-646-94318-3

Malthus, J., & White, M., (2021). Fashion forward … and back, in *Fashion FWD: Disruption through Design Exhibition Publication* (pp. 22–23). Dunedin: Otago Museum.

Malthus, J., White, M., & Barton, M. (2021). Together: The collaborative curatorial practices of a museum curator, dress historian and fashion design educator. *Scope (Art and Design)*, 22, 102–110.

McEwan, L. (2017). Investment piece: Co-design strategies to support the emerging designer sector of the New Zealand fashion industry. *Scope*, 15, 71–80.

McQuillan, H. (2019). *Zero waste design thinking*. Licentiate Thesis. Edited by L. Hallnäs. University of Borås. http://hb.diva-portal.org/smash/record.jsf?pid= diva2%3A1316575&dswid=-628

McQuillan, H., Archer-Martin, J., Menzies, G., Bailey, J., Kane, K., & Fox Derwin, E. (2018). Make/use: A system for open source, user-modifiable, zero waste fashion practice. *Fashion Practice 10*(1), 7–33.

Richards, H. (2021). Practices of cultural collectivity: Style activism, Miromoda and Māori fashion in Aotearoa New Zealand. *Critical Studies in Fashion & Beauty*, 12(1), 131–149.

Smith, N. and Radner, H. (2011), NOM*d: Conceptual couture in Dunedin. A study in visual style, from New Zealand to the international scene and back again. In Smith N., and H. Radner (Eds.), *NOM*d: The Art of Fashion* (pp. 13–34). Dunedin: University of Otago; Centre for Research on National Identity.

Sutherland, S., & Adams, M. (2019). Building on the definition of social and emotional wellbeing: An Indigenous (Australian, Canadian, and New Zealand) viewpoint. *ab-Original: Journal of Indigenous Studies and First Nations and First Peoples' Cultures*, 3(1), 48–72. DOI: 10.5325/aboriginal.3.1.0048

Tilson-Scoble, V. (2017). *The Misalignment between the expectations of fashion students, fashion tertiary educators, and the fashion Industry*. Thesis submitted for MA degree, University of Otago, Dunedin, NZ.

Topliss, A. (2021). *The Hidden History of the Smock Frock*. London: Bloomsbury Visual Arts.

Whitty, J. (2021). Fashion design for holistic systems in sustainable design. In Muthu, S. S., and M. A. Gardetti (Eds.), *Textiles and Fashion* (pp. 1–22). Singapore: Springer.

Chapter 4

Provenance and Production in Scotland's Fashion Sector

Shifting Stories

Karen Cross, Josie Steed and Yang Jiang

4.1 Introduction

Augmented Fashion is an Arts and Humanities Research Council (AHRC)-funded 36-month interdisciplinary research project involving academics and industry from the fashion, textiles and computing science disciplines in both the UK and China. The project seeks to explore ways to educate the consumer about the craftsmanship, heritage, value and sustainability of traditional fashion and textile products, using immersive technologies and Human-Computer Interactive (HCI) applications to engage with new generations of audiences. Research by Cross, Steed and Jiang (2021) established that fashion brands were using augmented (AR) and virtual (VR) technologies in three ways: creating virtual changing room try-on experiences, showing product and engagement in social life. There was little evidence of textile or fashion brands using immersive technologies to communicate craftsmanship or provenance, suggesting a 'missed opportunity in using human–computer interactions to communicate culture and place and in re-humanizing the making of clothing in the minds of contemporary consumers' (Cross, Steed and Jiang, 2021, p.489) by emotionally connecting maker and consumer, overcoming the invisibilisation of the producer and place of production. This presents an interesting opportunity to explore how immersive technologies can help to shape a sustainable future for the traditional textiles and slow fashion styles (Lynas, 2010; Strauss and Fuad-Luke, 2008; Fletcher, 2007) inherent in Scotland's fashion and textile industry and aligns with Textiles Scotland's (2016) assertion that a new cross-sector perspective with new ways of working together is required to see Scottish textiles as part of a high-value manufacturing sector. Given the scale of the fashion and textile industry worldwide and at a time when sustainability is high on the global agenda (Ahmed et al., 2019), the findings from this research will be important in helping to deliver UN Sustainable Development Goal (SDG) 12; ensure sustainable consumption and production patterns (United Nations, 2015).

DOI: 10.4324/9781032659053-4

4.2 Textiles, fashion, sustainability and Scotland

The scope of the fashion and textile industry is extensive; if it were ranked alongside individual countries' gross domestic product (GDP), the global fashion industry would represent the world's fifth-largest economy. It is the second biggest worldwide economic activity for intensity of trade, employing over 60 million workers in developing countries (Corner, 2014). In Scotland, there are approx. 550 companies employing around 9,000 people (Scottish Enterprise, 2021). Overall, 55% of Scottish textile companies have fewer than ten employees (Wilson, 2015) and Scottish textile jobs support the prosperity of many rural communities (Textiles Scotland, 2016), for example, the Harris Tweed hand-weavers in the Outer Hebrides. Scotland's traditional tweeds and tartans, cashmere and woollens continue to survive today, largely through small- to medium-sized enterprises (SMEs) producing luxury products with a focus on value rather than volume (Textiles Scotland, 2016). A 2015 study criticised the Scottish textile sector for lacking an overarching strategic vision in relation to the circular economy (Wilson, 2015). The research advised a focus on 'provenance, traceability, durability and quality'. In 2016, Textiles Scotland identified 'sustainable development' and 'environmental excellence' (2016, p.9) as a key opportunity for the Scottish textiles sector.

Increasing automation in the fashion and textile industry, moving away from artisan techniques involving the human hand, brings risk of losing intangible cultural heritage and craft skills. In recent history, the public have largely become unaware of how their clothing is produced, often showing little interest in the sources of materials and the manufacturing processes that generate them. In response, Strauss and Fuad-Luke's *reveal* slow design principle advocates revealing 'materials that can easily be overlooked in an artifact's existence or creation' (2008, p.3). Fast and effectively disposable fashion has seen clothing reduced to transient items, worn for a short period of time, then discarded (Serdari, 2018; Crewe, 2017), with the UK buying more clothes per capita than other European countries (Environmental Audit Commission [EAC], 2019). Fast fashion has pushed prices downwards, moving textile and clothing production to low-cost labour countries and decimating the traditional Scottish quality textile economy. The surviving Scottish textile companies find it difficult to attract young people to work with them (Textiles Scotland, 2016), leading to a skills shortage within the industry, recognised as a significant barrier to growth in UK fashion and textiles (Learning and Skills Council 2007). Fast fashion also drives consumer demand for newness, uses resources that are finite and potentially damaging to the environment and creates excessive and unnecessary landfill waste. The pressure to move towards a more sustainable fashion and textile industry has grown, with the UK government's EAC (2019) publishing a damning report on fashion and sustainability.

4.3 Methodology

As part of the Augmented Fashion project, a series of workshops were facilitated in October 2020; this chapter discusses the emergent themes from two of them, the 'Redesigning for Creative Recovery' (RCR) and 'Sustainable Fashion and Textiles in Scotland' (SFT) workshops. The RCR workshop was designed in direct response to the Covid-19 pandemic; a timely offer given Scottish Enterprise's August–December 2020 survey of Scottish textile companies, which confirmed that 82% of them saw Covid-19 as their biggest challenge. The SFT workshop was part of the Augmented Fashion project's original remit, which includes a focus on sustainability. The workshop participants and presenters comprised a purposive, key informant sample (Marshall, 1996), with participants invited based on their relevance to the Augmented Fashion research project. The RCR workshop brought together fashion, textile and creative industries' SMEs in Scotland, impacted by the Covid-19 pandemic. A total of 20 SMEs participated, discussing their experiences and issues encountered during lockdown. The SFT workshop invited three Scottish sustainable fashion and textile SMEs (Figure 4.1) and a circular economy consultant to present their sustainability stories, successes, experiences and aspirations. The workshop was attended by 55 participants, providing an opportunity for knowledge dissemination and exchange.

The workshops were 2 hours in length and delivered via Zoom due to Covid-19 lockdown restrictions. The workshops were recorded, providing rich, thick qualitative data for analysis, utilising an interpretive ontological worldview (Creswell, 2014). Three passes of the data were completed

Figure 4.1 Sustainable fashion and textiles in Scotland SMEs.

(Hanson, Balmer and Giardino, 2011), with narratives subject to initial coding, acknowledged as the first stage of a grounded theory approach (Saldana, 2016). Initially, these codes were in vivo, named using words from the narratives and preserving the participant voices (Richards, 2009). Pass two of the data compared and triangulated the findings from both workshops, clustering the initial codes into focussed codes (Charmaz, 2006) resulting in the following sections: Consumption, Production and Innovation. The final pass of the data builds towards more overarching theoretical explanations grounded in the data gathered, presented in the Conclusion section.

4.4 Discussion: Consumption, consumer awareness and citizen ethos

The RCR participants discussed the negative and positive impacts of Covid-19 on the Scottish fashion and textile sector. Island-based locations such as Shetland are highly dependent on tourism custom, brought to the island by cruise ships; these sales disappeared. Sales to tourists during the buoyant summer season sustain many craft practitioners and small businesses through long winters; participants described enduring 'three winters', with no summer sales to compensate. Physical retail sites were closed for a period, then opened with restrictions on how many customers could enter the store and limited opportunities to try on items, reducing both the hedonistic Romanticism (Campbell, 1989) and functional convenience of bricks-and-mortar shopping. Scottish SMEs supplying global clients through complex supply chains saw order books shrink, diminishing confidence and leading to some redundancies. On a more positive note, several participants noted that some consumers seemed to have more disposable income and time, noting engagement from new consumers via direct connections through online platforms. Higher engagement with ecommerce platforms and social media facilitated new routes to market for those businesses previously reliant on face-to-face selling, with one participant confirming, 'there has been a real shift to selling online and through social media'. For some participants, this necessitated a steep learning curve in terms of digital skills.

Consumption shifts due to lockdown lifestyle changes saw increased interest in comfortable, colourful and cosy products, crafted in local communities; products that epitomise Scottish fashion and textiles (Figure 4.2). Participants also noted increased consumer awareness of environmental issues and more interest in better made clothing with greater longevity. It could be that Covid-19 has engendered a more compassionate purchaser, in line with Geiger and Keller's (2017) study that links compassion to sustainable purchase behaviours. These involve both altruistic values (concern for others) and biospheric values (concern for nature), which lead to pro-environmental behaviours. Similarly, in the SFT workshop, presenters noted the increased desire among consumers for transparency, with certifications

Figure 4.2 Colourful, comfortable, cozy and crafted.

such as the National Living Wage, the Standard 100 by Oeko-tex and the Global Organic Textile Standard providing a form of reassurance. Joan Johnston, founder of the Ava Innes duvet brand, noted the importance of recognising what the customer is looking for. For Ava Innes, quality of sleep was identified as a key focus for the consumer, hence marketing activities prioritise this aspect along with the brand's sustainability messages.

In terms of consumption, social stigma was identified as a barrier to the re-use of clothing by circular economy consultant Lynn I Wilson. Teamed with the socio-economic pressure to shop for new products, finding ways to engage with the consumer and change consumption habits is a recognised and on-going issue. Scottish weaving mill Prickly Thistle uses social media to share stories of their sustainability ethos, employees and ethical customers, challenging clothing consumption habits and creating a like-minded online community. Knowledge exchange was seen as key to support a shift from a consumer ethos to a citizen ethos, with citizens defined by sociologist Bauman (2012) as those committed to the common interests of society. Prickly Thistle urges consumers to 'wear their values' and buy from brands that reflect their beliefs. The role of social desirability bias was discussed, acknowledging the attitude- or intention-behaviour gaps identified in several previous studies on sustainable clothing consumption (Jacobs et al., 2018; Park and Lin, 2018; Hassan, Shiu and Shaw, 2016). The UK's status as an individualistic society (Hofstede Insights, 2021) underpins gaps in sustainable purchase behaviour, where individualisation leads to a lack of solidarity, less commitment to society and more concern with individual, personal problems (Bauman, 2012). A citizen ethos towards clothing consumption could include sharing, renting and borrowing business models, encouraging consumers to re-circulate items in their wardrobes that they never wear. Prickly Thistle prioritises 'buy less' messages and both Prickly Thistle and Ava Innes stress the longevity of their products, directly challenging disposability and throwaway attitudes. Empowering consumers to become more involved with and responsible for the whole lifecycle of their clothes, shifting mind-sets from linear to circular models of use (Vehmas et al., 2018), also engenders a citizen ethos. Lynn I Wilson highlighted an interesting effect of the Covid-19 lockdown and reduced access to retail; the development of informal sharing systems on social media, where people posted items online that they were willing to pass on to those in need. Although there are existing models of resale (such as Depop and Vinted), this more informal sharing system fully embraces a citizen ethos.

The key issue the RCR workshop participants identified was the uncertainty around how shifts in consumption might evolve beyond the pandemic, leading them into reactionary practices rather than strategic planning. Thus, the concept of *the reactive practitioner* emerged. The SFT presenters were more certain; these *reflective practitioners* were focussed on their sustainability ethos and practices despite the challenges of Covid-19.

4.5 Discussion: Production, provenance and change

Reactionary practices were clear in the RCR workshop participants' production during this time. Access to materials was disrupted by both availability and cash flow. Some participants described working with new materials, often more locally sourced. Others adapted their product offer in response to constraints, for example, by pivoting their product offer from knitted items of clothing to selling yarns for hand-knitting instead. As volumes of production fell, some practitioners took the opportunity to embrace the flexibility of shorter runs, evolve new products more quickly and prioritise more sustainable production practices. Participants noted increased interest in provenance from some consumers, with details of material, origin and authenticity being sought (Figure 4.3), again aligning with Strauss and Fuad-Luke's (2008) *reveal* slow design principle and playing to the Scottish textile industry's strong reputation for the use of natural fibres, traditional textile techniques and high quality.

Production was also discussed in the SFT workshop, with Ava Innes noting that the source and journeys of her product components were a key consideration. Prickly Thistle focusses on what they can do now and what they can influence in the future. For example, there are limited raw materials that

Figure 4.3 Local, natural and authentic.

come from Scotland, so they are developing their own natural raw materials, taking into consideration the carbon cost of their supply chain sources and noting, 'it's cheaper to go elsewhere but that's not the point. We're committed to authenticity, integrity and provenance around our product'. Prickly Thistle also described their use of certifications to communicate their sustainable credentials, describing these as 'badges of honor'.

Linked with the shifts in consumption, the RCR participants were unsure about these rapid and reactionary changes to their production and expressed a desire to get back to more reflective and strategic planning. The rapid changes and uncertainty driven by Covid-19 (El Keshky, Basyouni and Al Sabban, 2020) accelerated the already unsettling speed of change in contemporary society (Bauman, 2012), underpinning the participants' uncertainty. Hirsh, Mar and Peterson state that uncertainty is experienced as anxiety, noting the 'critical importance' (2012, p.1) of managing uncertainty for an individual's well-being. Intolerance of uncertainty is linked to fear of the unknown (Carleton, 2016; Boswell et al., 2013), which many of these SMEs now face. The scale of change was highlighted by one participant, who stated, 'I am looking at making different things, working with different materials, offering different products with different price points, marketed in new ways… all this change means my story as a creative practitioner has had to shift'. Some participants had taken a more cautious approach, avoiding change where possible and waiting to see how shifts might settle before committing to change. A stronger narrative emerged from the SFT workshop, with presenters focussed on their sustainable strategies as a long-term commitment. Prickly Thistle stressed the importance of 'ability and willingness to change and adapt and to really embrace fear and not let that hold you back from what you're really passionate and committed to do'. Lippitt, Watson and Westley's (1958) Phases of Change theory posits that change is more likely to lead to stability if it spreads and is widely accepted. This suggests that the spread of customers seeking sustainably made products, combined with businesses adopting more sustainable production, could *evolve* (Struass and Fuad-Luke, 2008) into increased adoption of sustainable fashion and textile products, acknowledging slow design principles as agents of change.

Zero waste emerged as a theme within the SFT workshop, taking several forms: avoiding waste, regenerating waste and legislating for waste reduction. In terms of avoiding waste, zero waste pattern cutting was discussed and innovators in this field were identified, including Holly McQuillan, Timo Rissanen and Alison Gwilt. Prickly Thistle explained that they design out waste from the pattern cutting table, forming garments from block shapes and avoiding the use of buttons and zips, stating, 'it's been really exciting for us to bring that [zero waste design] to a finished product'. They have a minimum packaging policy, with all packaging made from recycled materials and garment care details provided via their website rather than being printed.

Loose yarn is composted on-site. Ava Innes regenerates the forgotten, coarse cashmere guard hairs, traditionally seen as a by-product of the cashmere industry, to create washable duvets, ensuring longevity to a product that sees 7.2 million cubic meters of duvets ending up in landfill every year, stating, 'we're just trying to do things better'. The UK's impending 'extended employer responsibility' scheme was highlighted (EAC, 2019), although it is not yet clear how this will impact the textiles and clothing sector.

In the SFT workshop, the importance of people in the production of more sustainable products was highlighted. Prickly Thistle focusses on creating employment in the Scottish Highlands, stating, 'this is a labor-intensive business model we're building'. They work with both Skills Development Scotland and the UK Fashion and Textile Association to develop their employees' skills. Founder, Clare Campbell, stated, 'I wanted to create jobs, which was my big focus, one of my personal drivers' and, 'we have people in our process and we look after them', noting that mass manufacture can remove the passion, pride and association with skill and craft in the making of clothing and textiles. For Prickly Thistle, people matter more than mass production or volume sales, addressing UN SDG 8, 'full and productive employment and decent work for all' (United Nations, 2015).

4.6 Discussion: Innovation, connection and communication

The RCR participants felt that innovation had been demanded in all aspects of their practice, in their production methods, end products, marketing, communication and distribution. There was sense of embracing a growth mindset, with one participant stating, 'what I've learned is don't be afraid to ask. Get out there, talk to as many people as you can to challenge what is known'. Upskilling, particularly digital upskilling was identified as an important form of innovation. For many of them, running meetings online, engaging with ecommerce platforms and marketing through social media were skills that needed to be acquired or enhanced speedily. Thus, an unintended benefit of the pandemic has been to accelerate digital skills acquisition and close a recognised digital skills gap (Scottish Government, 2021). Participants appreciated digital platforms as a means to communicate authenticity, noting the sustainability agenda as a driver of innovation in their practice due to pandemic-induced heightened consumer interest in the circular economy, aligning with the findings of Alexa, Apetrei and Sapena (2021). Again, many participants described their innovative practices as short-term, reactive solutions to immediate problems. Participants elucidated the challenge of this type of innovation, with one participant noting 'to be innovative and to innovate you have to be resilient … that requires inner energy and looking after your mental health'. This effort and energy required to be resilient aligns with El Keshky, Basyouni and Al Sabban's (2020) research into the impacts of the pandemic on the sustainability of psychological health and well-being. Several impacts on mental health were discussed by the RCR participants, including the blurred boundaries of home working and home life and the ability to maintain a level of creativity while isolated from peers and the studio environment. Perhaps due to these feelings of isolation, there was a strong desire for connection, with one participant stating, 'across the sector there are amazing stories of innovation, we need to make sure we connect them'. Participants expressed interest in capturing and sharing stories of change and examples of best practice, again aligning with Strauss and Fuad-Luke's (2008) *engage* slow design principle. They expressed a need to be seen as an inter-connected sector, rather than individual creative practitioners working in isolation. Similarly, in the SFT workshop, Joan Johnston, founder of the Ava Innes brand, noted the importance of networking and collaboration, stating that 'being part of a network of other innovators really helped with the drive to keep going'.

Despite the isolation of lockdown, the RCR participants noted the increased ease of connection with other places and people, through participation in webinars and international trade events, which they normally could not afford to attend in terms of time and cost. This aligns with Strauss and Fuad-Luke's *engage* slow design principle, which describes slow design as 'collaborative, relying on sharing, cooperation and transparency of information' (2008, p.6) and El Keshky, Basyouni and Al Sabban's (2020, p.10) recommendation that humanity takes 'a collective approach to avoid unnecessary harm to the environment'. In both workshops, digital routes proved important, providing a direct connection between customer and producer which in turn shifted production towards consumer needs and increased customisation. Allowing consumers an element of participation in the design process enhances a communitarian or citizen ethos (Bauman, 2012), embodying Strauss and Fuad-Luke's (2008) *participate* slow design principle. Indeed, Prickly Thistle elicited participatory responses right from its inception, using crowd-source funding to initiate their Highlands-based mill.

The RCR participants expressed appreciation for being involved in the workshop, noting an enhanced feeling of collective experience through hearing how other practitioners had been affected by the pandemic. The opportunity to share their stories was deemed important, not just in terms of supporting each other but also in the construction of stories about themselves as creative practitioners. Some highlighted how they feel closer to their markets and consumers, recognising that consumers were interested in the stories of their products, practices and brands and that they should probably pay more attention to how they tell those stories. This echoes Textiles Scotland's assertion that Scottish textile brands needed to 'become more customer-focused, more attuned to customer needs' (2016, p.11). This theme also emerged in the SFT workshop, with presenters asking, 'what products can we create in Scotland and what new markets can we create closer to home?'. Prickly Thistle noted that the pandemic had increased their sense of responsibility towards sharing what they had learned, their knowledge and their passion, feeling a need to *engage* (Strauss and Fuad-Luke, 2008) with communities and movements that they felt they could positively impact.

4.7 Conclusion

Scotland's dispersed and often rural fashion and textiles SMEs are increasingly working towards a slow design ethos, based on their provenance of small-scale, high-value, quality products. This is further driven by increasing consumer interest in more local, natural and sustainable products, propelled in part by the Covid-19 pandemic. A further impact of the pandemic was the disruption of supply chains, leading to use of more local sources, diversification of product offer and the disruption of in-person shopping, bringing producers closer to consumers via digital communications and sales. The findings identified two types of practitioners. The *reactive practitioner* is willing to adapt and uses upskilling as a form of innovation, with digital upskilling identified as a significant need. The *reflective practitioner* prefers to wait for shifts to settle before committing to significant change, remaining focussed on their sustainability ethos and practices despite the challenges of Covid-19 and uncertainty around how consumption will evolve post-pandemic.

The importance of storytelling emerged, with stories important to different audiences; stories for *communicating with consumers* and stories for *sharing among SMEs* (see Figure 4.4). For *communicating with consumers*, the importance of digital storytelling in enhancing accessibility, creating connection and overcoming distance was acknowledged. Consumers are showing increased awareness of environmental issues, driving interest in stories related to production, provenance and design. Sharing knowledge, educating and influencing the consumer to make better, slow fashion purchases is vital for a sustainable fashion future, described as a shift from a consumer ethos to a *citizen ethos*. Building a *collaborative community* between brand and consumer enhances engagement, both with the brand and its sustainability messages.

For *sharing among SMEs*, a need to see the creative industries sector as an inter-connected system, not just a set of creative practitioners and makers working in isolation, was deemed important, emphasising *collective experience* and being part of a *collaborative community*, in terms of both business development and the practitioners' personal well-being. Again, the role of digital is key in enabling connections between rural practitioners and access to events that are too far or too costly to travel to. Leveraging digital innovation to share stories of change, sustainability and success is vital to support Scotland's fashion and textile SMEs, especially those in rural locations.

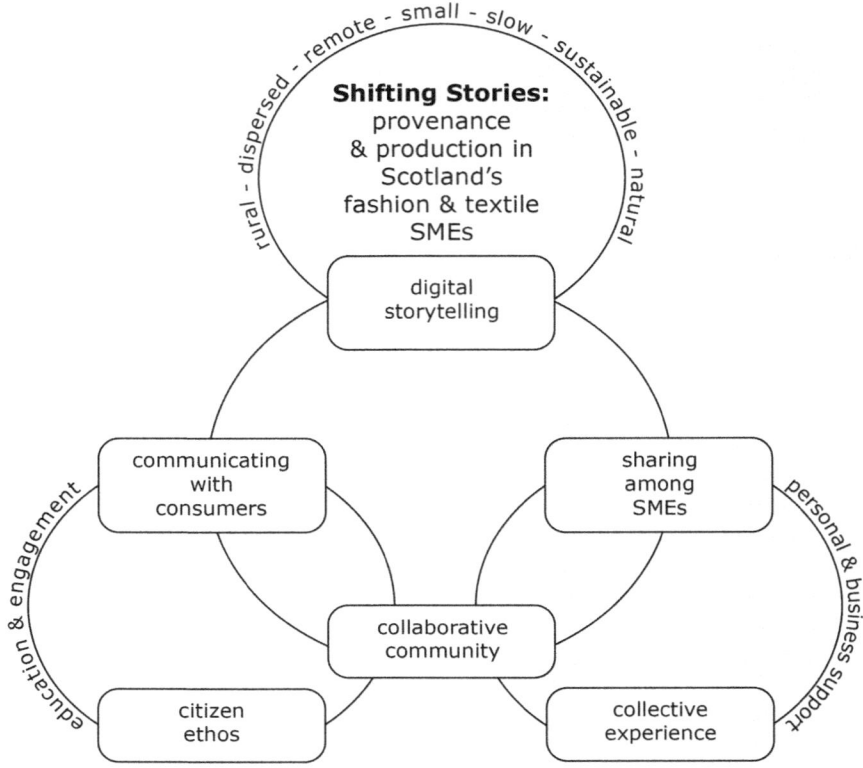

Figure 4.4 Shifting stories: provenance and production in Scotland's fashion and textile SMEs.

In terms of enhancing the sustainable ethos of Scotland's fashion and textile SMEs, this research suggests that there is a need to move the mind-sets of the *reactive practitioners* towards that of *reflective practitioners*. For some, an increased focus on sustainability has been driven by a period of rapid and disruptive change due to Covid-19. Supporting those businesses to transition from uncertainty and reactivity to sound sustainable strategies will be key to capitalising on the few positives to emerge from the pandemic. As noted by Textiles Scotland, 'sustainability is now an expected part of production and marketing—this will only continue to grow in importance for the textiles sector and Scottish companies must emphasise their distinctive quality in this area and tell a compelling story' (2016, p.7). In one participant's words, 'we have seen how everything is connected in new ways, we need to find new ways to tell these stories'.

This research, as part of the Augmented Fashion project, is a work in progress. The findings are limited by the small sample, representing a small proportion of current Scottish fashion and textile SMEs and therefore not generalisable to all. However, using a grounded theory approach, the findings provide direction for the theoretical sampling stage (Charmaz, 2006) of the Augmented Fashion project, which will seek to explore digital storytelling through creating immersive fashion experiences with a sustainability message as a new way to tell sustainability stories and communicate with consumers; providing collaborative and collective experiences and testing the effectiveness of these immersive interactions in encouraging a citizen ethos in fashion and textile consumption.

Acknowledgement

This work was supported by the UKRI, AHRC grant number AH/T011483/1.

References

Ahmed, I., Balchandani, A., Hedrich, S., Poojara, S. and Rolkens, F. (2019). 'The State of Fashion 2020', *Business of Fashion*, 21 November, www.mckinsey.com/industries/retail/our-insights/the-state-of-fashion-   2020-navigating-uncertainty. Accessed 10 January 2020.

Alexa, L., Apetrei, A. and Sapena, J. (2021). 'The COVID-19 Lockdown Effect on the Intention to Purchase Sustainable Brands', *Sustainability*, 13, pp.3241.

Bauman, Z. (2012). *Liquid Modernity*, Cambridge: Polity Press.

Boswell, J.F., Thomson-Ollands, J., Farchione, T.J. and Barlow, D.H. (2013). 'Intolerance of Uncertainty: A Common Factor in the Treatment of Emotional Disorders', *Journal of Clinical Psychology*, 69, pp.630–645.

Campbell, C. (1989). *The Romantic Ethic and the Spirit of Modern Consumerism*, Oxford: Basil Blackwell.

Carleton, R.N. (2016). 'Into the Unknown: A Review and Synthesis of Contemporary Models Involving Uncertainty', *Journal of Anxiety Disorders*, 39:2016, pp.30–43.

Charmaz, K. (2006). *Constructing Grounded Theory: A Practical Guide through Qualitative Analysis*, London: Sage.

Corner, F. (2014). *Why Fashion Matters*, New York: Thames & Hudson.

Creswell, J.W. (2014). *Research Design: Qualitative, Quantitative, and Mixed Methods Approaches*, London: Sage Publications Ltd.

Crewe, L. (2017). *The Geographies of Fashion: Consumption, Space and Value*, London: Bloomsbury.

Cross, K., Steed, J. and Jiang, Y. (2021). 'Harris Tweed; a Glocal Case Study', *Fashion, Style, and Popular Culture*, 8:4, pp.475–494.

El Keshky, M.E.S, Basyouni, S.S. and Al Sabban, A.M. (2020). 'Getting Through COVID-19: The Pandemic's Impact on the Psychology of Sustainability, Quality of Life, and the Global Economy—A Systematic Review', *Frontiers in Psychology*, 11:585897. doi: 10.3389/fpsyg.2020.585897

Environmental Audit Commission (EAC) (2019). 'Fixing Fashion: Clothing Consumption and Sustainability', *House of Commons*, 19 February, https://publi cations.parliament.uk/pa/cm201719/cmselect/cmenvaud/1952/1952. pdf. Accessed 10 October 2019.

Fletcher, K. (2007). 'Slow Fashion', *Ecologist*, 37:5, p.61.

Geiger, S.M. and Keller, J. (2017). 'Shopping for Clothes and Sensitivity to the Suffering of Others: The Role of Compassion and Values in Sustainable Fashion Consumption', *Environment and Behaviour*, 50:10, pp.1119–1144.

Hanson, J.L., Balmer, D.F. and Giardino, A.P. (2011). 'Qualitative Research Methods for Medical Educators', *Academic Paediatrics*, 11:5, pp.375–386.

Hassan, L.M., Shiu, E. and Shaw, D. (2016). 'Who Says There Is an Intention-Behaviour Gap? Assessing the Empirical Evidence of an Intention-Behaviour Gap in Ethical Consumption', *Journal of Business Ethics*, 136:2016, pp.219–236.

Hirsh, J.B., Mar, R.A. and Peterson, J.B. (2012). 'Psychological Entropy: A Framework for Understanding Uncertainty-Related Anxiety', *Psychological Review*, 119:2, pp.304–320.

Hofstede Insights (2021). 'United Kingdom', *Hofstede Insights*, www.hofstede-insig hts.com/country/the-uk/. Accessed 27 September 2021.

Jacobs, K., Petersen, L., Horisch, J. and Battenfeld, D. (2018). 'Green Thinking but Thoughtless Buying? An Empirical Extension of the Value-Attitude-Behaviour Hierarchy in Sustainable Clothing', *Journal of Cleaner Production*, 203:2018, pp.1155–1169.

Learning and Skills Council. (2007). The National Employers Skills Survey. Report produced in partnership with the Department for Innovation, Universities and Skills and the Sector Skills Development Agency.

Lippitt, R., Watson, J. and Westley, B. (1958). *The Dynamics of Planned Change*, New York: Harcourt, Brace and World.

Lynas, E. (2010). 'Textiles, Connection and Meaning', in C. V. Chaturvedi (ed.), *Fashion: Sustainability and Creativity Conference Proceedings*, 23 March, New Taipei City: Fu Jen Catholic University, pp.61–70.

Marshall, M.N. (1996). 'Sampling for Qualitative Research', *Family Practice*, 13:6, pp.522–526.

Park, H.J. and Lin, L.M. (2018). 'Exploring Attitude-Behaviour Gap in Sustainable Consumption: Comparison of Recycled and Upcycled Fashion Products', *Journal of Business Research*, 117:2020, pp.623–628.

Richards, L. (2009). *Handling Qualitative Data*, 2nd Ed, London: Sage Publications Ltd.

Saldana, J. (2016). *The Coding Manual for Qualitative Researchers*, London: Sage.

Scottish Enterprise (2021). 'Textiles Industry in Scotland', *Scottish Enterprise*, www.scottish-enterprise.com/learning-zone/research-and-publications/compone nts-folder/research-and-publications-listings/scotlands-textiles-facts. Accessed 26 September 2021.

Scottish Government (2021). 'A Changing Nation: How Scotland Will Thrive in a Digital World', *Scottish Government*, 11 March, www.gov.scot/publications/a-changing-nation-how-scotland-will-thrive-in-a-digital-world/pages/digital-educat ion-and-skills/. Accessed 27 September 2021.

Serdari, T. (2018). 'The Carloway Mill Harris Tweed: Tradition-Based Innovation for a Sustainable Future', in M. Gardetti and S. Muthu (eds.), *Sustainable Luxury, Entrepreneurship, and Innovation*, Singapore: Springer, pp.185–207.

Strauss, C.F. and Fuad-Luke, A. (2008). 'The Slow Design Principles: A New Interrogative and Reflexive Tool for Design Research and Practice', *slowLab*, 10 July, https://raaf.org/pdfs/Slow_Design_Principles.pdf. Accessed 3 July 2020.

Textiles Scotland (2016). 'Scottish Textile Industry Strategy 10 Year Plan', *Textiles Scotland*, www.textilescotland.com/resources/Pictures/Scottish%20Textiles%20Industry%20Strategy.pdf. Accessed 26 September 2021.

United Nations (2015). 'The 17 Goals', *United Nations*, https://sdgs.un.org/goals. Accessed 8 March 2019.

Vehams, K., Raudaskoski, A., Heikkila, P., Harlin, A. and Mensonen, A. (2018). 'Consumer Attitudes and Communication in Circular Fashion', *Journal of Fashion Marketing and Management*, 22:3, pp.286–300.

Wilson, L. (2015). 'The Sustainable Future of the Scottish Textiles Sector: Challenges and Opportunities of Introducing a Circular Economy Model', *Textiles and Clothing Sustainability*, 1:5.

Chapter 5

Designer Intent and Postmodern Fashion

A Postconservation Approach

Leanne Tonkin, Katherine Townsend, Jake Kaner and David Downes

5.1 Introduction: conserving the moment, authenticity in contemporary fashion

The use of postmodern materials in 21st-century fashion artifacts creates an ongoing archival challenge for many museums with dress archives. This chapter identifies 'Designer Intent' as a way of evaluating authenticity in the conservation of fashion artifacts incorporating postmodern, transient materials and technologies. The term Designer Intent, in the context of this research, refers to the wearer experience the designer intends to create. This new approach to conservation supports the idea of a dress object's 'continual identity', a notion that connects different archival stakeholders to sustain the cultural value of postmodern fashion. Establishing the authenticity of a postmodern fashion artifact, from a curatorial perspective, is to represent the creative output of a designer at a given point in time, as accurately as possible.

The postmodern fabrications of contemporary fashion are the outcome of crafted relationships between bodies, technologies and materials involving multi- and transdisciplinary approaches (Entwistle and Townsend, 2020). Such fabrications, whether engineered or cultivated, are challenging established understandings of material production, maker and user engagement by diversifying the traditional textile palette of the fashion designer. Fashion practitioners working 'at the edge' of the discipline have often sourced and created novel materials, surface details, and finishes to subvert convention, attracting the attention of curators of dress as being 'culturally significant' and therefore collected and conserved as fashion history (Evans, 2003). However, some of the most advanced materials may have transient properties, affecting the quality, hand and appearance of an artifact over even a relatively short time. Consequently, artifacts may quickly reach a point where the original aesthetic intention of the designer is no longer represented, sometimes leading to being isolated in an archive. This changes the artifact's ontological and material cultural value and meaning, impacting its conservation and interpretation within a museum context. The traditional reliance on the physical condition of an artifact by conservators may limit the scope

DOI: 10.4324/9781032659053-5

of interpretive fashion practice, impacting access to 'pioneering and nonconforming [and potentially] rematerialised' items of dress (Sadkowska, 2020, p.67) through the engagement of future cultural stakeholders.

Within this research, Material Engagement Theory (MET) by Malafouris (2013) is employed as a conceptual framework for artifact examination, defined as the 'in-between' space of the mind and the maker. In addition, the author undertook the thematic analysis of a series of interviews with professionals in the field of fashion collection care and conceptual fashion designers to accrue examples of current practice. MET and postphenomenology, a strand of philosophy that looks at the way artifacts mediate the relation between humans and the environment (van Dongen *et al.*, 2019, p.2), has been applied to identify material relationships (between designers, conservators and curators of dress objects) as a consideration to support a more holistic approach to conservation, one where the breaking down or physical degradation of fashion is acknowledged. This is particularly relevant due to the increasing use of (sustainable) biomaterials within fashion. Evolving perspectives on Designer Intent and debates on the authenticity of fashion requires continual interaction between collections care and future users of collections. To develop this discussion around evolving experiences with unstable products and related archiving protocols, three object studies are discussed to support links between Designer Intent, postmodern material characteristics and aesthetic experiences between the artifact and fashion cultural stakeholder, as criteria for supporting the conservation of postmodern fashion artifacts. The selected artifacts particularly demonstrate the impact that polymer-based materials, often favored by designers, have on the care of contemporary fashion. Studies of a duvet coat with a poly vinyl chloride (PVC) cover with a thermoplastic polyurethane (TPU) blend (de Sá, 2017, p.227) by Maison Martin Margiela, A/W 1999–2000, a kaleidoscopic perfectos dress made with a photosensitive print by Kunihiko Morinaga for ANREALAGE, S/S 2016 and a tailored coat with an aromatic PU cover by Raf Simons for Calvin Klein, A/W 2017 are presented. Analysis of these objects informs new criteria to conserve and interpret 'authenticity' through various aesthetic changes and archival time scales. Degradation of the plastic materials on the Margiela and Simons ensembles, the digital translation of the ANREALAGE dress and the consequences of these shifting material relationships encourage reappraisal of the aesthetics of fashion artifacts. Conclusions reveal the need to rethink the role of archives and dress conservation, suggesting a 'postconservation' model to support a 'postfashion' system, that re-evaluates how we create, conserve and value emergent forms of material culture.

5.2 Designer Intent and authenticity

The idea of Designer Intent and authenticity relating to fashion artifacts is an unfamiliar and undefined concept within conservation. The term 'authenticity', along with identity, values and interpretation, relating to the various disciplines of conservation has been thoroughly dissected and re-evaluated over the last two decades to help create more sustainable and axiological approaches in caring for mixed and multi-media cultural artifacts (van Saaze, 2013; Wharton, 2015). Authenticity and intent are acknowledged as being intertwined and performative elements through the continual existence of the material; 'issues of authenticity in conservation are better served by thinking of the debates in terms of conceptual, aesthetic, or material authenticity rather than a semiotic construct based on aims and context alone' (Scott, 2015, p.294). This interrelationship is affected by different cultural stakeholders, like collection care staff, viewers of the artifact and others. 'An object's journey involves multiple interactions and multiple values and its authenticity is created by viewers via their own individual relationship with the object. It becomes an individual concept understood through many layers of knowing, certainties and uncertainties' (Sweetnam and Henderson, 2022, p.4). Experiencing the material is becoming a recognized form of interpretation that helps construct meaning in conservation practice (Llamas-Pacheco, 2020, p.5) that allows for the elements of authenticity and intent to become less materiality dependent when documenting and conserving an artifact.

Contemporary fashion is subject to retranslation through the processes of acquisition, examination and display, despite not undergoing any physical or aesthetic change. The link to the designer remains an important transferable asset toward the 'new translation', making the artifact distinguishable, valuable and sustainable in fashion collections by embedding a constant cultural meaning that continues to socialize the work of the designer. 'Fashion, with its affinity for transformation, can act out instability and loss but it can also and equally, stake out the terrain of "becoming", new social and sexual identities, masquerade and performativity' (Evans, 2003, p.6). The notion of Designer Intent can become paradoxical when combined with a cultural landscape because of the change in context in which the artifact was created. The 'material consciousness' (Malafouris, 2014, p.149) of the designer through their creative process can be reappreciated by cultural heritage stakeholders who collect artifacts that represent the materialization of the creative ideas of the designer in a specific time and place. Often the value of intent resides with the direct link to the designer based on reputation but is still subject to institutional interpretation and (artifact) expectations. The designer's use of postmodern materials can impact these institutional values because they 'archivally act' differently to traditional textiles (e.g. wool, cotton, silk) because of their distinct material characteristics and instabilities (e.g. 3D-printed composites) and, therefore, challenge traditional archival parameters. This shifts the paradigm of 'materiality dependent' values in dress conservation and calls for a new approach to fashion artifacts made from postmodern materials which (sometimes unexpectedly) change or are dependent on technological iterations in the future. The dynamics inherent within postmodern material properties can therefore change the originality of a design, as captured on the catwalk or in the media, broadening the meaning of Designer Intent.

Postmodern materials offer unlimited opportunities for designers to explore, experiment and push beyond conventional textile forms, introducing unpredictable and surprising aspects into their creative process. This freedom of artistic creative expression is crucial to fashion design and the need to form a reciprocal Material Conservation Theory (MCT) that will expand and support this area. MET acknowledges the 'constant search' to identify a 'true vision of things' (Malafouris, 2013, p.52); there is no fixed perception of material engagement; it is an enabler of awareness, interpretation and understanding of the elements being investigated. MET identifies a paradoxical situated phenomenon of objectivity relating to the subjectivity of human experience, and when there is a shift toward objectivity, there is 'less attachment' to a specific quality of a material; in fact, it distances our perception of the 'true vision'. In other words, a desire to capture originality as the moment of creation only represents a single version of what the maker was experiencing at the time.

> intentionality is construed as a strictly internal phenomenon of human consciousness with no counterpart in the realm of things.
> (Malafouris, 2013, p.137)

As such, MET encapsulates the designer's philosophy, while the term Designer Intent represents a snapshot worthy of documenting at the time of acquisition and is an indeterminable point of authenticity, a mobile concept that allows multiple viewpoints to co-exist. This type of fluid documentation steers away from an isolated, fixed representation of Designer Intent toward one that is transferable to a wider range of fashion uses and users.

5.3 The characteristics of postmodern materials

Identifying the right moment to collect a designer's work is part of the authenticating process for museums. Curators sometimes follow patterns of influence and timing in a designer's career that shows uniqueness or reflects significant trends that resonate with the fashion press and public. For example, Iris van Herpen's snake dress from her Capriole collection, A/W 11/12, as worn by the singer Björk for the Roskilde Festival in 2012 (van Herpen, 2021), catapulted this distinctive style specific to the designer. The dress was subsequently collected by the dress curators at the V&A as an iconic artifact of fashion heritage. These moments make the design worth collecting by curators; they become important material anchors, acting as distributed cognition in supporting these choices, perceptions and priorities

(Malafouris, 2013, pp.67, 72). 'Material signs' (Ibid, p.117), such as those moments that for no particular reason capture our imagination, can be read and enacted to substantiate the 'aura' of a garment, elevating it as a collectable clothing concept. A catwalk presentation provides a translation of the designer's work situated in seasonal formats, thematic performances and a series of individual, connected looks, which are often presented as physical arrangements (Entwistle and Rocamora, 2006, p.744). The curator often engages with this presentation as a key event in identifying moments of fashion heritage to collect and conserve and is often part of a spatial, temporal and experiential occasion that acknowledges social relations between actors in the fashion system. When a curator selects a look from the catwalk, this could be acknowledged as a 'material sign' that has emerged from the various parameters of the catwalk performance. This is part of a fashion engagement process which occurs when the 'material sign' initially engages the curator through epistemological rather than a hermeneutical action (Malafouris, 2013, p.117). The curator has meaningfully engaged with the look before any actual historical meaning has emerged. Kate Fletcher (2019, p.49) describes this 'fashion moment' as 'an electric experience, unpredictable, unschooled, emergent'. Within that moment are attempts of sense-making, a possibility of historical meaning, as a 'temporally emergent property of material engagement' (Malafouris, 2013, p.117) between curator and the fashion look. When the artifacts are selected through the decision of the curator, it enters a heritage landscape to undergo 'museumization', where it is transformed into the confinement of an archive (Calefato, 2019, p.38) and it is here in the museum that a sense of cultural identity and representation is realized within a historical setting. This recontextualization glorifies fashion artifacts that become 'denuded of any dynamism' (Ibid, p.39) in becoming an active part in fashion history which causes the museumization of Designer Intent. The action of curatorial selection can 'provoke a disconnection between preserving the design and the original designer's intent' (Tonkin, 2017, p.165). Working with the designer, their house and the acquisition process can be curatorially driven which creates further disconnection; the notion of authenticity becomes materially bound to the conservator dependent on curatorial advice and interpretation. This situation can be limiting and in relation to fashion artifacts constructed from transient materials, through a lack of mutual understanding and disparate motivations between the curator and conservator. And while cutting-edge fashion designers such as Kawakubo, Chalayan and Margiela have explored 'dereliction' and 'patina' as artistic strategies (Evans, 2003; Verhelst and Debo, 2008), in conservation there is no recollection of the 'numinous' quality the artifact (Clavir, 2002, p.30) has collected since its inception and catwalk appearance. Material authenticity is the main priority for inclusion and survival in the archive, increasing the cautiousness in gaining knowledge and understanding of unknown material trajectories. Contemporary fashion shows refer to the situation of collecting artifacts, which is a 'social construct' (Clavir, 2009, p.139) of cultural significance. In interviews with Edwina Ehrman, independent dress historian (and former senior curator, fashion and textiles, V&A), Alexandre Samson, curator, Haute Couture and Contemporary Design, Palais Galleria and Kaat Debo, director and chief curator, ModeMuseum (MoMu), Antwerp (October to November 2019) reflected on how subjective and risk-taking acquiring fashion can be and identified the challenge of the right time to capture that design moment. Ehrman (2019) reaffirms timing is crucial, 'we often don't get the designers at the right stage in their careers. We wait too long'. This highlights the narrow window, and language fashion artifacts are often translated through. In conserving the authenticity of fashion, conservation needs to consider the subjective nature of the acquisitioning process and the variable criteria which affect the decisions around product durability and cultural value in relation to postmodern fashion artifacts.

5.3.1 Authenticities and postmodern fashion artifacts

Conserving the authenticity of fashion brings with it debate. The pristine, as new, condition of a dress object is often perceived as its original condition when it was made. Recently, this approach has been considered too objective and scientifically determined, creating a fictitious aim to follow a 'truth-enforced operation' (Muñoz Viñas, 2005, p.81). Personal choice or subjectivity can also be employed to determine the material authenticity of an item, enacted through engaging with the artifact through conservation practice (Muñoz Viñas, 2020, p.29). Material engagement between the conservator and the artifact can be complex, and the process of engagement is often not documented, the preferencing of perpetuity being the most valued outcome of conservation (Henderson, 2020, p.10). Attempting to conserve postmodern fashion encompassing transient properties with a view to longevity can be a rigorous and resource rich task. The freshness and newness of a fashion artifact are elements that can be reinstated to a degree through physical intervention, repair or reproduction (Morris and Keneghan, 2011, pp.111–117). However, these acts of simulation do not reverse the 'signs of time' (Verhelst and Debo, 2008) nor do they return the artifact to its moment of inception. The artifact has undergone various changes, both physical and conceptual, through acts of performance, merchandizing, wear and conservation, after the designer's intention has been realized, gathering different authenticities. The future authenticity of fashion artifacts may be considered temporal moments of material engagement where museum staff recollect and reinterpret designers' work knowing that elements of the artifact have or are expected to change with time (Hölling, 2016, p.17).

5.4 The aesthetic experiences of postmodern materials

Postmodern material properties and qualities, like those found in fashion artifacts entering the cultural landscape, reconfigure aesthetic expectations. For example, 'when polyurethane (PU) materials become part of museum collections, degradation problems emerge and in a short period of time PU starts to show its inherent material instability' (de Sá et al., 2014, p.195). And in a similar vein, 'new materials in art may involve the risk of creating a work which, due to material problems, deviates immediately after its creation' (Jadzinska, 2016, p.189). While 'fashion' constantly reinvents itself, so is transient in terms of its conception, there is a paradoxical, cultural expectation that its physical outcomes should remain fixed. As a result, conservators are pressured by the instantiation of fashion. The expectation for beauty in fashion is high and is an inherent property of aesthetic value which is subject to constant change and differences in interpretation. Joanne Entwistle states in her essay 'The aesthetic economy: the production of value in the field of fashion modeling' (2002),

> Aesthetic economies have their own particularity. They are more nebulous since at first glance they seem far more 'subjective', immaterial or effervescent and thus far less 'stable' and 'qualities of aesthetic content change, as any history of art or design illustrates'.
>
> (p.321)

These ideas are reflected in a postmodern cultural era that has influenced fashion through the emergence of wider and more inclusive understandings of aesthetic appreciation 'through its rejection of tradition, its relaxation of norms, its emphasis on individual diversity and its multiplicity of styles. The result was diminished shared meanings of styles' (Tseëlon, 2016, p.220). Contemporary designers working with state-of-the-art materials can present challenges to professionals in fashion heritage who have the responsibility to conserve and interpret the aesthetics of their work to a wider cultural community. This potential scenario can influence a museum's decision not to acquire an item, selection for display or subsequent archival treatment, even if the artifact is in good condition, based on material properties (Samson, 2019). Pre-empting changes in a fashion artifact based on material-led values, therefore creates barriers leading to the isolation of particular substrates due to potential loss of aesthetic agency (Malafouris, 2011, p.126).

Toward the development of the MET, Malafouris produced an essay on 'The aesthetics of material engagement' (2011, pp.123–139) which explores a less epistemological approach to reimagine 'our aesthetic presumptions, in the common sense of taste and beauty' which 'can be a great obstacle when examining the aesthetic agency of things or artworks' (Ibid, p.126). This approach helps the effectiveness of developing a MCT for postmodern fashion artifacts because it appreciates a wider and more inclusive understanding of aesthetics as recognized through the evolvement of style in 'the postmodern stage' (Tseëlon, 2016, p.220) of fashion. Malafouris (2011) encourages 'a situated aesthetic approach' that enables different forms of aesthetic experiences to exist and to be inhabited to achieve fuller, wider and extended material engagement from an artifact (Ibid, p.126). An MCT that acknowledges this new ontological basis as a way of engaging with aesthetics helps to prevent fixed and somewhat unsustainable notions of aesthetics in fashion conservation and interpretive practice. MCT could support ideas that work toward a more sustainable model in the archiving of postmodern fashion that accepts material change as integral and interpretable characteristics of postmodern materials. Introducing this new approach may enable wider aesthetic beliefs to co-exist with changing materials that could extend the aesthetic life of an object. A recognition in the aesthetics of material engagement, as explored by Malafouris, could involve different levels of material analysis, definitions, classifications and, therefore, discussions within the collections care of fashion artifacts that recognizes 'the temporal dynamics' and 'embodied aspects of aesthetic experiences' (Ibid, p.127). The designers, their teams and assistants have actively engaged in creating the aesthetic appeal of a fashion artifact. They have contributed to what could be considered an 'act of embodiment' (Ibid, p.131) sharing experiences and conceptions of the artifact with different audiences an act of 'embodied aesthetics', a term that describes the metaphysical distance between the experiences of aesthetics from other senses reliant on vision, hearing and listening (Montero, 2018, pp.892, 899). This encourages less focused engagement with the original aesthetic of an artifact as experienced by the curator during the catwalk show, to one that can be shared and reflected upon by diverse cultural users.

Jo Cope, a conceptual designer, expresses how she actively engages with materials through her skills in cordwaining, which provides some insight into her aesthetic experiences that may be considered 'embodied aesthetic' practice.

> What's really interesting about the material, it's like I allow myself to imagine whatever is [present] in my mind's eye, I have to work out how I make [the artefact]. And I really like that approach. It's hard because I'm starting from scratch every time. Sometimes, it's like, I've got to find a new way of working, [therefore] I've got to find a new material. [...] Things like leather can create that stretch and relate to skin, can become seamless. I'm extending traditions. But I'm making materials do things that they're not necessarily meant to do. And each time the challenge [is thinking] I don't know how to make it, but I'll find a way of making it. And then I work through the materials.
>
> (Cope, 2019)

Designers like Cope want the wearers of their creations to relate to the mental and physical craftsmanship involved, metaphorically and practically, by delivering a heightened experience which may involve dynamic new materials. In constructing a 'situated aesthetic approach', Malafouris describes an aspect of this approach of 'enactive discovery' (Malafouris, 2011, pp.130–131) that acknowledges the 'act of embodying' as 'situated praxis as a trajectory of material engagement'. In other words, the mental and physical stages of creative practice are intertwined and inseparable and cannot be represented as a fixed end-product. Through an 'enactive discovery' approach, different aesthetic connections could allow for fashion conservation and interpretation to transcend from the immediacy of the original aesthetic of the fashion artifact. Kate Fletcher (2016) acknowledges that aesthetic obsolescence is the main product of contemporary fashion that becomes enmeshed in changing social and cultural conditions. The notion of 'aesthetic' (changing appearance renders existing products obsolete) and 'In the fashion sector the primary, though not exclusive, tool of obsolescence is aesthetics' (Ibid, p.194). Cultural investment in keeping alive the original aesthetic choices of contemporary designers raises challenges for postmodern materials entering established practice in fashion conservation. On the other hand, cultural investment could raise other possibilities that the high skill sets and talents of fashion conservators, novel testing systems to help support practice, problem solving, decision-making processes and ability to deliver exhibitions en masse can be redirected to a postconservation model. One that does not present fixed illusions of aesthetic engagement.

5.5 Object studies

The following object studies help illustrate and combine ideas of Designer Intent, postmodern material characteristics and aesthetic experiences between fashion artifacts and cultural user(s). These criteria help consider and support the conservation of postmodern fashion artifacts through the impact of collecting polymer-based materials and their instabilities which often presents challenges to dress archives.

Object No 1: Plastic cover from the duvet coat. Mode Museum (MoMu), Antwerp, Belgium. *Attribution*: Part of the Maison Martin Margiela 'artisanal' line of the 1990s attributed to their white phase of design (Figure 5.1). *Description*: Separate transparent plastic cover that covered a soft white duvet jacket filled with feather down. *Materials*: Cotton and down-fill (duvet), poly (vinyl) chloride (PVC) and thermoplastic polyurethane (ester) (TPU) blend (transparent plastic cover) (de Sá, 2017, pp.227–228). *Condition*: Significant yellow discoloration caused by photodegradation.

Designer Intent: The PVC and TPU blended cover has undergone significant discoloration and is far removed from its original white concept as presented by Margiela in 1999 (MMM shows, 2020; Verhelst and Debo, 2008,

Figure 5.1 Plastic cover from the duvet coat designed by Maison Martin Margiela, Autumn–Winter 1999. The current condition of the plastic cover is now showing significant yellowing. Image: Mode Museum, Antwerp. c. 1999 (T99/32). © Frédéric Boutié, MoMu, Antwerpen.

pp.9–10). The spectrum of changes from the original white design aesthetic creates a sense of loss in value and aesthetic forming a distance between the designer and the artifact influencing its translation and configuration of the past practices of Margiela. The yellowing could be considered an unexpected 'material sign' changing the direction of fashion interpretive practice to one that builds on ideas around authenticating the discoloration. This type of material engagement offers active and transient engagement through exploration between the cultural users and current and future conditions of the artifact.

Material relationships: The changes that have occurred to the plastic cover go beyond the original intentionality of Margiela because 'things cannot exhibit intentional states' (Malafouris, 2013, p.137) and have become parts of the material authenticity. Caroline Evans (2003) uses concepts of 'Now-Time' (Ibid, p.293) to include elements of 'unexpectedness, ephemerality and mortality' and 'Spoiling' (Ibid, p.307) to recognize 'abjection, alienation and decay' as notions that actualize engagement with artifacts and their environments. Similarly, cultural environments, like MoMu, could consider the yellowing of the cover as a mediator between their museum users and the material properties and qualities as an ethical and honest way to conserve and interpret the changing PVC, TPU blended duvet cover that culturally contributes to fashion as a subject of 'modernity and post-modernism' (Evans 2003, p.304). This approach offers different material values to emerge, providing cultural stakeholders with a sense of the 'true materialism' (Fletcher, 2016, p.140) of the duvet cover. Showing 'a deep appreciation and respect for intrinsic material qualities' (Ibid, p.140) of postmodern materials that encourages MoMu's gallery spaces to be 'a truly material society, where materials and the world they rely on are cherished' (Ibid, p.141) keeping the duvet coat 'a true point of pride' (Samson, 2018, p.86), an important link to the contribution of Margiela to postmodern fashion culture.

Aesthetic experiences: Salvador Muñas Viñas (2005) positions aesthetic enjoyment as relative. 'It is not aesthetic enjoyment what is expected, but a different experience' that people expect when engaging with an original artifact (Ibid, p.84). The effects of the degrading duvet cover can be viewed as creating aesthetic relationships between the artifact and the attention of the viewer, placing emphasis on the notion of 'attentional values' for the cultural user (Llamas-Pacheco, 2020, p.4). Identifying the existence of these interrelationships acknowledges 'it is not the object alone that carries the artwork' (Ibid) but the continual aesthetic experiences of the duvet cover.

Object No 2: Dress made of kaleidoscope perfectos with photosensitive prints. Palais Galliera, Paris, France. *Attribution*: Ready-to-wear collection, by Kunihiko Morinaga, REFLECT collection (Figures 5.2 and 5.3). *Description*: Short cream dress made from six motorcycle jackets. *Materials*: Cotton canvas coated with kaleidoscopic-inspired pattern made visible with a camera flash. *Condition*: Yellow discoloration has occurred on the outer surface.

Designer Intent: The kaleidoscopic inspired pattern on the dress is viewed using an iPhone with a flash. This digital-material interface is an 'embodied and situated' (van Dongen *et al.*, 2019, p.2) experience for the curator who employs a postphenomenological approach through mediation between artifacts, human experiences and the environment (van Dongen and Toussaint, 2020, p.113). The roles of human (the conservator, curator and owner/wearer/viewer) and nonhuman (the iPhone) are technologically bound and essential for recording, archiving and interpreting, creating different anthropological histories and 'embodied practices' (Ihde, 2009, p.42; van Dongen *et al.*, 2019, p.1) of fashion artifacts. The realization of the artifact's visual and material qualities as intended by the designer is reliant on the application of digital technology. The notion of immediacy and temporality in fashion becomes apparent because of the 'cognitive demands' on the user (Howells and Negreiros, 2019, p.332) to view the decorative patterning of the dress. These elements are part of the designer's creative process where activating peoples' desires and emotions is key to the experience of fashion.

Material relationships: The digital method to comprehend the patterning of the material to enact curatorial decision-making about a moment in design

Figure 5.2 Front of kaleidoscopic perfectos dress (natural light) designed by Kunihiko Morinaga, ANREALAGE, Spring–Summer 2016 (GAL2019.4.2.1 à 10). © Palais Galliera/Ville de Paris. 2019.

history, a moment that is a sign of contemporary collecting could be useful for a conservator to document. Identifying different levels of the material characteristics could be part of the future care of the dress. Tim Ingold (2007) highlights the importance of material qualities as central to creativity, 'it is not only the properties of materials that an artist or craftsperson seeks to express, but rather their qualities' (Ibid, p.13). This consideration extends the conservator's remit of understanding postmodern materials by conserving the objective and subjective responses to the artifact. The dress exemplifies the need to develop new, more open approaches to conservation and curation that mirror the responsive nature of the artifact as a digital social phenomenon, rather than storing something lifeless (Calefato, 2019, p.38).

Aesthetic experiences: Recording the experiences of the catwalk show could see that contemporary fashion artifacts exist as an idea without the need for continuous materialization (Llamas-Pacheco, 2020, p.8). Similar concepts are being explored in fashion design theory where the relationships between 'products and attention' through seasonal changes acknowledge the role of ongoing and intertwined narratives (Roubelat *et al.*, 2015,

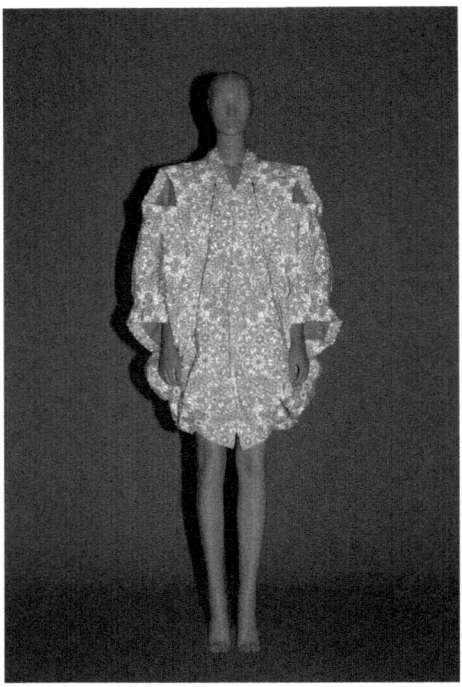

p.8). Documentation could engage within the digital realm developing practices in design conservation and interpretation beyond the physical materiality of the artifact. This would make the dress a phenomenologically transparent object (Colombetti, 2018, p.583), whereby experiences of the ANREALAGE dress by participants, as consumers or viewers, could be documented as material-digital narratives as part of the authentic state of the dress.

Object No 3: Monochromatic tweed coat with clear plastic cover. MoMu, Antwerp, Belgium. *Attribution*: Ready-to-wear Raf Simons for Calvin Klein (Figure 5.4). *Description:* Long double-layered coat with separate clear plastic top layer. *Materials*: Wool (under coat), aromatic PU (plastic cover). *Condition*: The PU is showing signs of clouding/whitening making the clear plastic opaque (Figure 5.5).

Designer Intent: 'When ready-to-wear fashion becomes part of a museum collection, most of the previous assumptions change, these garments gain a new form of authenticity' (de Sá, 2014, pp.199–200). The ensemble could

Figure 5.4 Tailored tweed coat with clear plastic cover designed by Raf Simons for Calvin Klein, Autumn–Winter 2017. Mode Museum, Antwerp. c.2017 (T17/877AB). © Collectie Modemuseum Antwerpen, Image: Stany Dederen.

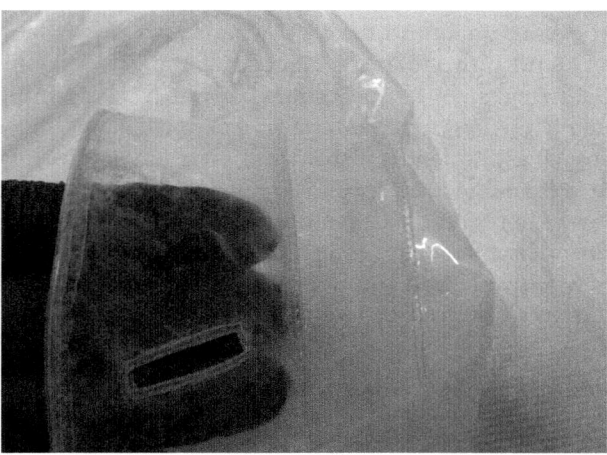

Figure 5.5 Current condition of the clear plastic cover showing the loss of transparency due to chemical reactions with the tweed jacket as documented in July 2020. Designed by Raf Simons for Calvin Klein, Autumn–Winter 2017. Mode Museum, Antwerp. c.2017 (T17/877AB). © Frédéric Boutié, MoMu, Antwerpen. 2020.

not be presented for exhibition because of the risk of further damage to the PU cover. Stabilizing and maintaining the authentic state of the material becomes reliant on conservation strategies, for example, the decision not to exhibit because of the risk of further chemical reactions to support the status of the artifact. Conserving the authenticity of Designer Intent of the Simons ensemble could shift the paradigm of documentation because of anticipated and quickening change in the PU material. Diverse forms of documentation may become essential and could include notions of a 'continuity through change' (Hölling, 2015, p.88), a term used to document ongoing changes in components in multi-media artifacts in archives, to replace fixed ideas of authenticity.

Material relationships: In this case, replacing the plastic cover may not be a viable option because the designer, Raf Simons and his team no longer design for Calvin Klein. The ensemble is part of Simons' debut collection for the house and signifies a place in Belgian design history which was epistemologically collected by Debo as part of the collection policy for MoMu. Contemporary fashion collecting, like the Raf Simons fashion ensemble, made with a component from postmodern materials likely to change, would benefit from a model of 'continual identity' to support design histories that will otherwise risk not being collected or being lost to an archive.

Aesthetic experiences: The visual, chemical and anthropological changes in the PU cover connect those transcending ideas of Simons, as enmeshed and related aspects of the designer's material choices. This transitional aspect of Designer Intent can be aligned with cultural uses and users, whereby the material engagement is not representational but embodiment relations (Ihde and Malafouris, 2019, p.205). The viewer is free to engage with the changing material properties and qualities of the PU where aesthetic experience becomes 'a quality of mind rather than of object and things', becoming a part of sense-making (Arteaga, 2017, p.2) allowing the (re)conception of degrading and changing postmodern materials. Acknowledging different approaches to experiencing aesthetics, instead of static understandings of aesthetic objects, may encourage a more active material engagement where aesthetic processes evolve, progress and live on display. This is part of the plastic's material authenticity, supporting the notion of 'continual identity' with fashion artifacts where expected and unexpected material changes may not hinder any 'exhibition value'.

5.6 Conclusion: toward a postconservation approach

Postmodern materials present new considerations for dress archives that support fashion heritage. Exploring an ontological approach, while utilizing a postphenomenological and MET-informed epistemology that supports a theory of 'continual identity', may help diversify and extend stories of the designer and their choices in postmodern materials. Developing broader definitions of material aesthetics and how they are experienced may recognize the existence of closer engagements with 'the real nature of the phenomenon' (Malafouris, 2013, p.53) which acknowledges the temporal dynamics and embodied aspects of aesthetic experiences. This approach shows a commitment to relational ontology, where humans and artifacts are inseparably linked (Ihde and Malafouris, 2019, p.201). Alternative forms of documentation, including that of an MCT, may support ongoing ideas to conserve and value postmodern materials and fashion as a cultural asset. The MCT (as evidenced with the object studies) would recognize the intangible aspects of fashion artifacts, like Designer Intent, material relationships and aesthetic experiences, as conservation paradigm which acknowledges 'continual identity' as a valued and sustainable 'cultural currency' (Fletcher, 2016, p.142). These considerations help reposition notions of authenticity in contemporary fashion. When 'revealing the material core' (Malafouris, 2013, p.12) through its changing material circumstances (degradation, physical breakdown), it becomes an active source of material culture recognizing the important moment, material choices and modernity in fashion history the artifact derives. Contrary to the 'assumption that there is a fundamental good in prolonging the existence of cultural property' (Henderson, 2020, p.10) extends 'continual identity' to others widening the benefits of the artifact. A suggested postconservation model may consider the aesthetic desires of the designer, the museum stakeholders and users of fashion artifacts as 'creating platforms for envisaging fashion futures with a diversity of voices' (Fletcher and Tham, 2019, p.44), creating new documentation of the Designer Intent which will add to object records, the object itself, and encourage a more people-centered approach (Giliberto) to conserving dress archives.

References

Arteaga, A. (2017). Embodied and situated aesthetics; an enactive approach to a cognitive notion of aesthetics. *Artnodes*, 20, pp.20–27. doi:10.7238/a.v0i20.3155

Calefato, P. (2019). Fashionscapes. In: Geczy, A., and Karaminas, V., eds., *The End of Fashion: Clothing and Dress in the Age of Globalization*. London: Bloomsbury Publishing, pp.31–45.

Clavir, M. (2002). *Preserving What Is Valued: Museums, Conservation, and First Nations*. Vancouver: UBC Press.

Clavir, M. (2009). Conservation and cultural significance. In: Richmond, A., and Bracker, A., eds., *Conservation: Principles, Dilemmas and Uncomfortable Truths*. Oxford: Routledge, pp.139–149.

Colombetti, G. (2018). Enacting affectivity. In: Newen, A., de Bruin, l., and Gallagher, S., eds., *The Oxford Handbook of 4E Cognition*. Oxford: OUP Oxford, pp.571–587.

Cope, J. (2019). Jo Cope: Interview with Leanne Tonkin, Nottingham, 11 November 2019.

de Sá, S. (2017). *What does the future hold for polyurethane fashion and design? Conservation studies regarding the 1960s and 1970s objects from the MUDE collection.* PhD. thesis, Universidade Nova de Lisboa.

de Sá, S., Ferreira, J. L., Ramos, A. M., Coutinho, B., and Macedo, R. (2014). How to keep what was intended to be temporarily functional? reflections on decision-making for the conservation of polyurethane ready-to-wear fashion. In: Gordon, R., Hermens, E., and Lennard, F., eds., *Authenticity and Replication: The 'Real Thing' in Art and Conservation.* Proceedings of the International Conference held at the University of Glasgow, 6–7 December 2012. London: Archetype. ISBN 9781904982999pp.193–203.

Debo, K. (2019). Director and chief curator, Mode Museum, Antwerp: Interview with Leanne Tonkin, telephone, 18 October 2019.

Ehrman, E. (2019). Senior curator of textiles and fashion, V&A, London: Interview with Leanne Tonkin, London, 25 November 2019.

Entwistle, J. (2002). The aesthetic economy: the production of value in the field of fashion modelling. *Journal of Consumer Culture*, 2(3), pp.317–339. doi:10.1177/146954050200200302

Entwistle, J., and Rocamora, A. (2006). The field of fashion materialized: a study of London fashion week. *Sociology* 40(4), pp.735–751. https://doi.org/10.1177/0038038506065158

Entwistle, J., and Townsend, K. (2020). On fashioning anatomy. In: Townsend K., Solomon, R., and Briggs-Goode, A., eds., 2020. *Crafting Anatomies: Archives, Dialogues, Fabrications*. London: Bloomsbury Visual Arts, pp.289–304.

Evans, C. (2003). *Fashion at the Edge: Spectacle, Modernity and Deathliness.* London: Yale University Press.

Fletcher, K. (2016). *Craft of Use: Post-Growth Fashion.* Abingdon: Routledge.

Fletcher, K. (2019). *Wild Dress: Clothing and the Natural World.* Devon: Uniformbooks.

Fletcher, K., and Tham, M. (2019). *Earth Logic: Fashion Action Research Plan.* London: JJ Charitable Trust.

Gilibero, F. (2021). Reducing Inequalities and Decolonising Heritage Practices: People-Centred Approaches [online]. Heritage and Our Sustainable Future Series, 4. Available at: https://mailchi.mp/unesco/2019-regional-workshop-on-unesco-designations-and-sustainable-development-italy-8270572?e=f0d545accc (Accessed: 17 October 2021).

Henderson, J. (2020). Beyond lifetimes: who do we exclude when we keep things for the future? *Journal of the Institute of Conservation*, 43(3), pp.195–212. doi:10.1080/19455224.2020.1810729

Hölling, H. (2015). The archival turn: toward new ways of conceptualising changeable artworks. *Acoustic Space*, 14, pp.73–88.

Hölling, H. (2016). The aesthetics of change: on the relative durations of the impermanent and critical thinking in conservation. In: Hermens, E., and Robertson, F., eds., *Authenticity in Transition: Changing Practices in Art Making and Conservation.* London: Archetype, pp.13–24.

Howells, R., and Negreiros, J. (2019). *Visual Culture.* Hoboken, NJ: John Wiley & Sons.

Ihde, D. (2009). *Postphenomenology and Technoscience: The Peking University Lectures.* New York: Suny Press.

Ihde, D., and Malafouris, L. (2019). Homo faber revisited: postphenomenology and material engagement theory. *Philosophy & Technology*, 32(2), pp.195–214. doi:10.1007/s13347-018-0321-7

Ingold, T. (2007). Materials against materiality. *Archaeological Dialogues*, 14(1), pp.1–16.

Jadzinska, M. (2016). Artists' experiments with new materials in works of art: how to preserve intent and matter. In: Hermens, E., and Robertson, F., eds., *Authenticity in Transition: Changing Practices in Art Making and Conservation*. Cambridge: Cambridge University Press, pp.189–196.

Llamas-Pacheco, R. (2020). Some theory for the conservation of contemporary art. *Studies in Conservation*, pp.1–12. doi:10.1080/00393630.2020.1733790

Malafouris, L. (2011). The aesthetics of material engagement. In: Manzotti, R., ed., *Situated Aesthetics: Art beyond the Skin*. Exeter: Imprint Academic, pp.123–139.

Malafouris, L. (2013). *How Things Shape the Mind a Theory of Material Engagement*. London: The MIT Press.

Malafouris, L. (2014). Creative thinging: the feeling of and for clay. *Pragmatics & Cognition*, 22(1), pp.140–158. doi:10.1075/pc.22.1.08mal

MMMShows (2020). Maison Martin Margiela Fall 1999–2000 [online]. Dailymotion. Available at: www.dailymotion.com/video/x5sb18f [Accessed: 8 October 2020].

Montero, B. (2018). Embodied aesthetics. In: Newen, A., de Bruin, l., and Gallagher, S., eds., *The Oxford Handbook of 4E Cognition*. Oxford: OUP Oxford, pp.891–910.

Morris, R. and Keneghan, B. (2011). Cold war fashion: two case studies from an exhibition at the Victoria and Albert Museum. In: Bechthold, T, ed., *Future Talks 009: The Conservation of Modern Materials in Applied Arts and Design, Munich, October 23-45 2009*. Munich: Die Neue Sammlung, The Design Museum, pp.111–117.

Muñoz Viñas, S. (2005). *Contemporary Theory of Conservation*. London: Routledge.

Muñoz Viñas, S. (2020). *On the Ethics of Cultural Heritage Conservation*. London: Archetype Publications.

Roubelat, F., McAllum, M., Hoffmann, J., and Kera, D. (2015). Probing ephemeral futures: scenarios as fashion design. *Futures*, 74, pp.27–36. doi:10.1016/j.futures.2015.05.004

Sadkowska, A. (2020). Pioneering, nonconforming, and rematerializing: crafting understanding of older men's experiences of fashion through their personal archives. In: Townsend K., Solomon, R., and Briggs-Goode, A., eds., *Crafting Anatomies: Archives, Dialogues, Fabrications*. London: Bloomsbury Visual Arts, pp.67–88.

Samson, A. (2018). *The Women's Collection 1989–2009: Martin Margiela*. New York: Rizzoli Electa.

Samson, A. (2019). Haute Couture and contemporary design curator, Palais Galliera, Paris. Interview with Leanne Tonkin, telephone, 27 November 2019.

Scott, D. A. (2015). Conservation and authenticity: interactions and enquiries. *Studies in Conservation*, 60(5), pp.291–305.

Sweetnam, E., and Henderson, J. (2022). Disruptive conservation: challenging conservation orthodoxy. *Studies in Conservation*, 67(1–2), pp.63–71. doi: 10.1080/00393630.2021.1947073

Tonkin, L. (2017). Visionary design practices: preserving plastics and designers' intent in collections of modern and contemporary fashion. *Journal of the Institute of Conservation*, 40(2), pp.152–167.

Tseëlon, E. (2016). Jean Baudrillard: post-modern fashion as the end of meaning. In: Rocamora, A., and Smelik, A., eds., *Thinking Through Fashion: A Guide to Key Theorists*. London: Bloomsbury Publishing, pp.215–232.

van Dongen, P., and Toussaint, L. (2020). In touch with the now: stimulating mindfulness through a smart denim jacket. *APRIA Journal*, 1(1), pp.112–119. doi:10.37198/APRIA.01.00.a16

van Dongen. P., Wakkary, R., Tomico, O., and Wensveen, S. (2019). Towards a postphenomenological approach to wearable technology through design journeys. In: Textile Design Research Group, eds., 2019. *Textile Intersections, Loughborough University, London, September 12-14 2019* [online]. London: Loughborough University. Available at: https://repository.lboro.ac.uk/articles/Towards_a_Postphenomenological_Approach_to_Wearable_Technology_through_Design_Journeys/9724649 (Accessed: 30 October 2020).

van herpen, I. (2021). *News: Björk at Roskilde in Snake Dress* [online]. Available at: www.irisvanherpen.com/news/bjork-at-roskilde-in-snake-dress (Accessed: 24 October 2021).

van Saaze, V. (2013). *Installation Art and the Museum: Presentation and Conservation of Changing Artworks*. Amsterdam: Amsterdam University Press.

Verhelst, B., and Debo, K. (2008). *Maison Martin Margiela: 20: The Exhibition*. Antwerp: MoMu.

Wharton, G. (2015). Artist intention and the conservation of contemporary art. *American Institute for Conservation of Historic & Artistic Works. Objects Specialty Group Postprints*, 22, pp.1–12.

Chapter 6

Overconsumption in the Global Fashion Industry

Desire, Power and Capitalism

Michelle Blair Gabriel

A common refrain heard about the global fashion industry from professionals and employees operating within it, journalists commenting on it and communities affected by it is that it has a *big* problem. It might be more accurate to say that the industry has *many* big problems which are simultaneously discrete and intertwined.

In the last 30 years, the global fashion industry has created, amplified and had to contend with a number of issues related to its operational practices including human rights abuses, unsafe working conditions, ecological disasters from manufacturing practices, greenhouse gas emissions, hazardous chemical usage, overproduction, product dumping and lack of waste management practices, to name a few. A throughline can be found across the issues of the fashion industry; overconsumption supports the myriad problems the fashion industry faces today as the scale and scope of the industry is a major factor in tackling any isolated issue. Overconsumption is necessary to make growth possible in a saturated fashion market.

A conversation has emerged about the role of consumption in the challenges of and possible solutions for the industry. Examples can be seen in the slow fashion movement, in fashion brands such as Cuyana, Mara Hoffman and Patagonia asking consumers to buy less but better and by advocacy organizations such as ReMake and Fashion Revolution telling social media followers that 'ALL YOU NEED IS LESS'. Despite these examples, we find very few discussions seeking to unpack the complicated and nuanced relationship consumers have to fashion companies, the use of power in that relationship and the role of desire in consumers' ability to effect change in their consumption habits and thus assessing their role within the greater culture of consumption and effectively reducing their own consumption behaviors.

Power is a master key to understanding consumption dynamics within fashion contexts. This discussion utilizes the complementary theories of Roland Barthes and Michel Foucault to investigate the intersection of power and fashion. Barthes' *The Language of Fashion* (2013) contextualizes clothing and fashion in semiotic terms and elevates fashion to a language in and of itself. Foucault's work in *The History of Sexuality, Volume 1: An*

DOI: 10.4324/9781032659053-6

Introduction (1980) argues at length for the understanding of language and discussion as significant tools for the utilization of power. With these theories as tools for understanding, we can see fashion as a language and as a language a powerful tool for the use of power. Power itself must be understood if its schemes are to be uncovered.

Through these theories, we can understand the role desire plays within fashion broadly and specifically within the dynamic of fashion consumption. Once these layers have been unpacked and better understood, we can see how the interaction of fashion and capitalism takes a consumption dynamic already energetically charged and pushes it into overdrive. Much like a matryoshka doll, you may feel you have investigated thoroughly down to the source of these concepts only to find there are still dolls within dolls to open. By investigating by layer, starting first with fashion as language, then power employed through language and fashion, followed by how to find and measure power and ultimately the role desire has in fashion consumption, we can see fashion as a system interested in and supportive of overconsumption in and of itself. In this we can discuss capitalism as its peer, not its parent, in that behavior.

6.1 Fashion as Language

The first step we must take to understand fashion overconsumption dynamics is to define what is fashion and understand what cultural phenomena construct this definition. Fashion is a concept that holds many meanings. The different spheres of experience—the individual, the institutional, the societal and the global—all apply their own layers of meaning, resulting in fashion as a deeply contextual concept (Entwistle, 2000; Rocamora & Smelik, 2015; Wilson, 2019). Rocamora and Smelik (2015) provide a comprehensive definition with support from Kawamura (2005, p.2):

> We understand fashion as both material culture and as symbolic system Kawamura (2005). It is a commercial industry producing and selling material commodities; a socio-cultural force bound up with the dynamics of modernity and post modernity; and an intangible system of signification. It is thus made of things and signs, as well as individual and collective agents, which all coalesce through practices of production, consumption, distribution and representation.

In this definition, we can see that fashion is both conceptual and practical, defining 'intangible systems' on one hand and an entire global industry on the other.

Through Roland Barthes' work *The Language of Fashion* (2013), we can understand and utilize fashion as a meaningful and functional language. Barthes (2013) dissects the components of what makes up fashion—clothing, accessories, stylings, trends—into signs and linguistic components. He argues that fashion as language and tool for discussion is made up through the interaction between these tangible components and between the wearer and other members of a society. Clothing only evolves to be understood as fashion and thus moves from the realm of function to the realm of meaning, when it is situated within a social context. For clothing to become fashion, it requires both a speaker (or wearer in this context) to construct a statement in clothing and a listener (or observer of the wearer) to perceive the clothing statement. This begins a discussion with clothing as the shared language. This discussion is what transforms disparate clothing elements into fashion.

For Barthes (2013), the collective belief in fashion and use of fashion as a language makes it greater than the sum of its parts. The component items of clothing are limited and have an inherent ephemerality which supports the illusion of constant newness in the fashion dynamic. In reality, we recycle and reconfigure the same limited components of this language to form the dialog. This process works because the meaning—which is created through the dialog—is in the fashion combinations themselves, not in the individual clothing items (Barthes, 2013). According to Barthes, there is a tension in the development of dialog and meaning in fashion; in order to participate in the language and culture of fashion, an individual cannot avoid using mass-produced clothing items. These mass-produced items are inherently unoriginal, are subject to coded rules of the culture under which they are produced and thus are finite in their use within the language of fashion (Barthes, 2013). Stated plainly: 'you have to imitate that which is in fashion in order not to be imitable' (Barthes, 2013, p.81). This describes a tension present in the use of fashion: the individual utilizes fashion to try to construct a unique identity within a given social dynamic and fashion and the fashion industry strive to strike a balance between making items of clothing broadly available through mass production while signaling that fashion provides unique opportunities upon which to build an individual identity.

Fashion has, however, always had a powerful tool at its disposal which assists in striking that balance: the speed of style innovation. Barthes (2013) defines fashion as 'the collective imitation of regular novelty' (p.63). Fashion is marked by an extreme focus on the present at the expense of both the past and the future. This results in exceptionally finite temporal relevance for clothing items, which in turn supports the definition of fashion itself. Again, we can look to Barthes (2013) for incisive commentary:

> Fashion experiences itself as a Right, the natural right of the present over the past ... with long-term memory abolished and with time reduced to the duo of that which is rejected and that which is inaugurated, pure Fashion, logical Fashion is never anything other than the amnesiac substitution of the present for the past.

(pp.110–111)

With this infatuation with the present, abandonment of the past and willful blindness to the future, fashion forces a rapid pace of change. What fashion *is* today is gone tomorrow, requiring a new idea of what *is* fashion to be continually constructed in the present. This reliable pace of fashion change does not require participants or society to know what is fashionable, strictly speaking, but only that which is unfashionable; according to Barthes (2013), fashion has the unique quality of being understood through what it is not (p.63). This comparison is important and completes the transformation of utilitarian clothing into fashion, as 'what makes meaning is not repetition but difference' (Barthes, 2013, p.74). Barthes' (2013) interpretation of fashion is key to understanding the transformation of utilitarian, individual items of clothing through socio-cultural construction to be meaningful components in the shared language and phenomenon of fashion.

6.2 Understanding Power

To understand what motivates, maintains and expands fashion consumption behaviors, it is necessary to understand power: how it operates, how it is leveraged and how it can be found. In understanding these qualities of power, we can discuss how power is utilized in fashion contexts, who holds power in fashion consumption dynamics and how power is leveraged to drive fashion overconsumption.

A commonly used definition of power (Gruenfeld et al., 2008; Magee & Galinsky, 2008) comes from French and Raven (1959) who define 'power in terms of influence' (p.260) We can look to Foucault's *The History of Sexuality, Volume 1: An Introduction* (1980) to understand how power is utilized. The combination of Foucault (1980) and Barthes (2013) creates a framework for understanding power within fashion through Barthes' theory of fashion as language and an understanding of language and discussion as a tool for power through Foucault. Foucault (1980) argues that power's greatest means for employment is language and language is the manner of power's hold on sexuality. 'Discourse transmits and produces power; it reinforces it' (Foucault, 1980, p.101). Fashion and clothing are in service of and served by both sexuality and power. The global fashion industry is an approximately 2.5 trillion USD business (United States Joint Economic Committee, n.d.) that, at its core, sells sexuality (Hunter & Davis, 1992). Sexuality is deeply embedded in the culture and ideas of fashion and is necessary to the adoption of fashion concepts and products (Barthes, 2013; Entwistle, 2000). Language and desire are important tools at sexuality's disposal for power's implementation. In understanding fashion as a language, we can see fashion and clothing as discursive tools used in the employment of power.

Foucault (1980) makes clear the direction of power within a discourse: 'the agency of domination does not reside in the one who speaks (for it is he who is constrained), but in the one who listens and says nothing' (p.62). He goes on to say, however, that 'power is tolerable only on condition that it masks a substantial part of itself. Its success is proportional to its ability to hide its own mechanisms' (Foucault, 1980, p.86). Power may be with the listener, but power has its greatest effect when it hides its true intentions; subtlety and sophistication are important. For example, in using discourse to engage with fashion consumers, fashion corporations may give the illusion that the consumer is powerful by supporting the consumer's belief that fashion is an empowerment tool, giving the illusion that the corporation in power has loosened its grip. In actuality, the fashion corporation, already in a position of power relative to the consumer, has taken a greater hold on power through increased knowledge and greater supervision of the consumer. This knowledge is utilized to more intimately understand the consumer to sell more goods while packaged as power and freedom for the individual consumer. Power exerted over an individual packaged as empowerment of that same individual is power in its most compelling form (Foucault, 1980).

As a discourse, fashion functions as Foucault theorizes—as a tool seemingly in service of the 'speaker', or in fashion's case the performing wearer of fashion who is using fashion to construct identity, but fashion is actually in service to the partner in that discourse, the provider of fashion, the fashion corporation in this case. In the wearer's need to craft identity, self-express and participate in the greater culture of fashion, they give up more than they gain, including autonomy (by participating in fashion, the wearer has entered into a discourse which relinquishes them of agency), true individualism (as mass-produced fashion items are inherently unoriginal) and economic freedom (with the power relation present in the discourse between wearer and corporation, the wearer enters into a consumption dynamic which is designed to capture the wearer in a cycle of consumption which is very challenging to exit once begun).

Arguably, Foucault's most salient point in his discussion of power is the subtle nature of power. When power moves from overt *will* to more subtle mechanisms, it embodies itself in the more covert *norm*. Bolder *will* can be undermined and rebelled against. A *will* can be pointed to and isolated. Will is exercised by the singular or few, the *them* to the *us*. Norms, however, are applied by many points and are woven deeply into the fabric of societies, institutions, classes, communities and individuals. A norm is not easily isolated and often cannot easily be discussed directly but must be talked around. An example of this within fashion contexts can be seen when a teenager rebels against a school dress code. The institution seeks to exert its power over desire, sexuality and fashion by requiring girl's skirts to be a certain length. Reliably, students will roll their skirt waists to shorten and subvert the rule, which, if never made a rule by the school, might not be cause for rebellion from the students. In contrast, if a teenager's peers collectively determine that short skirts are simply outside of the norm of 'coolness', the teenager would not dare to shorten their skirt nor to question the unstated rule of such sartorial norms. In this example we can see that power from one point, the school in this example, is limited and weak. Power that is made omnipresent through normalization, by peers setting unspoken standards of 'cool' in this example, is asserted from all directions and is capable of evolution, which assists in its efficacy. These qualities make countering or subverting a norm complicated and challenging.

Fashion and sexuality are normative concepts and are strong tools at power's disposal. The norm of consumptive behavior within the fashion industry is perpetuated by the conceptualization of fashion and is further supported by the corporations in power whose existence is predicated on the continued consumption patterns of those who seek to be fashionable and express themselves through clothing. To isolate this norm is exceptionally challenging.

6.3 Desire

With fashion as a language and with an understanding that power, when paired with sexuality, uses language effectively to extend its influence, we can see fashion as an effective employment tool for power. Desire is a feedback loop which aids in power's effectiveness and ensnares individuals. Foucault (1980) makes clear, 'Where there is desire, the power relation is already present' (p.81).

The concept of fashion and the fashion industry are both fueled by desire: desire for individual expression, desire to be desired, desire to consume to construct identity, desire to drive consumption to perpetuate fashion businesses and a desire to accumulate wealth through the business of fashion (Entwistle, 2015; Horton & Payne, 2018). The consumption culture which exists within both the culture and industry of fashion offers a promise to satiate desire. The dynamic of newness inherent to the concept of fashion and to the operations of the fashion industry creates a reliable revolving door of desire; when one item ceases to be desirable as it inevitably and reliably becomes 'old' and out of fashion, a new item rooted in the present comes through the door to jump-start a new cycle of desire. Modern life is predicated upon purchasing and consumption; it exists through a complicated web of production and consumption with the systems of sexuality, desire and fashion serving to reinforce that web. Fashion is an extreme example of this paradigm. These cycles of desire within fashion capture participants in a never-ending loop that does not resolve in satisfaction for the participant (Szocik et al., 2018; Fletcher, 2010).

The greatest underlying motivation to desire for the fashion consumer is to be desired (Horton & Payne, 2018; Szocik et al., 2018); sexuality has an overt role in desire for the consumer, but the desire to be emulated by those around them and the desire to be found relevant by the prevailing culture is not to be understated as reason for fashion consumption. In utilizing desire, those in positions of relative power (fashion corporations, in this case) assure their own interests (continued consumption). Szocik et al. (2018) put a fine point on the discussion:

> The ethics of consumption are defined through pleasure, relaxation and fun. Consumption and consuming have become a domain of free time … With the wide offer in the market, the question arising is not whether you want to own a product, but rather which one best 'describes' you.
>
> (p.2109)

Desiring and purchasing to satiate that desire gives the fashion consumer the opportunity to express themselves and construct identity in exchange for handing power to the fashion corporation. This transaction is not framed as a means of economic enslavement for the consumer, but as a tool for the liberation of the individual. In Foucault's (1980) estimation, the idea of constructing identity through consumption is leveraged by power to assure continued participation in a capitalistic cycle that is not necessarily in the individual consumer's best interest. The consumption of fashion as a pathway to identity building is a self-reinforcing cycle foundationally built on desire. The cycles and seasons of the fashion industry maintain a perpetual rhythm to support this pursuit of identity crafting.

Szocik et al. (2018) also argue that the act of consumption, specifically in fashion contexts, is itself a form of discussion, arguing that production is no longer the focus of capitalism but is replaced by management of 'consumptive demand', which takes power from consumers and gives it to producers (Szocik et al., 2018). We understand language and dialog are tools primarily in service of power's employment (Foucault, 1980); if consumption itself is a mechanism for discursive power employment, it is the corporation which benefits and the consumer who relinquishes power. The consumer is relieved of power through the act of discussion, both in the form of engaging in the dialog of fashion and through the act of consumption and by entering into a desire dynamic which entraps them and reliably relieves them of power.

Within the fashion consumer-corporation relationship and through the understanding of desire, one can understand that the fashion corporation has greater power relative to the consumer as the consumer is tethered to their desire and the corporation itself is made up of individual fashion-desiring consumers who make decisions in their role within the corporation. In this dynamic, the corporation can choose to produce or not produce, sell or not sell a specific fashion item, but a consumer, once trapped in the pursuit of their desire, relinquishes power in order to have the opportunity to fulfill their desire through the mechanism of fashion. Once a consumer enters this desire dynamic, they hand over power to the corporation and become an enabler to their own unchecked consumption behavior fueled by a spiral of increasing desire. This spiral of ever-increasing desire is exceedingly challenging for consumers to extricate themselves and does not end in satisfaction for the consumer (Magee & Galinsky, 2008; Szocik et al., 2018).

6.4 Consumer Interviews

Effective power structures are supported from all directions and innumerable touchpoints, not exclusively from the direction of those who are in the positions of relative power (Foucault, 1980; French & Raven, 1959; Magee & Galinsky, 2008). Magee and Galinsky (2008) discuss that individuals at all levels of a power hierarchy tend to be invested in the maintenance of that hierarchy, including those in less advantaged positions. If fashion consumers are in positions of less relative power in their dynamic with fashion corporations, are they aware of their disadvantaged position? Are consumers able to see the machinations of power and desire which influence their fashion consumption behaviors? Or are consumers blind to the dynamics of power and desire within the culture and industry of fashion and thus are unable to participate meaningfully in behaviors which might change the dynamics of power and ultimately allow them to reevaluate their current consumption behaviors?

In understanding the theories and systems which support clothing overconsumption, it is prudent to understand the experiences of fashion consumers who do the daily task of performing within these theoretical constructs and whose perceptions and actions activate the behaviors of the systems.

One hundred subjects were chosen at random by two interviewers, one female and one male, over a three-day period in high fashion consumption areas of New York City in May of 2019, including 5th Avenue near 59th Street and Rockefeller Center in midtown Manhattan and Troutman and Wyckoff Avenues in Bushwick, Brooklyn. Subjects were approached by an interviewer and asked to participate in a five-question interview with an estimated completion time of 2 minutes. Subjects were asked permission to be recorded on the interviewer's iPhone. Subjects were chosen at random; however, some guidelines were utilized. A conscious effort was made to choose subjects of varying assumed ages, ethnicities and gender identities within the 100 interviewees and potential subjects with conspicuous shopping bags were favored. Potential subjects were avoided who were assumed younger than 18 years of age.

Each random subject was asked five questions in the order below. To ensure each subject was in fact a fashion consumer, Q1 was offered as a screening question to challenge any assumptions about consumption habits despite the ubiquity of clothing consumption in the United States.

Q1: Have you bought an item of clothing, shoes or accessories in the last 6 months?

Q2: What power do you believe you have as a fashion consumer?

Q3: Do you believe that fashion brands to which you are loyal care about your preferences?

Q4: Do you believe that you have the ability to change the way that a fashion brand operates?

Q5: Do you believe that consumers acting together can have a measurable effect on the behavior of corporations?

The aim of conducting short form interviews with a wide range of unprepared subjects was to capture the greatest basic understanding of consumers' perception of their power when they were likely to offer the greatest amount of candor to the interviewer while in a setting of close physical proximity to the manifestations of clothing consumption.

6.5 Findings

Each individual response was first reviewed and categorized as 'yes', 'no' or 'maybe', including the arguably most subjective question Q2, before being analyzed for themes and patterns across participants. Despite Q2's open-ended structure, interview subjects consistently responded as if the question had asked *whether* they felt they had power which allowed for the responses to Q2 to be coded as 'yes', 'no' or 'maybe' (Table 6.1).

Analysis of the 100 interviews yielded many nuanced results, but the general consensus from consumers was that the majority did not feel they hold power as individuals relative to fashion corporations. This sentiment

Table 6.1 Quantitative responses to interview questions

	Yes (%)	No (%)	Maybe (%)
Q1: Have you bought an item of clothing, shoes or accessories in the last 6 months?	98	2	0
Q2: What power do you believe you have as a fashion consumer?	47	53	0
Q3: Do you believe that fashion brands to which you are loyal care about your preferences?	36	60	4
Q4: Do you believe that you have the ability to change the way that a fashion brand operates?	31	65	4
Q5: Do you believe that consumers acting together can have a measurable effect on the behavior of corporations?	92	2	6

generally increased as the questions progressed. The only area where consumers overwhelmingly agreed and believed in their own power was when discussing the power held by consumers acting together.

Although there were varied perspectives within the Q2 'yes' responses, the 53% of respondents who answered 'no' were nearly uniform in their answers with responses such as 'none', 'zero', 'not much' and 'very little' dominating the response data. This negative response trend regarding the individual consumer's perception of power progressively increases across the interview questions through Q4, increasing from 53% in Q2 to 60% in Q3 and topping off at 65% in Q4.

In reviewing the qualitative responses to the five interview questions, trends were easily correlated. For Q3 responses, the most robust trend within 'no' responses was the idea that 'brands do their own thing and do not care about what I want as a consumer'. Throughout responses to Q2, Q3 and Q4, consumers consistently referenced their power of choice and/or exit. The greatest portion of the responses in this trend occur in Q2. However, Q2 qualitative responses illustrate a discordant perception from consumers; several initial responses which were categorized as 'yes' continued in a dissonant way, undermining their initial positive response. An example from Respondent 98 to Q2: 'I have the power to choose where I spend my money. I don't think that necessarily dictates the kind of factories or the work that is done but it's something' (R98, Q2). Although participants recognized the power of collective action, they also recognized the challenge of bringing disparate consumers together to combat a global industry as seen in Respondent 65's response to Q5: 'Together, yes. But the problem is getting them together' (R65, Q5).

Ultimately the response data confirms that fashion consumers do not recognize their opportunities for power and ultimately do not effectively use the power that might be available to them including the power of collective action or the power to ultimately exit the consumption dynamic entirely. Per Foucault (1980), power cannot be utilized unless it is acknowledged or used with specific intent (p. 94). With this understanding, we can see power in fashion settings overwhelming in favor of the fashion corporation.

6.6 Discussion

In understanding fashion as a discursive tool, the power dynamic present in a fashion context and the amplifying role desire plays in that context, this theoretical analysis makes clear that consumers do not have power within fashion. In uncovering the way fashion consumers see themselves relative to fashion corporations and their perceptions of their own power within fashion contexts, the interviews with fashion consumers suggest that fashion consumers are deeply enmeshed within consumption dynamics and do not recognize or utilize tools that might offer them power in their relationship to fashion and specifically to fashion corporations. In this, consumers support the consumption motivations of fashion corporations and the fashion industry. They do not see their opportunities for exit nor do they see themselves outside of the consumption dynamic.

What is evident is that the fundamental nature of fashion is itself an engine of consumption. The moment clothing becomes fashion, through the meaning-making process discussed by Barthes, the consumption engine has been initiated. The embedded systems of desire and power motivate the system and ensure a steady production of new fashions not because of any consumer demand, but because the elevation of clothing to the status of fashion requires an ephemerality; a newness for newness' sake, only serving to create a new definition of fashion for the present so the past, in contrast, can be seen as out of fashion. The motivating forces of innovation and fleeting relevance are what define clothing as fashion. This reliable fashion engine can drive consumption and overconsumption all by itself; it is only for an industry or an economic system to take advantage of such a powerful engine to take the already reliable consumption dynamic and push it to hyperdrive.

The Industrial Revolution was the impetus for the creation of the world's first capitalist industry: the fashion industry. At the nascent stage of both fashion and capitalism, we see an early recognition of a mutually beneficial dynamic between the two ideologies; Barbon wrote in 1690 in his *A Discourse of Trade*, 'Fashion or the alteration of dress, is a great Promoter of Trade, because it occasions the Expanse of Clothes, before the old ones are worn out: It is the Spirit of Life of Trade' (Barbon, 1690, in Briggs, 2013, p.188). Fashion and capitalism have long been intertwined in a mutually beneficial feedback loop which supports the growth, expansion and power of one another (Briggs, 2013; Wilson, 2019). Wilson (2019) puts it neatly: 'Fashion speaks capitalism' (p.14), and in turn it might be said that capitalism feels most itself when speaking the language of fashion.

While desire and fashion work together to drive consumption (Entwistle, 2015; Horton & Payne, 2018), fashion and capitalism work closely to both produce and grow the industry of fashion. Fashion and capitalism share many common ideas, the greatest of which is the 'logic of continual change and novelty' (Horton & Payne, 2018, p.3). Foucault (1980) suggests that power, sex and capitalism have been intertwined since the early stages of the Industrial Revolution. The economic growth that accompanied industrialization was dependent on the creation of goods at an ever-increasing scale which necessitated a shift in consumption habits for all members of the industrialized society (Galbraith, 1958; Goodwin et al., 2008; Edwards, 2014) from need based to want based (Katona, 1964; Edwards, 2014). Newly christened 'consumers' entered a paradigm of working for the express purpose of acquiring funds to purchase more goods (Goodwin et al., 2008). Accordingly, a shift took place during this period, where goods were purchased increasingly because of the want of the consumer and not the outright need (Galbraith, 1958; Katona, 1964).

Fletcher (2010) points out that the value of growth at the expense of other considerations is shared by capitalism and the fashion industry, stating that 'in the fashion sector, the logic of growth is well established as the basis of power and prosperity. The system that grows fastest is considered best and is sustained because people believe in it' (Fletcher, 2010, p.260). Both the system of fashion and the system of capitalism measure success by growth and speed and both are sustained by the belief in the validity of these metrics by participants in the systems (Fletchers, 2010). This illustrates fashion's ideological and historical alignment to capitalism but also a deep operational alignment to the 'growth and profit at all costs' mindset often perceived to be native to capitalism. Wilson (2019) describes this dynamic between fashion and capitalism well:

> Capitalism maims, kills, appropriates, lays waste. It also creates great wealth and beauty, together with a yearning for lives and opportunities that remain just beyond our reach. It manufactures dreams and images as well as things and fashion is as much a part of the dream world of capitalism as of its economy. We therefore love and hate fashion and we love and hate capitalism itself.
>
> (Wilson, 2019, p.14)

Modern life is predicated upon purchasing and consumption; unending want, propelled by the presence of desire, is fueled by the nature of fashion itself—newness for its own sake—which, when paired with capitalism, creates the opportunity for excessive production (Fletcher, 2010). This shared value of growth and the mutually beneficial dynamic of fashion's newness cycle result in a unique relationship between fashion, capitalism and consumption. The power both fashion and capitalism hold allow the growth of one another and ensure the adoption of their ideologies in the broader culture in the form of norms, which are challenging to disrupt.

6.7 Conclusion

With increased consumption and the rise of consumer culture in the twentieth century, the fashion industry witnessed an increase in style production and turnover, largely within the confines of biannual seasonal offerings. This dynamic moved into high gear with the advent of 'fast fashion' in the late twentieth and early twenty-first centuries with brands such as Forever 21, H&M and Zara innovating in the space (Briggs, 2013; Fletcher, 2010). According to Briggs (2013), by 2004, Zara had moved to 20 seasons a year and was receiving new goods in store twice a week. This 'coincided with a drop in clothing prices of 14 percent and an increase in the consumption of garments by 37 percent' within four years (p.188).

The hedonism of fast fashion takes capitalism's drive toward profit maximization and greater efficiency and the definition of fashion itself—'dress in which the key feature is rapid and continual changing of styles' (Wilson, 2019, p.3)—and thrusts consumption into overdrive. In a modern society, buying for buying's sake becomes a socially acceptable, common addiction and irrational self-sustaining behavior for fashion consumers (Szocik et al., 2018) which results in exponential consumption without satisfaction.

If consumers have almost no power relative to fashion corporations, especially specific to questioning consumption habits, if consumption is a component deeply intrinsic to the systems of both fashion and capitalism and if consumption is managed and employed through the manipulation of desire to reliably drive consumption behaviors where need is not a consideration, how can consumers effectively support any reduction or reevaluation of their own consumption behaviors? This theoretical analysis indicates and the exploratory consumer interview confirms that consumers lack meaningful power to overcome the patterns of overconsumption.

The problem of overconsumption requires policy at global, national, regional and local levels in the form of regulation of overproduction, dumping of product, tax structures, advertising claims and end of life considerations for the fashion industry. Overconsumption is supported by myriad incentives within both fashion and capitalism and leverages many fundamental components of the psychology of consumers and, as such, must be tackled from many points simultaneously if it is to be reduced. And given the fundamental nature of fashion, reduction might be all we can hope for. As long as clothing is reliably transformed and utilized as fashion—as a means to construct identity, as a tool for communication and as a mechanism for liberation—it will inevitably enslave us in consumption, manufacturing desires in the turnover which defines fashion itself.

References

Barthes, R. (2013). *The Language of Fashion* (M. Carter & A. Stafford, Eds.; A. Stafford, Trans.; Bloomsbury Revelations). Bloomsbury.

Branch, L. (2004). Plain Style, or the High Fashion of Empire: Colonialism, Resistance and Assimilation in Adam Smith's Lectures on Rhetoric and Belles Lettres. *Studies in Scottish Literature*, 33(1), pp.435–453.

Briggs, A. (2013). Capitalism's Favourite Child: The Production of Fashion. In S. Bruzzi & P. Church Gibson (Eds.), *Fashion Cultures Revisited: Theories, Explorations and Analysis*. Routledge, pp. 186–199.

Denegri-Knott, J., Zwick, D., & Schroeder, J. E. (2006). Mapping Consumer Power: An Integrative Framework for Marketing and Consumer Research. *European Journal of Marketing*, 40(9), pp.950–971. https://doi.org/10.1108/03090560610680952

Edwards, J. M. (2014). Consumer Power and Market Control: Exploring Consumer Behaviour in Affluent Contexts (1946–1980). *The European Journal of the History of Economic Thought*, 21(4), pp.699–723. https://doi.org/10.1080/09672 567.2012.708767

Entwistle, J. (2000). *The Fashioned Body: Fashion, Dress and Modern Social Theory*. Cambridge: Polity Press.

Entwistle, J. (2015). *The Fashioned Body: Fashion, Dress and Modern Social Theory*. Cambridge: Polity Press.

Flacher, D. (2005). Industrial revolutions and consumption: a common model to the various periods of industrialization. Working Papers 5078, Economic History Society

Fletcher, K. (2010). Slow Fashion: An Invitation for Systems Change. *Fashion Practice*, 2(2), pp.259–266. https://doi.org/10.2752/175693810X12774625387594

Foucault, M. (1980). *The History of Sexuality, Volume 1: An Introduction*. Vol. I (Vintage Books Edition). Vintage Books.

French, J. R. P., & Raven, B. (1959). The Bases of Social Power. In *Studies in Social Power*. Institute for Social Research, pp. 259–269.

Galbraith, J. K. (1958). *The Affluent Society*. Houghton Mifflin Company.

Goodwin, N., Nelson, J. A., Ackerman, F., & Weisskopf, T. (2008). Consumption and the Consumer Society. In *Microeconomics in Context*.

Goux, J.-J. (1990). *Symbolic Economies: After Marx and Freud*. Cornell University Press.

Gruenfeld, D. H., Inesi, M. E., Magee, J. C., Galinsky, A. D., & Dovidio, J. F. (editor). (2008). Power and the Objectification of Social Targets. *Journal of Personality and Social Psychology*, 95(1), pp.111–127. https://doi.org/10.1037/ 0022-3514.95.1.111

Hirschman, A. O. (1970). *Exit, Voice, and Loyalty*. Harvard University Press.

Horton, K., & Payne, A. (2018). Imagination Wove This Flesh Garment: Fashion, Critique and Capitalism. In *Undesign: Critical Practices at the Intersection of Art and Design*, pp.186–197. https://doi.org/10.4324/9781315526379-16

Hunter, A. G., & Davis, J. E. (1992). Constructing gender: An exploration of Afro-American men's conceptualization of manhood. *Gender & Society*, 6(3), pp.464–479. https://doi.org/10.1177/089124392006003007

Jameson, F. (1991). *Postmodernism, or, the Cultural Logic of Late Capitalism*. Verso.

Jansen, M. A. (2020). Fashion and the Phantasmagoria of Modernity: An Introduction to Decolonial Fashion Discourse. *Fashion Theory: The Journal of Dress, Body and Culture*, 24(6), pp.815–836. https://doi.org/10.1080/1362704X.2020.1802098

Katona, G. (1964). *The Mass Consumption Society*. McGraw Hill.

Kawamura, Y. (2005). *Fashion-ology: An Introduction to Fashion Studies*. Berg.

Labrecque, L. I., Vor, D. E., Mathwick, C., Novak, T. P., & Hofacker, C. F. (2013). Consumer Power: Evolution in the Digital Age. *Journal of Interactive Marketing*, 27(4), pp.257–269. https://doi.org/10.1016/j.intmar.2013.09.002

Magee, J., & Galinsky, A. (2008). Social Hierarchy: The Self-Reinforcing Nature of Power and Status. *The Academy of Management Annals*, 2(1), pp.351–398. https:// doi.org/10.1080/19416520802211628

Mishan, E. J. (1969). *The Costs of Economic Growth*. Penguin.

Polanyi, K. (2001). *The Great Transformation: The Political and Economic Origins of Our Time* (2nd ed.). Beacon Press.

Rocamora, A., & Smelik, A. (2015). *Thinking through Fashion: A Guide to Key Theorists*. Bloomsbury Publishing.

Rofel, L., & Yanagisako, S. J. (2019). *Introduction. In Fabricating Transnational Capitalism: A Collaborative Ethnography of Italian-Chinese Global Fashion*, Duke University, pp. 1–34.

Slater, D. (1997). *Consumer Culture and Modernity*. Polity Press.

Su, K. A. (2021). Clothed in Meaning: Literature, Labor, & Cotton in Nineteenth Century America. *Fashion Theory: The Journal of Dress, Body and Culture*, 25(5), pp.715–719. https://doi.org/10.1080/1362704X.2021.1885151

Szocik, K., Gemzik-Salwach, A., Cywiński, Ł., & Inglot-Brzęk, E. (2018). Fashion Effects: Self-Limitations of the Free Will Caused by Degeneration of the Free Market. *Economic Research-Ekonomska Istraživanja*, 31(1), pp.2100–2115. https://doi.org/10.1080/1331677X.2018.1544087

United States Joint Economic Committee. (n.d.) The Economic Impact of the Fashion Industry—The Economic Impact of the Fashion Industry. Retrieved 28 September 2021, from www.jec.senate.gov/public/index.cfm/democrats/2019/2/the-economic-impact-of-the-fashion-industry

Wilson, E. (2019). *Adorned in Dreams: Fashion and Modernity* (Updated edition). Bloomsbury Visual Arts.

Chapter 7

Holistic Sustainability in Fashion(?)

The Case of *Vogue Talents*

Nadica Maksimova

7.1 Introduction

In November 2019, Condé Nast joined United Nations Framework Convention on Climate Change (UNFCCC)'s Fashion Industry Charter for Climate Action. It was an official declaration of the commitment "(to) play a more proactive and meaningful role in informing (their) readers about the climate emergency and inspiring them to take practical actions" (Condé Nast, 2019). In January 2020, the issue of *Vogue Italia* was entirely dedicated to sustainability and creativity. Even before this act, perceived as an official declaration of commitment, the Italian fashion magazine was involved in renewed initiatives such as the scoutings organised in collaboration with Marangoni Institute "Towards a Responsible Future". Moreover, there is a consistent investment in the affluent, sustainability-dedicated section on the *Vogue* website. In February 2019, the supplement to *Vogue Italia* issue n. 822, *Vogue Talents*, was titled *The New Frontiers of Awareness*. From its first publication in September 2009, the supplement was conceived as a platform for the showcase and support of young designers from around the world; it was dedicated to the creatives able to change the system for good. Still, the February issue was the first entirely dedicated to environmentally sensitive and socially responsible fashion practices. The supplement's attention to creative diversity and the apparent engagement in fashion decentralisation were crucial for the decision to broaden the already undertaken content analysis of the entire *Vogue Italia* archive that aimed to individualise the salient sustainability-related contents. The pages of *Vogue Talents* offer a much broader perspective on what sustainability is, or better, how it is presented in the fashion media context.

Fashion's environmental impact and social consequences are certainly a topic of discussion for decades now (Black, 2008; Fletcher, 2014 [2008]; Black et al., 2013; Hethorn & Ulasewicz, 2015 [2008]; Gwilt & Rissanen, 2011). Nevertheless, there is still no evidence of fundamental shifts. As a society, we still lack a holistic understanding of the problems linked to the

DOI: 10.4324/9781032659053-7

fashion system. We have been seeing sporadical individual efforts for years now, but we lack concrete action for a systemic move forward. The analysis of the supplement's contents is important insofar as it could shed light on the evolution of the sustainability-related discourse. Furthermore, it could provide critical insight regarding the sustainability engagement of the fashion media giants. Finally, the *Vogue Talents* content observations are to be discussed in comparison with the more restricted in scale perspective of the Italian fashion realities.

At the beginning of 2021, with Flavia Piancazzo, a colleague and PhD candidate at the Department for Life Quality Studies at the University of Bologna, we decided to investigate the directions that the contemporary born-sustainable Italian fashion brands are taking regarding sustainable and responsible practices. The research project aimed to understand what fashion sustainability means in the Italian context today. It sought to analyse how Italian fashion brands dedicated to sustainability embrace the *Earth Logic* concept, as discussed by Fletcher and Tham (2021 [2019]). The results of this preliminary research, which were presented during the Fashion Tales 2020+ 1 Conference and on which we wrote extensively in the conference proceedings (Maksimova & Piancazzo, 2022), served as a counterpoint perspective on what sustainability can mean in the localised fashion context, as opposed to the broader dimension of the fashion magazine.

By delving into the new ways of fashion production and consumption, presented through the brand stories on the pages of *Vogue Talents*, the study orientates towards understanding and describing the contemporary creative and production processes with a focus on the integration of the different sustainability aspects, the environmental safeguarding, social responsibility and protection of cultural diversities. In order to understand the levels of integration in sustainability representations, the contents of the supplement issue *Vogue Talents* are analysed in light of the values and the holistic landscapes proposed in the *Earth Logic Fashion Action Research Plan* (Fletcher & Tham, 2021 [2019]). The scope of this framework is to add a critical perspective and open for discussion on the possible improvements based on the concepts of degrowth, re-centring, scaling and diversification in the learning, communicating and governing fashion. Fashion as a manufacturing industry, still relying on modernist ways of production, should rethink and improve its practices. As a creative and communication industry, fashion should not forget its educative and awareness-raising role. As fashion agents, we all should engage in an active reimagining of how fashion is understood, practised and recounted today. This imagination act could open a path for the very needed paradigm shift towards a sustainable, inclusive and ethical society with respect for all life forms on this planet we call home. Ultimately, the grounded imagination, as opposed to misleading fantasy, could be fashion's role in saving the world.

7.2 Fashion and sustainability—the paradox

The presentation of sustainable fashion case studies has always been an integral part of academic publications on the topic. In one of the first works dedicated to the relationship between fashion and sustainability, *Eco-Chic: The Fashion Paradox*, Black (2008) writes about numerous practitioners, activists and brands that had contributed to the gradual introduction of eco-fashion. Even though the "eco" prefix implies a focus on environmental issues, the publication showcases positive examples regarding many aspects of sustainable fashion, from the use of certified organic materials and unharmful processes to fair trade and respect for the people producing the garments. The importance of taking a stance and speaking out to the injustices and the commitment to safeguarding the local traditions and skills are also an integral part of the discourse. Black is one of the first authors to provide a defined path towards a more responsible, ethical and sustainable fashion system. She suggests rethinking design in the spirit of multifunctionality and longevity of the style, reclaiming and reusing waste materials through recycling, upcycling, repairing, remodelling and recreating (Black, 2008). Many of the academic works written on the relationship between fashion and sustainability dissect in detail the consecutive stages of the product lifecycle: textile production, sourcing, making, distribution, use, disposal, providing essential information to improve each one of them (Fletcher, 2014 [2008]; Gwilt & Rissanen, 2011; Fletcher & Grose, 2012). In the early 2010s, fashion sustainability is also the focus of some cumulative works. The publication edited by Hethorn and Ulasewicz *Sustainable Fashion: Why Now?* (2008) and then republished as *What's Next?* (2015) opened a conversation centred on three venues of sustainability exploration: people, production and economic processes and planet. Furthermore, Section VII of *The Handbook of Fashion Studies* (Black et al., 2013) was also dedicated to sustainability in the fashion context with contributions related to corporate responsibility, sustainable design and alternative business models.

Most importantly, the paradoxicality of "sustainable fashion" is acknowledged. Over-consumption and planned obsolescence are the drivers behind an industry constantly increasing in size, with a growth rate estimated at 2.1% between 2017 and 2022 (Euromonitor, 2017, cited in Rinaldi, 2019). The complexity of the matter implies a need to address the system rather than the individual parts (Fletcher, 2014 [2008]). While Black optimistically speaks of a "paradigmatic shift (towards) a new era of ethical consumption" (Black, 2008), Tham relying on the concept of *Languaging* understood as "a continuous and co-dependent process of understanding through saying and defining and by saying and defining, in turn, shaping our world" explains why the attempts to change the intrinsic culture of the words "consumer" or "consumption" by transferring to their properties concepts like "ethical" or "conscious" are fundamentally wrong (Tham, 2010). She continues by stressing how "sustainability" could not and should not be simply force-fully attached to fashion. Instead, we should change our approach, and by investigating the immaterial manifestations of fashion, "we might find sustainability latent within the capabilities and qualities of fashion" (Tham, 2010, 17). Sustainability as a concept is inherently opposed to the capitalist and consumerist paradigm. The logic of unlimited and perpetual economic growth is not in tune with the natural flows; thus, simplistic juxtapositioning of the concepts of fashion and sustainability is not possible.

What is possible instead is a paradigmatic shift towards the logic of the Earth, based on eight values: *Multiple centres* of attention and action, *Interdependency* between all of the diverse actors, openness to *Diverse ways of knowing*, *Co-creation* involving active collaboration, listening, dialogue and linking, *Action research* because our time to research without acting has passed, *Grounded imagination* as opposed to the fantasy of escaping the conditions of the world, concerned with how to join the world within its limits, *Care of the world* and *Care of self* for engaging with profound change means recognising loss (Fletcher & Tham, 2021 [2019]). To bring the concept of sustainability and the predominant fashion system closer, the system itself has to be changed from within. Fletcher and Tham propose six holistic landscapes, "each containing an imperative to reformulate industry away from the physical accumulation of goods and towards care and maintenance" (Fletcher & Tham, 2021 [2019]). The primary solution, and our only option, is to grow out of growth and simply produce *less*. The fashion industry produces 53 million tonnes of textiles every year (de Castro, 2021). There are 8.1 billion of us on this planet, 75 % of the produced textiles are discarded and a question remains: Is there a reasonable need for so many textile products? We live in different climate conditions; we have different social and cultural backgrounds; we experience different personal interests, needs and aspirations. Thus, fashion should be re-centred, ideated, produced and practised *locally*. Moreover, it should come from a variety of places, emphasising the *plurality* of our existence, celebrating the variety of perceptions, ideas and forms that humankind is conceiving and creating. To shift towards *Less*, *Plural* and *Local* fashion system, we will have to engage with new ways of *Learning*, *Governance* and *Languaging*. We will have to open for new knowledge and skills, rethink organising fashion, change our mindsets and open up for updated communication practices.

Although we are witnessing the academic effort to stress the necessary holistic shift, the fashion system is still very much embedded in the capitalist paradigm. There is still a gap between what theory argues and the levels of environmental and social engagement when there are attempts to implement that theory. Focusing on the 15 industry's most prominent players and investigating their performance across six categories, *The Business of Fashion* states that "fashion is falling short of ambitions to operate in a more environmentally and socially responsible manner". They also find that "companies demonstrate progress in analysing and understanding their impact and in setting targets ... [while] waste and workers' rights are the weakest categories" (Kent for BoF, 2021). Although studies have shown that there is a significant "gap between incumbent fashion companies willing to innovate their business model toward sustainability and born-sustainable startups striving to make their business model replicable and scalable" (Todeschini et al., 2017), the question remains on the so-called sustainable champions, small, born-sustainable companies. How do they approach sustainability? Is it holistic, considering the different aspects of sustainability, or is it still the well-known business-as-usual practice dressed in green?

Aimed at proposing an opinion on these questions, during the Fashion Tales 2020+1 Conference in June 2021, the initial results of the pilot project "Culture and Sustainability: An Interplay on the (contemporary) Made in Italy Landscape" (Maksimova & Piancazzo, 2021) were presented. Methodologically, the project was based on a grounded qualitative analysis of 60 Italian fashion realities, evaluated in the light of the values and landscapes presented in the *Earth Logic Fashion Action Research Plan* (Fletcher & Tham, 2021 [2019]). The results showed significant discrepancies regarding the holistic understanding of sustainability in fashion. In the Italian context, the lack of *Multiple centres* is sadly evident. It was shown that only 3 out of 54 brands are openly inclusive of marginalised communities, while only 2 are built with attention to non-Western perspectives. The focus is on the environment, while community engagement and social responsibility are latent for most of the analysed Italian born-sustainable brands. One of the most prominent values is the *Diverse ways of knowing*, even though limited to the territorial know-how, without considering the broader understanding of the concept as integration of all of the available knowledge, wisdom, capabilities and creativities (Maksimova & Piancazzo, 2022).

The preliminary project, however, was focused on the Italian fashion context alone. It is a good starting point, but it should not result in generalisations. The following pages, dedicated to the fashion media perspective presented through the analysis of the pages of *Vogue Talents*, will hopefully provide insightful reflections resulting from critical thinking. In doing so and aimed at the improvement of the contemporary fashion system, the present contribution wants to deepen the discussion on how fashion can paradigmatically change the world.

7.3 Methodology

Following the above-discussed issues related to sustainability in the fashion context and the limited research in sustainability discourse analysis in the context of fashion media brought forward by recent contributions by Laing (2023, 45–74), Denisova (2021), Jones (2019), Jones and Hawley (2017), an in-depth content analysis of the *Vogue Italia* archive was conducted. The initial content analysis was broadened to include the *Vogue Talents* supplement contents. For the study, a cover-to-cover content analysis for a total of 15 *Vogue Talents* issues was conducted, covering the issues from September 2010 to September 2021. Since missing from the consulted collection, the issues from September 2009, September 2014, September 2016 and February 2017 were not explored. The complete list of the analysed issues with general information, such as issue number, date, page format, number of pages (without covers), title and subtitle, can be consulted in Appendix 7A.1. During the content analysis, the focus was undoubtedly on identifying sustainability-related content. Still, other information that was found relevant was also noted. Pertinent for the delineation of the sustainability discourse, contents were selected to illustrate the developments in sustainability representation. For a facilitated referencing process, Appendix 7A.2 contains all the *Vogue Talents* sustainability-related contents used in the *Findings*. This table contains the issue number, date, page, section and title or brand name. Functional to the contextualisation and the Critical Discourse Analysis that followed, contents from the *Vogue Italia* archive, individualised during previous analysis, were also included. In Appendix 7A.3, a list of these contents with respective general information, content type and title can be found.

The findings of the content analysis are presented on the following pages. In an observation-driven discussion, the insights on how the globally orientated fashion magazine supplement represents sustainability are exposed. Thus, a view on the evolution of the sustainability discourse will be offered. Consequently, the discrepancies in the holistic approach to sustainability, on both global and local levels, will lead to final considerations, informed by the importance of fashion media representations for rising awareness and encouraging consumers' well-reasoned decision-making.

7.4 How fashion become responsible, an ongoing evolution

At the beginning of the 1990s, a series of Moschino advertisement campaigns reflected the persistent socio-cultural issues: drug culture, racism, violence and wars (Appendix 7A.3, 1–4). From the point of sustainability discourse, much more reviling were the slogans such as "Stop! Don't use the sea as a WC" (Appendix 7A.3, 3) or "Leave my plants alone!" (Appendix 7A.3, 4). Seeing a seal with the question "what about me?" (Appendix 7A.3, 2) must have had a strong impact, especially in an industry that at that time still boldly relied on the use of natural furs. Not to talk about the images of children asking, "What about us?" (Appendix 7A.3, 3). These were manifestos against the culture of consumerism, stating that the "advertisements could provoke damage to your brain and your pocket" (Appendix 7A.3, 2). It was the fashion system turning on itself: "Stop the fashion system!" (Appendix 7A.3, 1). Even though Moschino stated that "being in the latest fashion means being as aware as possible of the harm that can be done to nature, to our planet, to ourselves" (Appendix 7A.3, 5), the 1990s were also the years of uncontrollable acceleration of the fashion system. The production practices changed pace and location, the new markets opened for unexpected possibilities, the fashion was becoming democratised. The greater demand meant only one thing—an even greater offer and consequently terrible side effects. Still, fashion's relation to environmental problems and social injustices was not a point of discussion. Even though environmental issues and possible actions towards sustainable living were featured on the pages of *Vogue Italia* in the early 2000s (Appendix 7A.3, 6–12, 14–16), it will take decades for the actual discourse on sustainable fashion to evolve. One of the first articles on ethical fashion dates December 2009, and it recounts the cases of fashion brands engaging in projects empowering communities in developing countries (Appendix 7A.3, 13). In the following decade, numerous articles, brand showcases and discussions on sustainability in both fashion and not will make it to the pages of one of the most influential fashion magazines. The year 2009 was also when the first issue of the *Vogue Talents* supplement was published.

Vogue Talents—*research for the talented and the responsible*

Right from the beginning, *Vogue Talents* was conceived as a platform for showcasing the new creatives of the fashion industry. For the first five years, the supplement was regularly published once a year in September (Appendix 7A.1, 1–4). The well-recognisable format contained four mandatory sections: Graduated from, Womenswear, Menswear and Accessories, plus the expected shoutouts to academic fashion institutions, scouting contests, prices, articles on where to find and buy emerging brands or simply talent-related updates. In the first section, the presentation of the newly graduated designers was divided per academic institution and country; only name and contact information for each designer were provided. Here the display was supported by photos and other visual materials. No specific explanations of the creative process or information on production were available. Thus, only the aesthetic choices, often inspired by cultures and perspectives different from the dominant Eurocentric codes, can be discussed here. It could be argued that the globalised style of the designers' solutions and the showcasing of a multitude of perspectives were talking about *Vogue Italia*'s awareness of the needed decentralisation of fashion, yet it would come as rather forced deduction. The Womenswear, Menswear and Accessories sections were dedicated to already operating brands, providing more detail on each brand's identity and collections. In these brief descriptions, we see the first although distant signs and mentions of sustainability and responsible fashion practices (Appendix 7A.2, 1).

In September 2010 issue, Christopher Raeburn stated that he is mixing sustainability and fun; for him, "fashion (was) opportunity to create clothing and products in an intelligent, sustainable, greener way" (Appendix 7A.2, 3). Marco Corso was inspired by the environmental crisis (Appendix 7A.2, 4). Still, in neither of the two cases, additional information is given. The reader could only imagine what does this mean in practice. We see the first slightly more detailed info on some responsible practices a year later when Partsparts Imseonic gives a partial description of their processes and explains how those respond to the production waste problem (Appendix 7A.2, 11). In the short overview on womenswear of the same issue, the editor highlights the "eco-conscious dying techniques" (Appendix 7A.2, 6). While some designers were proudly emphasising that they were using "ecological fur only" without actually explaining what it is or what they meant by "ecological" (Appendix 7A.2, 9–10), others like Vincent Billeci were completely immersed in the exploration of the traditional craftworks via collaborations with artisans, silversmiths and leather goods manufacturers (Appendix 7A.2, 8). The latest is maybe one of the first examples of *localism*, attention to the crafts of a specific place and openness to *diverse ways of knowing* and learning. In line with the traditions, but also with respect to the environment, were the vegetable-tanning skills employed in the production of the accessories by Nasha Mekraksavanich and PB0110 (Appendix 7A.2, 14, 15). Furthermore, the founder of PB0110 stated, "I believe in the significance of the beloved objects, in things that develop an individuality through daily use" (Appendix 7A.2, 15). This statement, so as the philosophy of "creating editions and not collections; clothes, objects and accessories that outlive the cycle of a season" (Appendix 7A.2, 7) and thus could be used for a very long time, reflects the message of the *Loved Clothes Last* (de Castro, 2021). While designers were promoting an eco-friendly attitude towards fashion, reflected in their "modular composition and (creation of) garments (that) can be assembled and disassembled to create different solutions" (Appendix 7A.2, 12) or were creating collections starting from an elaborated vintage leather jacket (Appendix 7A.2, 2), *Vogue Talents* was investigating the fashion capitals of tomorrow. Significant for the decentralisation of fashion, Dublin's Redress initiative was also a symbol of encouragement for "better ethics and sustainability" (Appendix 7A.2, 5). In these initial years of the supplement publication, no specific reference on the growing-out-of-growth logic is noted. Most of the brands' activities appear to be best positioned within the mainstream business frameworks, whereas sustainability-related characteristics such as revisited design, use of allegedly sustainable materials and attention to local crafts are to be understood as a plus, a feature useful for finer brands' positioning.

In December 2013, a special issue of *Vogue Talents* was published, and it was dedicated, as the title states, to "The ones who have succeeded" (Appendix 7A.1, 5). Fashion is understood as "a bridge between cultures" while adhering to the ethical fashion programme of the The International Trade Centre (ITC) of the United Nations is presented as the right path to undertake (Appendix 7A.2, 16). Yet, the title suggests an alignment with the predominant system. Starting from 2015, the February edition of *Vogue Talents* was introduced, and it was initially dedicated to talents from around the globe. The format was also changed, giving more space to the individual presentation. Consequently, we learn more about designers' personal paths, philosophy and inspirations. The analysis of the section "Scouting for Africa" showed that many brands acknowledging the need for more socially responsible fashion practices were actively engaged in community empowerment. Differently from what is observable in the first *Vogue Italia* article on ethical fashion where there were the Western designers to engage with the communities in the developing countries, here, we see African designers engaging with local communities, empowering women, providing educational workshops and skill-learning opportunities (Appendix 7A.2, 17, 19). Not less importantly, they are promoting African fashion products and aesthetics. The focus was on preserving traditional techniques and promotion of the local crafts (Appendix 7A.2, 18, 19, 26, 30). Still, no discussion on cultural inspiration, as opposed to cultural appropriation, is present on these pages. Fashion was perceived and used as an empowering tool to lift people out of poverty (Appendix 7A.2, 19, 26, 27, 28). The *Plural* landscape proposed by Fletcher and Tham undoubtedly involves honouring of the numerous non-Western perspectives. In this line, the "focus on the countries to watch for new talented emerging designers" issue of *Vogue Talents* does a great job in featuring the new generation of creatives from Nigeria, Sudan, Ghana, Senegal, Mozambique, but also from Ukraine, China, Lebanon, Saudi Arabia, United Arab Emirates, Kuwait, Qatar and Russia. What is to highlight are not only the different geographies, represented in the issue in question by individual designers, but also the crafts and traditions which are usually suppressed by the pervasive, capital-driven system. In that sense, it could be argued that *Vogue Talents* is coming short in setting fashion free from its prominent association with consumerist ideals, mainly because the success stories are always contextualised within the predominant fashion system. Nevertheless, on the pages dedicated to the African creatives, the problem of the second-hand Western clothing market also pops up (Appendix 7A.2, 29). Donating the clothes that we do not care for anymore to charity does not help the underdeveloped communities; on the contrary, it additionally damages the local industry and burdens the waste management of the countries of arrival. In this sense, donating to charity is the same as discarding; the only difference is that it is not the landfill near one's home but another, kilometres away. Still, it is on the same planet, and featuring these problems, even though sporadically, on a platform as *Vogue Italia* was undoubtedly a very needed step. It is to admit though that the neo-colonial aspects of fashion are sadly underrepresented and not enough talked about in the mainstream fashion media. For this reason, the new frontiers of fashion activism must discuss revisited ways of organisation and governance, proposing and learning, as well as unlearning outdated common senses.

Moving to the September issue of the same year, we see the comeback of the classical *Vogue Talents* format, this time enriched by a selection of 20 emerging designers chosen by the combined efforts of *Vogue Italia* editors and the readers of Vogue.it. The keywords with which these brands are described are customisable, handcrafted, collaborative, craftsmanship, tradition, handwork (Appendix 7A.2, 31). The stance away from the industrialised production processes characteristic of the fashion system is underlined. It is in this issue that the first, even though implicit, features of degrowth, understood as "purposefully slow[ing] things down in order to minimize harm to humans and earth systems" (Kallis et al., 2020), can be perceived. In the Womenswear section, the editor emphasises the need for agency regarding socio-cultural concerns and engagement for traceability in the supply chain (Appendix 7A.2, 32), whilst an updated view of luxury is also proposed, imagined as "quality and traceability rather than a logo" (Appendix 7A.2, 33). Moreover, the editorial choice to boldly present practices related to artisanal and handmade methods is reflected in articles such as *Italians handcrafting innovation* (Appendix 7A.2, 34), where examples of brand collaborations with experienced craftspeople are showcased. In these examples we can observe traces of values such as *Co-creation, Grounded imagination*, reliance on *Diverse ways of knowing*, characteristic for the *Earth Logic*. Clearly, that is only what can be perceived from the representations in the supplement, while the actual integration of these values by the brands would require an additional, in-depth analysis.

The traditional skills and local craftsmanship continued to be topics of interest and action for the brands featured in *Vogue Talents* also two years later (Appendix 7A.2, 37–42, 50). Eco-sustainability was increasingly emphasised (Appendix 7A.2, 39, 41, 46–48), but alternative fashion practices were also consistently more present. Upcycling was becoming a thing, with designers "going to vintage shops, choosing items and then re-elaborating them" (Appendix 7A.2, 36, 44). Brands were becoming more attentive to minimising or eliminating production waste (Appendix 7A.2, 36, 41) also by introducing the make-to-order principle (Appendix 7A.2, 43). These practices that shift away from the conventional relying on virgin materials, the more resource-wise design approaches and the active listening of the community are all features that could be well located within the *Less* landscape. Ultimately, however, *Less* means living within a framework of decreased production and consumption. Thus, it "is the largest provocation associated with the transition to sustainability" (Fletcher & Tham, [2019] 2021, 45), especially within the context of capitalist realism where "capital's 'need of constantly expanding market' [and] its 'growth fetish' mean that capitalism is by its very nature opposed to any notion of sustainability" (Fisher, 2009, 18–19). In fact, all of the featured steps towards a more sustainable fashion system were reasonable and appreciable but not enough. Unfortunately, the results of the questionnaire administered to 950 young people from 53 countries showed that 90% of them are interested in sustainability "but thought that saving on fabric cuts and fewer seams is enough." Only "Few believed it is necessary to tackle the entire production chain with a holistic approach and be transparent with consumers" (Appendix 7A.2, 45).

While emerging brands were gradually exploring different approaches to sustainability, *Vogue Talents* initiated to emphasise sustainable fashion brands. As the September issues changed, still featuring the newly graduated designers but introducing the Scouting section, which replaced the well-known Womenswear, Menswear and Accessories divisions, the "Sustainable" label was also placed alongside brands that were considered sustainable (Appendix 7A.1, 9). Out of 46 brands featured in the Scouting section, seven were marked as "Sustainable". The analysis showed that these brands were mainly focused on small production (Appendix 7A.2, 53, 57, 59) and the use of natural, ethically sourced materials (Appendix 7A.2, 51, 59), or however materials that would be otherwise burned or destinated to landfill (Appendix 7A.2, 56, 57, 60). Furthermore, the brands showed attention to transparency and traceability (Appendix 7A.2, 51) and engagement in collaborations with artisans and craftspeople (Appendix 7A.2, 53). In contrast to this practice, the neo-colonialist approach of many luxury brands, which take inspiration from the traditional work of minority cultures without giving back to the interested communities, was also contested (Appendix 7A.2, 62). Sustainable practices were observed in the description of six additional brands, which were not emphasised as "sustainable" most likely because of their focus on social and ethical questions with the environmental engagement being not clearly expressed. This mode of representation is questionable since the focus on community, local artisans and craftsmanship (Appendix 7A.2, 55), the preservation of the traditional culture (Appendix 7A.2, 58), as well as the small production and workers' rights (Appendix 7A.2, 52, 54) are all building blocks of a righteous fashion system. This eco-centred approach in the sustainability presentation as detached from the socio-ethical and cultural issues is rather problematic, and it brings about perpetuation of fashion injustices. Starting from 2019, this will change, moving towards a more holistic understanding of the fashion system's impact and consequential presentation of positive brand examples.

In the editorial message from February 2019, Sara Sozzani Maino writes, "From today, we must strive to change the way we produce, distribute and consume. ... our commitment is to highlight some of the designers and enterprises that are seeking to improve the present system". "Now we must try to encourage creatives of the future to tread a more sustainable path" (Appendix 7A.2, 63). Indeed, the supplement pages became a platform for awareness-raising and education, featuring responsible brands, which here are not an exception but the norm. An increasing number of articles dedicated to sustainability enriched the traditional showcase of emerging designers whilst highlighting the complexity of the fashion-sustainability relationship (Appendix 7A.2, 64, 66–68). Community engagement and eco-friendly practices were presented as equally important (Appendix 7A.2, 72, 73, 77–81, 83–85). While in 2015, the information was still sporadic, without an evident *fil rouge*, featuring only some isolated responsible actions or sustainable practices, here we see the combination of "sustainability" with "social commitment". The need for an integrated, transparent and traceable approach is also underlined. The concept of *Less*, as discussed by Fletcher and Tham (2021 [2019]), is reflected in upcycling processes where creativity is conditioned by the available second-hand objects or dead-stock materials (Appendix 7A.2, 74–76, 82). Other caring practices such as repairing (Appendix 7A.2, 77) and designing carry-over pieces (Appendix 7A.2, 79) are also featured. The selection is enriched by texts with tips on "what can we do, follow, visit" or "where to study sustainability" (Appendix 7A.2, 69, 71, 65).

The commitment to encourage responsible fashion practices continued in the following issues of *Vogue Talents*. It was at the centre of many competitions, awards and projects presented in the supplement (Appendix 7A.2, 86–90). The new talents representing the hope for a just world (Appendix 7A.2, 91–93) were "refusing to be implicated in the waste, destructiveness and lack of care for workers which the clothing industry wreaks on the planet". "Upcycling, responsible sourcing and localism (were) becoming the new normal" (Appendix 7A.2, 93). This statement is reflected in the *New Avantgarde* section of the same issue (Appendix 7A.2, 94–97) and the February issue the following year (Appendix 7A.2, 99–113). Following *Vogue Italia*'s "Sustainability and Creativity" issue from January 2020, the February supplement boldly stated the commitment for a better future. The issue started with the "10 Reasons for Radical Change" by Matteo Ward (Appendix 7A.2, 98) and continued with the already mentioned selection of designers integrating the different aspects of sustainability in their practice. The next issue underlines the importance of fashion media and the redesign of communication practices (Appendix 7A.2, 117), actively emphasising the importance of the *Language* and *Learning* landscapes, as proposed by Fletcher and Tham ([2019] 2021). The focus is on upcycling and reusing with brands counteracting the business-as-usual approach (Appendix 7A.2, 118–121) while centring on alternative practices based on values like *Care, Co-creation* and *Interdependency* (Appendix 7A.2, 123). More so, a reflection of the editorial choices to limit the industry's impact are the editorials such "Morning light, the origin of everything"—a celebration of responsible fashion brands (Appendix 7A.2, 116) and "Tender is the Night" completely illustrated by Yuliya Yg (Appendix 7A.2, 124). The latest was designed to save precious resources, usually needed during photo shootings—something that *Vogue Italia* also did for the January issue of the same year. It also recalls the past magazine practices when fashion was not so accelerated, harmful and unjust. Articles on "Europe's best practices" (Appendix 7A.2, 122) and "Amsterdam's sustainability offer" (Appendix 7A.2, 115) only broaden the understanding of how sustainability should be integrated into the larger context. In the latest issue, Sara Sozzani Maino wraps up the reasons behind the editorial decisions and provides an undoubtable definition of what fashion today should be:

> Along with a commitment to more environmentally friendly fashion industry, (the) inclusive sense of responsibility also embraces society, artisans, people and local territories, conveying thought-provoking messages that raise awareness in present and future consumers.
>
> (Appendix 7A.2, 125)

7.5 Discussion and conclusion

As presented in the *Findings*, the sustainability-related contents are not a recent feature of *Vogue Italia*; still, the more concrete delineation of the relationship between fashion and sustainability is observable after 2010. Specifically, in the context of the supplement *Vogue Talents*, this relation demonstrates a clear evolution and developments in regard to the meanings associated with the oxymoron "sustainable fashion". From the ungrounded use of the word "sustainable" in the early 2010s to the holistic understanding of what it means to be responsible in the fashion industry visible in the latest issues, we saw how the manifestations of social responsibility and ethics were gradually integrated with the environmentally centred aspects, the latest, for a long time being perceived as the only association to sustainability in the fashion context. The ways in which the global perspective is presented by the emerging designers of all continents highlight the power of the decentralisation of fashion, while opening for a discussion on the underrepresented nuances of plurality. Significantly, in the *Vogue Talents* context, the first appearances of social responsibility and community engagement are almost exclusively related to the non-Western realities speaking volumes of the importance of the opening to *Multiple centres*—a dimension that was observed as lacking among the Italian born-sustainable fashion brands. Here we observe an incrementing representation over time. The supplement's contents, reflective of the gradual, yet implicit, introduction of the degrowth logic, add towards developments in a responsible direction, even though the road is still to be traced. Speaking to this is the lack of observable implications of updated forms of *Learning*, *Governing* and *Languaging*, which would undoubtedly demonstrate how the revisited understanding of where and who could envision, practise and recount fashion today builds towards a more just and holistically sustainable fashion system.

Moreover, it is to be underlined that the context of *Vogue Talents* is an isolated one in terms that it is ideated from the beginning to feature only a selection of progressive fashion brands. Furthermore, here the focus is on the presented contents, not the featured individual brands. Thus, the results regard what is represented, not the actual integration of sustainability-related aspects by the brands. What is to highlight is that throughout the decade, we observe the evolution of both the meaning of the term "sustainability" and the quantity and the quality of sustainability-related representations. If in 2010 there was only one unclear mention of "sustainability", starting from 2019, the pages are dedicated to born-sustainable fashion practices. Here, it is useful to remember that, as we saw through the qualitative analysis conducted during the pilot project "Culture and Sustainability: An Interplay on the (contemporary) Made in Italy Landscape", born-sustainable does not always mean holistically integrated. The in-depth analysis revealed discrepancies in regard to the *Earth Logic* values and landscapes. Although in the present study we observe a gradual development of a holistic approach to sustainability, represented by an integrated understanding and presentation of the various sustainability aspects on the fashion magazine level, there are no practical frameworks able to efficiently convey the various levels of sustainable action undertaken by single concerns. In order to understand one brand's levels of sustainability-oriented commitment, the information available in *Vogue Talents* is not sufficient and we must further investigate the brand. The global perspective comprises plenty of local points of view, place-specific needs and responses to those needs, yet, as anticipated earlier, the multiverse of local pluralities is still unexplored. Bearing this in mind, it is essential to investigate and to actively foster new modes of understanding, organising and communicating fashion in a more systemic manner, also because we saw those aspects significantly underrepresented.

The latest issue of *Vogue Talents* reveals yet another layer. It is called Fearless Generations, and it somehow implies that future generations, those that have nothing to lose, have to bear the burden or at least the responsibility to change the system for good. In order to paradigmatically shift the predominant system, we need the contribution of everyone, certainly including the efforts of those who have many things to lose. And here, everyone is to be understood, not as implicit of multiple individual efforts, but as a call for collective subjectivity, required, as discussed by Fisher, in facing systemic issues (Fisher, 2009).

In conclusion, we must acknowledge the fact that the concept of sustainability presented in the fashion media context is not yet a reflection of the actual situation. In practice, as it is discussed in Vol.12 n.2 of *ZoneModa Journal* (Maksimova & Piancazzo, 2022), there is still much focus on the environmental aspects, at least in the Italian context. The field analysis unravels inconsistencies and much room for improvements. In this line, it is of importance to offer a critical and more reflective thought, also within the mainstream media. For that matter, proposing consistent frameworks, also in the context of fashion media, would add to the role of fashion as a creative and communication industry, which integrated with its revisited fashion-as-industry (Payne, 2021) praxis could be able to show the path towards a more responsible, inclusive and respectful society. Maybe only afterwards fashion will be a step closer to saving the world. In the meantime, we as a society should continue to engage consistently in a bolder manner to underline the complexity of sustainable thinking and action, growing past the simplistic associations of sustainability with environmental or social responsibility.

Appendix 7A.1

No	Issue	Date	Page format	No of pages	Title	Subtitle + Heading
1	721	Sep. 2010	A3	34*	Fidenza Village is proud to support Vogue Talents	160 emerging designers
2	733	Sep 2011	A3	34*	Fidenza Village and Vogue Talents explore a world of new talents	180 emerging designers
3	745	Sep 2012	A3	34*	Fidenza Village and Vogue Talents discovering fashion's future generation of talents	190 emerging designers
4	757	Sep 2013	A3	34*	Samsung and Vogue Talents present a new generation of fashion designers and Samsung Accessories Talents Scouting	200 emerging designers
5	760	Dec 2013	A3	8	The Dubai Mall and Vogue Talents present "The ones who have succeeded... The new generation of fashion designers"	--
6	774	Feb 2015	A3	26**	The Dubai Mall and Vogue Talents present "A focus on the countries to watch for new talented emerging designers"	New countries to watch out for
7	781	Sep 2015	A3	34*	Camera Nazionale della Moda Italiana and Vogue Talents present spotlight on 2015's fashion designers	200 emerging designers
8	810	Feb 2018	A3	30***	Camera Nazionale della Moda Italiana and Vogue Talents present countries to watch for new talented designers	Vogue Italia Talents
9	817	Sep 2018	A3	36****	Vogue Talents Spotlight on 2018's fashion designers	–
10	822	Feb 2019	A3	30***	Vogue Talents – The New Frontiers of Awareness	–
11	829	Sep 2019	21×28.5	88	Vogue Talents 10 (anniversary)	–
12	834	Feb 2020	21×28.5	48	Vogue Talents – The New Frontiers of Awareness	–
13	840	Sep 2020	21×28.5	56	Vogue Talents – Strength of purpose	–
14	845	Feb 2021	21×28.5	48	Vogue Talents – The New Frontiers of Awareness	–
15	852	Sep 2021	21×28.5	64	Vogue Talents – Fearless Generations	–

Notes: *36 with the internal covers; **28 with front and back cover; ***32 with front and back cover; **** with front and back cover

Appendix 7A.2

No	Issue	Date	Page	Section	Title or brand name*
1	721	Sep 2010	19	Womenswear	Short description
2	721	Sep 2010	21	Womenswear	*ERRO
3	721	Sep 2010	26	Menswear	*Christopher Raeburn
4	733	Sep 2011	20	Womenswear	*Marco Corso
5	757	Sep 2013	2	Articles	The Fashion Capitals of Tomorrow
6	757	Sep 2013	22	Womenswear	Short description
7	757	Sep 2013	22	Womenswear	*Cristaseya
8	757	Sep 2013	22	Womenswear	*Vincent Billeci
9	757	Sep 2013	23	Womenswear	*Kamenskakononova
10	757	Sep 2013	23	Womenswear	*Alcoolique
11	757	Sep 2013	26	Womenswear	*Partsparts Imseonoc
12	757	Sep 2013	27	Womenswear	*FlaviaLaRocca
13	757	Sep 2013	28	Menswear	*Tigran Avetisyan
14	757	Sep 2013	31	Accessories	*Nasha Mekraksavanich
15	757	Sep 2013	32	Accessories	*PB0110
16	760	Dec 2013	7	/	*Stella Jean
17	774	Feb 2015	3	/	*Ituen Basi
18	774	Feb 2015	6	/	*Maki Oh
19	774	Feb 2015	7	/	*Studio One Eighty Nine
26	774	Feb 2015	16	Scouting for Africa	*A A K S by Akosua Afriyie-Kumi
27	774	Feb 2015	17	Scouting for Africa	*Loza Maléombho
28	774	Feb 2015	19	Scouting for Africa	*Orange Culture
29	774	Feb 2015	18	Scouting for Africa	*Mafrika by Sadia Mustafa
30	774	Feb 2015	18	Scouting for Africa	*O 'Milua by Olajumoke Ademilua
31	781	Sep 2015	1	Supported by	-whole section
32	781	Sep 2015	18	Womenswear	Short description

(Continued)

33	781	Sep 2015	23	Womenswear	*Etienne Deroeux
34	781	Sep 2015	24	Article	Italians handcrafting innovation
36	810	Feb 2018	06	/	*Kozaburo
37	810	Feb 2018	07	/	*Problem
38	810	Feb 2018	15	/	*Yohei Ohno
39	810	Feb 2018	17	/	*Moon Choi
40	810	Feb 2018	22	/	*Etiqueta Latina
41	810	Feb 2018	25	/	*Chain
42	810	Feb 2018	25	/	*Kenneth Ize
43	810	Feb 2018	27	/	*Proudrace
44	810	Feb 2018	28	/	*Style wars
45	810	Feb 2018	10	Article	ITS is back
46	810	Feb 2018	19	Scouting for India	*Bav Tailor
47	810	Feb 2018	19	Scouting for India	*N&S Gaia
48	810	Feb 2018	20	Scouting for India	*Shift
49	810	Feb 2018	21	Scouting for India	*Ara Lumiere
50	810	Feb 2018	20	Scouting for India	*Urvashi Kaur
51	817	Sep 2018	13	Scouting	*Soster Studio
52	817	Sep 2018	15	Scouting	*Victor Von Schwarz
53	817	Sep 2018	17	Scouting	*Phipps
54	817	Sep 2018	18	Scouting	*Kay Kwok
55	817	Sep 2018	19	Scouting	*Armando Takeda
56	817	Sep 2018	24	Scouting	*Germanier
57	817	Sep 2018	28	Scouting	*Nathalie Ballout
58	817	Sep 2018	30	Scouting	*Emmy Kasbit
59	817	Sep 2018	33	Scouting	*Gabriella Coll Garments
60	817	Sep 2018	32	Scouting	*Tiziano Guardini
61	817	Sep 2018	33	Scouting	*Grassi 10000 by Anna Grassi
62	817	Sep 2018	35	Scouting	*Alama

No	Issue	Date	Page	Section	Title or brand name*
63	822	Feb 2019	2	Article	New Frontiers of Awareness
64	822	Feb 2019	2	Article	Waterworld: Everything the sea has to offer
65	822	Feb 2019	3	Article	Where to study sustainability?
66	822	Feb 2019	19	Article	What is the future of our planet? What can we do to safeguard it?
67	822	Feb 2019	23	Article	The Challenge to Climate Change and the Cooperative approach to production
68	822	Feb 2019	24	Article	Natural Mimesis
69	822	Feb 2019	27	Article	How to be sustainable. 15 resources to go greener while buying or making fashion
70	822	Feb 2019	29	Article	Success Stories
71	822	Feb 2019	31	Article	What's going on. Summits, Awards and Exhibitions during 2019
72	822	Feb 2019	4	Scouting	*Bethany Williams
73	822	Feb 2019	4	Scouting	*Soster Studio
74	822	Feb 2019	5	Scouting	* Germanier
75	822	Feb 2019	5	Scouting	* Helen Kirkum
76	822	Feb 2019	8	Scouting	* Ahluwalia Studio
77	822	Feb 2019	8	Scouting	*Maggie Marilyn
78	822	Feb 2019	9	Scouting	* Hazza
79	822	Feb 2019	9	Scouting	*Bite Studios
80	822	Feb 2019	10	Scouting	*Cara Marie Piazza
81	822	Feb 2019	10	Scouting	* Escudo
82	822	Feb 2019	20	Scouting	*Matthew Needham
83	822	Feb 2019	21	Scouting	*Cora Bellotto
84	822	Feb 2019	21	Scouting	*John Alexander Skelton
85	822	Feb 2019	21	Scouting	*Cesta Collective
86	829	Sep 2019	3	Vogue Talents for	NABA
87	829	Sep 2019	5	Vogue Talents for	CNMI
88	829	Sep 2019	28–29	Vogue Talents for	Fashion 4 development

89	829	Sep 2019	40–43	Vogue Talents for	Woolmark company (award)
90	829	Sep 2019	74–75	Vogue Talents for	Fidenza Village
91	829	Sep 2019	6	Voices on talents	Federico Marchetti
92	829	Sep 2019	8	Voices on talents	Sara Mower
93	829	Sep 2019	6	Voices on talents	Clare Press
94	829	Sep 2019	62	The New Avantgarde	*Carlota Berrera
95	829	Sep 2019	68	The New Avantgarde	*Duran Lantink
96	829	Sep 2019	71	The New Avantgarde	*Salim Azzam
97	829	Sep 2019	71	The New Avantgarde	*Oloapitreps
98	834	Feb 2020	4	Article	10 Reasons for Radical Change
99	834	Feb 2020	6	The New Avantgarde	*Vitelli
100	834	Feb 2020	8	The New Avantgarde	*Sevali
101	834	Feb 2020	12	The New Avantgarde	*Leandi Mulder
102	834	Feb 2020	14	The New Avantgarde	*Collina Strada
103	834	Feb 2020	16	The New Avantgarde	*Amesh
104	834	Feb 2020	20	The New Avantgarde	*Morphine.online
105	834	Feb 2020	21	The New Avantgarde	*re;code
106	834	Feb 2020	22	The New Avantgarde	*Weiyu Hung
107	834	Feb 2020	24	The New Avantgarde	*Style wars
108	834	Feb 2020	25	The New Avantgarde	*Kowtow
109	834	Feb 2020	28	The New Avantgarde	*Kidsuper
110	834	Feb 2020	29	The New Avantgarde	*Vanta Design Studio
111	834	Feb 2020	32	The New Avantgarde	*Fantabody
112	834	Feb 2020	33	The New Avantgarde	*Mama Tiera
113	834	Feb 2020	34	The New Avantgarde	*Manuel Manufactures
114	834	Feb 2020	30–31	Vogue Talents for	African Fashion Foundation
115	834	Feb 2020	36–37	Article	Walking in Amsterdam: The home of sustainability
116	834	Feb 2020	39–46	Editorial	Morning light, the origin of everything

(Continued)

No	Issue	Date	Page	Section	Title or brand name*
117	840	Sep 2020	4	Article	Communication as a force of change
118	840	Sep 2020	6	New Generation	*Av Vattev
119	840	Sep 2020	10	New Generation	*Arturo Obegero
120	840	Sep 2020	23	New Generation	*Florentina Leitner
121	840	Sep 2020	24	New Generation	*Vaquar
122	840	Sep 2020	26	Article	From energy to culture: Best practices in Europe
123	840	Sep 2020	43–46	Artisans and Community	Entire section
124	840	Sep 2020	49–53	Editorial	Tender is the night
125	852	Sep 2021	3	Editorial	Fearless Generations

Note: *36 with the internal covers.

Appendix 7A.3

N°	Issue	Date	Page	Type	Original title
1	478	Apr 1990	33	Adv.	Moschino
2	499	Mar 1992	135	Adv.	Moschino
3	506	Oct 1992	133	Adv.	Moschino
4	510	Feb 1993	91	Adv.	Moschino
5	529	Sep 1994	105	Adv.	Moschino
6	637	Sep 2003	200	Article	Eco awards
7	637	Sep 2003	206	Article	Philosophy: consumo etico?
8	687	Nov 2007	112	Article	Eco
9	688	Dec 2007	96	Article	Eco-ansia
10	703	Mar 2009	182	Article	Ecoterapia
11	704	Apr 2009	20	Article	Sostenibilità
12	704	Apr 2009	92	Article	Earth Day
13	712	Dec 2009	84	Article	Goodwill fibres
14	716	Apr 2010	52	Article	Sure this is not a wonderful world
15	716	Apr 2010	80	Article	L'insostenibile leggerezza dello spreco
16	717	May 2010	52	Article	Il tempo sostenibile

References

Black, S. (2008). *Eco-Chic: The Fashion Paradox*. London: Black Dog Publishing Limited.

Black, S., de la Haye, A., Entwistle, J., Rocamora, A., Root, R. A. and Thomas, H. (Eds.). (2013). *The Handbook of Fashion Studies*. London-New York: Bloomsbury.

Ciuni, L. and Spadafora, M. (2020), *La rivoluzione comincia dal tuo armadio* (The revolution starts in your wardrobe) Tutto quello che dovreste sapere sulla moda sostenibile, Milano: Solferino.

de Castro, O. (2021). *Loved Clothes Last: How the Joy of Rewearing and Repairing Your Clothes Can Be a Revolutionary Act*. London: Penguin Random House.

Denisova, A. (2021). *Fashion Media and Sustainability*. London: University of Westminster Press.

Fisher, M. (2009). *Capitalist Realism. Is There No Alternative?* UK: Zero Books.

Fletcher, K. (2014 [2008]). *Sustainable Fashion and Textiles. Design Journeys*. London-New York: Routledge.

Fletcher, K. and Grose, L. (2012). *Fashion & Sustainability, Design for Change*. London: Laurence King Publishing Ltd.

Fletcher, K. and Tham, M. (2019). *Earth Logic: Fashion Action Research Plan*. London: The JJ Charitable Trust.

Gwilt, A. and Rissanen, T. (Eds.). (2011). *Shaping Sustainable Fashion: Changing the Way We Make and Use Our Clothes*. London-Washington: Earthscan.

Hethorn, J. and Ulasewicz, C. (Eds.). (2015). *Sustainable Fashion. What's Next?* London-New York: Bloomsbury.

Jones, K.B. and J.M. Hawley. (2017). 'Chic but Scrupulous, Down to the Very Last Stitch': 'Style Ethics' in American Vogue. *Fashion Practice*, 9:2: 280–302.

Jones, K.B. (2019). "American Vogue and Sustainable Fashion (1990–2015): A Multimodal Critical Discourse Analysis." *Clothing and Textiles Research Journal*, 38(2): 104–118.

Kallis, G., Paulson, S., D'Alisa, G., and Demaria, F. (2020). *The Case for Degrowth*. Cambridge: Polity Press.

Kent, S. (2021, March 22). "The Sustainability Gap: How Fashion Measures Up". *Business of Fashion*,. https://cdn.businessoffashion.com/reports/The_Sustainability_Index_2021.pdf

Laing, M. (2023). "Animals 'Occupy' Vogue Italia: Sustainability, Ethics and the Fashion Media." In L. Wallenberg and A. Kollnitz (eds.) *Fashion Aesthetics and Ethics. Past and Present*. London-New York-Dublin: Bloomsbury Publishing Plc.

Maksimova, N. and Piancazzo, F. (2021, June 17–19). *Culture and Sustainability: An Interplay on the (Contemporary) Made in Italy Landscape* [Conference presentation]. Fashion Tales 2020+1 Conference, Milan, Italy.

Maksimova, N. and Piancazzo, F. (2022, December). Culture and sustainability: An interplay on the new made in Italy landscape. *ZoneModa Journal*, 12(2): 57–82. https://doi.org/10.6092/issn.2611-0563/15813

Payne, A. (2021). *Designing Fashion's Future: Present Practice and Tactics for Sustainable Change*. London: Bloomsbury Visual Arts.

Rinaldi, F. R. (2019). *Fashion Industry 2030. Reshaping the Future through Sustainability and Responsible Innovation*. Milan: Bocconi University Press.

Tham, M. (2010). Languaging fashion and sustainability: Towards synergistic modes of thinking, wording, visualising and doing fashion and sustainability. *Nordic Textile Journal*, 3(1): 14–23.

Todeschini, B.V., Cortimiglia, M.N., Callegaro-de-Menezes, D. and Ghezzi, A. (2017). Innovative and sustainable business models in the fashion industry: Entrepreneurial drivers, opportunities, and challenges. *Business Horizons*, 60: 759–770. DOI: 10.1016/j.bushor.2017.07.003

Chapter 8

Educating Fashion for a Sustainable Future

Naomi Braithwaite and Lisa Trencher

8.1 Introduction

The complex relationship between fashion and sustainability at all levels of the industry is well documented. Despite the negative impacts that fashion has had on the environment, the industry has taken a lead in moving towards securing sustainable practices, from ethical production to sustainable consumption. The accelerated growth in sustainable business strategies throughout the global fashion industry has created opportunities for fashion education to play an integral role in nurturing the skills and knowledge that will support a more ethical and sustainable industry. The development of sustainability knowledge in higher education has been evolving over many years (Haigh, 2005). While there are important examples of fashion design education supporting sustainable practices within the curriculum (Armstrong and LeHew, 2013; Murzyn-Kupisz and Holuj, 2021), there is a defined opportunity to further embed sustainable practices within the curriculum for fashion business courses that can support the further implementation within industry practice. As lecturers in fashion business courses at two UK Higher Education Institutions, Manchester Metropolitan University (MMU) and Nottingham Trent University (NTU), the authors have responded to this opportunity by exploring two distinct pedagogical approaches that could equip their students with the knowledge and skills to become champions for a sustainable fashion future. This chapter discusses the rationale and implementation of the authors' respective pedagogical approaches and reflects on the impact it has had on their students. While the approach was started independently, discussions and reflections have enabled collaboration through shared experiences with the aim of disseminating these approaches within the institutions' respective curriculums.

The challenges of embedding sustainability in business courses which tend to focus on economic models of growth including marketing for sales, profit maximisation and consumption have been examined (Fisher and Bonn, 2011; Armstrong and LeHew, 2013). In the case of fashion business where there is an increased shift towards sustainable practices, including achieving a more

DOI: 10.4324/9781032659053-8

circular approach (Vogue, 2020), fashion education has an important contribution to instil the knowledge and skills that will support the employability of students in the industry of the future. At an institutional level education for sustainable development (ESD) has facilitated a reappraisal of how and what students learn, with the intention of vesting them with the knowledge and skills required to become sustainable citizens along with encouraging sustainable behaviours (Egan, 2004). The role of ESD is to build competencies, skills, attributes and values in relation to specific subject knowledge and knowledge of sustainable development (QAA, 2021). Initiated in 2014 and revised in 2021 ESD aims to encourage the skills and values in students that will support them in taking an active lead in the transition towards a sustainable society (QAA, 2021).

While there are some examples of studies that have embedded sustainability in various marketing, management and business programmes (Stubbs and Cocklin, 2008; Benn and Dunphy, 2009), there is little detail of pedagogical approaches where students have taken the lead in developing sustainability in the curriculum as the co-creators of knowledge (Radclyffe-Thomas, Varley and Roncha, 2018). Barber et al. (2014) have discussed the merit for applying an integrated approach in business courses to support the development of skills and knowledge for students, enhancing their graduate attributes. To implement a student-centred approach to learning, the authors have applied a constructivist pedagogy (Taber, 2011) with the intention of actively engaging students in co-creating sustainability knowledge that enhances their potential as future fashion industry leaders and as sustainable citizens. The objective was to further embed sustainable practice within the institutions' fashion business curricula through the outcomes of student-led research. The chapter reflects on these outcomes as case studies of best practice and considers their role in the curriculum of the future.

8.2 Sustainability in Higher Education—The Context for Fashion Business Students

In 2016 the Business of Fashion predicted 'sustainability expert' to be one of the key fashion careers of the future (Chitrakorn, 2016). Documented evidence that sustainable literate students are more employable (Radclyffe-Thomas, Varley and Roncha, 2018) supported the rationale for the authors pedagogical approaches. Drawing from Armstrong and LeHew's (2013) analysis of the ESD framework, the study has focused on developing the construct of sustainable literacy. According to Armstrong and LeHew's (2013) framework, sustainable literacy implies the following: understanding sustainability, its implications and the need for change, including the knowledge and skills needed to empower individuals to make change and move others to make change (Forum for the Future, 2004).

Within the two institutions different approaches to facilitate the embedding of sustainable literacy within the curriculum have been developed. At MMU the focus was predominantly on industry practice and identifying the skills required to support a career in industry. Students worked together to collate job specifications of current industry roles in relation to responsible fashion business and sustainability. Through this task they were analysing the skills and attributes required to develop an understanding of current industry challenges and best practice. The intention was to create a resource that could then be used and added to by future students on the courses.

The approach at NTU focused on issues surrounding sustainable consumption, engaging students in reflections on their own, along with their peers' attitudes and behaviours, towards fashion and clothing, with the aim of gaining greater understanding of what motivates consumption and behaviours towards clothing through its life span. Goldberg (2009) recognised that while many people including students are passionate about sustainability and ethics, it is important to understand what the wider issues are that people are concerned about as this will shed deeper insights about what drives motivations and behaviour. In the context of fashion consumption, this is significant as it is important to understand how individuals feel about clothing and why they buy as this can highlight the barriers and opportunities for more sustainable consumption. By engaging fashion students in this sharing of personal attitudes and values towards clothing, the objective was for them to gain insights about what mattered to them in the context of clothing and how this could enhance a greater understanding of how sustainable consumption could be achieved in the future. While the applied approaches were very different, they supported the ESD model by facilitating opportunities to create skills, knowledge and reflect on values, attitudes and behaviours that will encourage students to become agents of change, both as consumers and industry professionals.

Sustainability has been core to the authors' teaching for many years. Recent drives to embed the United Nations (UN) Goals of Sustainable Development within the respective curriculums have encouraged reflection on how to better immerse students in these debates. Recognising the importance of equipping students for the future, the pedagogical approaches respond to the growing importance of corporate social responsibility and ethical practices (Wong et al., 2021) as graduate attributes. Radclyffe-Thomas, Varley and Ronchas' work explored the development of a model for responsible fashion education (2018). They noted that sustainability in the curriculum has been most visible in courses that focus on fashion design and production, rather than business management courses. In the context of embedding sustainable literacy, the Higher Education Academy (HEA)'s Future Fit Framework (Sterling, 2011) has detailed strategies for sustainable development which promote active, participatory and experiential methods that engage students in ways that will make a significant difference to their knowledge and understanding, enabling them to become active facilitators of change (Radclyffe-Thomas, Varley and Roncha, 2018). Goldberg (2009) proposed that the development of sustainable literacy comes through students being able to identify their own behaviours and motivations, as this becomes a platform for their own reflection and transformation.

Both approaches align with the growth in student-centred pedagogies within higher education (Sterling, 2011). Drawing from Dewey (2011) students were encouraged to become actively involved in the development of sustainability within the curriculum. Applying an interactive approach enabled a move away from the more usual passive transmission of information about sustainability and instead applied a student-led research approach to build knowledge in the context of corporate social responsibility and consumer behaviour with reference to how personal values drive consumer behaviour and attitudes. To support the different approaches, a central research question was defined which asked how students could take an active role in developing sustainability in the curriculum and what impact does this have on their learning experience. The approaches were then implemented, followed by a subsequent reflection on what the participating students had gained from the experiences. Further discussion enabled consideration of the development of these approaches in the respective institutions and through the sharing of knowledge.

8.3 Developing the Pedagogical Approaches

The approach at MMU is founded in a student-centred curriculum (SCC) project at MMU which puts the student at the heart of curriculum design encouraging the development of student experiences beyond their academic course; this is titled as the RISE project. A key element of the SCC project is to support the development of confidence building and employability skills. The MMU author is the employability lead for Manchester Fashion Institute, working closely with industry, and has a strong understanding of the current landscape and the value of sustainability as a core graduate attribute. The objective of the approach at MMU was to affirm the value of knowledge and attitudes of students/graduates for responsible business practice and sustainability as a defined employability skill. Manchester has a thriving fashion industry with multiple head offices located within the city and though there are several exceptions the area is seen as predominantly 'fast fashion.' A high percentage of fashion graduates remain in the North West and are employed by these fast fashion companies. The wider industry is looking for change and this appears to be reflected in student attitudes as they embed sustainable elements within their work. The approach at MMU involved a research project that explored the opportunities for careers in responsible fashion. By valuing students as research partners in this area, there is an opportunity to develop resources to be shared with other students promoting peer learning.

The SCC at MMU encourages students to participate in extra-curricular activities which include opportunities for collaboration tailored to their studies (RISE). These activities can engage students in a wide range of experiences, earning degree credits and developing new skills that help shape their future careers. The rationale for this was founded by a previous experience where the MMU academic had undertaken a RISE internship the previous academic year: Careers in the Fashion Industry, in relation to two specific courses at Manchester Fashion Institute. In this internship students had explored the variety of potential roles available to graduates in relation to their area of study. Having reflected on this in terms of the student learning outcomes, there was strong evidence of increased knowledge and confidence, along with the provision of a valuable resource to share with peers. This outcome provided motivation for developing another project which was an extra-curricular approach that encouraged the development of skills and knowledge around careers in responsible fashion. The internship involved four students who worked collaboratively with an academic and library subject specialist to research, develop and produce an online resource to share with their peers. The students focused their research on the following key activities:

- Sourced live roles in the area of sustainability.
- Devised questions and conducted interviews with senior fashion industry personnel.
- Explored companies considered to be implementing responsible business practice as part of their ethos.
- Worked as part of a team with academic and library staff to select resources to develop knowledge in this area.
- Researched and provided employability resources to support students seeking roles.
- Developed knowledge of responsible business practice and fashion sustainability.

Through their research the students designed and produced a digital resource that their current and future peers could use to understand the skills and knowledge required for sustainability at industry level. The objectives of their research were as follows:

- Identification of the key issues/challenges faced by the fashion industry in this area and initiatives.
- Collated resources/reading to develop knowledge in this area.
- Identified current live roles/opportunities in the industry.

- To gain an industry perspective of what recruiters are looking for.
- To understand a student approach and skills required in a graduate job search.
- To present findings to a small group of staff/online conference.

The project ran for ten weeks across the third term. The team met weekly via Microsoft Teams; the students spanned three of the courses within Manchester Fashion Institute across first-year to final-year students and promoted peer learning. The students were tasked with presenting at an online sustainability conference at Manchester Fashion Institute organised by the academic. This was to promote the RISE initiative and their project. This enabled reflections of what the students had gained from the process and how this process could inform the curriculum at MMU. The created resource would become a valuable tool to share with students and staff across the fashion business courses at MMU. This project places students as future industry leaders and decision makers on how sustainable the fashion industry will be. Through this voluntary research-informed approach, students have generated data that has the potential to inform current and future sustainable business practices within the curriculum.

The value of experiential and interactive approaches is recognised as significant in ESD as they encourage collaboration, peer learning and reflection, particularly in terms of critical reflection, or transformational learning (Sterling, 2011). This can encourage students to reflect on their own and each other's values and consider opportunities for change. Like the student-led approach at MMU, the NTU academic applied a peer-led approach to gain deeper insights regarding sustainable consumption. Both institutions found that taking a student-led approach was an opportunity to create data that informs the curriculum while developing student knowledge around sustainable business and consumption.

The NTU academic rationale for the approach was a noted rise in student projects that focus on sustainability, which has been steadily increasing over the last five years. These projects had a particular leaning towards the issue of overconsumption and how to understand the values and motivations of consumers. While the fashion industry works to achieve a more sustainable supply chain (Turker and Altuntas, 2014) and moves towards circulatory through initiatives such as recycling and leasing models (Braithwaite and Schlemann, 2018), there is an urgency to understand consumption drivers and where opportunities for change lie. It is the need to elicit further understanding of consumer behaviour and attitudes to fashion that underpins the approach employed at NTU. Overconsumption in society is documented practically (Cole, 2010) and academically (Ianole and Cornescu, 2013). In response the approach at NTU asked students to focus on their own clothing and consumption motivations to draw out what values underpinned their decisions.

In support of Goldberg's work (2009), the intention was to flesh out a deeper understanding of what drives fashion consumption and where there may be barriers and opportunities to facilitate more sustainable practices.

Research into the sustainability knowledge and behaviour of fashion students is not unique. Hiller Connell and Kozar (2012) analysed changes in undergraduate student knowledge of sustainability and fashion at a higher education institution in the Midwestern USA. The authors found that an increase in knowledge derived from the curriculum did not translate into a significant change in purchasing behaviour (Hiller Connell and Kozar, 2012). Rhee and Johnson (2019) applied a practical approach to engage their students in discussion around their attitudes towards clothing. They termed this the wardrobe diet. The objective of their work was to get students to wear a total of six garments over 30 days. The implications of their study were to encourage greater awareness amongst the students of their clothing attitudes which would initiate through reflection a shift in their consumption habits. The NTU approach took two different methods which engaged first, final-year undergraduate and postgraduate students across several fashion business courses. The first approach, initiated in 2020, was titled Fashioning Change and involved object-based workshops. Students were asked to undertake an inventory of owned garments, excluding underwear, socks and hosiery, in their wardrobes before the workshop. The inventory asked them to categorise garments according to frequency of wear. This research was exploratory using object-based workshops to explore attitudes, behaviour and meanings through specific items of clothing. Rather than opening questions which explicitly asked about sustainability, the project used discussions around clothing to explore the individual's relationship to sustainability. Each student was asked to bring four garments to the workshop for discussion. These included something they had owned for a long time, an item that was worn frequently and something rarely or never worn. Finally, they were asked to bring a recent purchase, with the focus on what drove the purchase decision and how that garment was now valued in the use phase.

Workshops were selected as an interactive means to develop discussion around the students' garments. The exploratory process highlighted attitudes towards garment ownership and how this linked to sustainable behaviours. The research objective was to understand what values students placed on their garments. The workshop used a process of show and tell as students shared garment stories, revealing what things meant and how that influenced the experience of wearing and keeping. The students were asked to document their findings and in subsequent sessions they worked together to draw out key insights and use them to create a thematic map related to different values, motivations and behaviours. While their insights drew out the complexities of achieving sustainable consumption, they also emphasised that in the most part clothes can be invested with deep emotional attachments that offer clear opportunities for longevity, even in the context of fast fashion garments, which are frequently considered to be more disposable.

The second approach 'Fashion Stories' was undertaken with postgraduate students. Here students were asked to select any item of clothing or an accessory that was meaningful to them and photograph it. They were then tasked with uploading the photograph to an online form on Padlet. The image was then supported with a written narrative response to why this garment was meaningful to them and how wearing it made them feel. Coming together in a workshop session the students shared their posts with peers drawing out the deeper meanings around things. They used these to identify personal values related to clothing ownership. Through peer discussions they co-created knowledge related to clothing consumption and ownership that brings a deeper understanding of what drives motivations and behaviours. In addition, the images and narratives will become an ongoing dataset of values and meanings that can be used by future cohorts for understanding the attitudes and behaviours that underpin consumers. The NTU approach took a personalised approach by focusing on students own clothing, behaviours and attitudes and through research and reflection, the students have created greater knowledge of the wider issues that impact sustainability.

8.4 Findings and Discussion

The key impact of the project at MMU was the creation of a valuable and innovative resource that focuses specifically on responsible fashion careers. As a model for embedding sustainability within the curriculum of fashion business courses, this is a significant tool as it is student led and industry focused. While it fosters skills and knowledge in the participating students, it has an integral role in the education of future cohorts as they gain greater insights of industry perspectives along with the opportunity to continue the development of the resource through RISE projects.

Following the internship students were required to write a reflection on their experience. In the context of education and work-based learning, reflection is integral to knowledge development (Helyer, 2015). Students noted the value of the resource they had created and their increased knowledge around responsible business practice. They also acknowledged the value of the student perspective when developing a resource for peers as they understood how students would engage.

> I can definitely see the value of this resource for students, particularly the employability resources and industry perspectives. I think this resource serves as a good opening for students into sustainability within the industry, sparking interest and beginning conversations.
>
> (P1 2021)

I saw the project as a valuable resource in providing an in-depth look as to what roles and areas of businesses are out there for students who aspire to a career with a sustainable focus within the industry.

(P2 2021)

I do hope other students get the chance to use our resource as it includes key starting points when researching into responsible fashion and employability.

(P3 2021)

Students noted increased motivation to develop work experience opportunities whether that be new work experience or further developing current roles to incorporate more responsible approaches.

This has allowed me to consider how my current [graduate] role within marketing, could be incorporated into a sustainable focus and so allowing me to consider a future career, which encompasses both areas that I have an interest in.

(P2 2021)

In terms of student confidence, all students noted the positive impact of the project.

Conducting interviews helped me improve my ability to ask questions effectively and has helped me gain confidence and valuable industry connections.

(P3 2021)

I feel this experience boosted my confidence when speaking to others from the industry … I think this will help when you are being interviewed for a job in the future.

(P2 2021)

The [industry] interviews also gave me the opportunity to have discussions and develop my knowledge as to why an eco-friendlier approach to fashion is needed. This in turn provided a chance for gaining confidence, in asking questions and stating your opinions.

(P3 2021)

One of the students noted the value of working collaboratively.

During the Rise project I was able to develop my communication skills, through both collaborating and working with the rest of the team, in addition to conducting interviews with individuals within the industry. Furthermore, this enabled me to build industry connections, whilst understanding and gaining first-hand insight into what businesses and employers are looking for in potential new candidates.

(P2 2021)

In terms of knowledge of sustainable practices, students noted an increase.

[the project] has made me aware of the specific areas I already have experience in, that play a role within the sustainable movement and particularly how these roles might change and adapt in the future.

(P3 2021)

I have also widened my vocabulary in regard to sustainability, learning about concepts such as circularity and gaining a better understanding of different environmental terms.

(P4 2021)

In relation to the development of employability skills, softer skills such as confidence have already been acknowledged; there were some interesting comments regarding what students took away from the project.

Whilst I don't think [the project] has influenced my career yet, I am optimistic that the connections I have made completing the project will be excellent stepping stones for future opportunities, whether it be internships, placements, or advice, as well as being a unique addition to my CV that will help me stand out to future employers.

(P3 2021)

Throughout this project I have learnt many new valuable skills, including navigating LinkedIn and Wakelet, to websites used within industry.

(P3 2021)

One student discussed how the project had provided motivation and when seeking voluntary work in the charity sector noted the organisation was interested in her CV content relating to the project. This made the student further realise the value of the project.

From an academic perspective it was clear that the project had increased confidence in the students, developed throughout the internship. At the outset the dynamic of the group was very much led by the final-year students with the less experienced students being very quiet and not showing so much initiative due to their lack of confidence. However, as the project progressed the final-year students graduated and secured employment. This allowed the less experienced students to take the lead. Over the weeks the students became more confident. This confidence was further enhanced by industry exposure when conducting interviews. Students appeared empowered following the interviews after initially being nervous; however, they linked their writing of questions prior to the interview as helpful and became more confident as they conducted more interviews. The less experienced students presented at the conference and the academic promoted this on LinkedIn and this was an important opportunity to further disseminate the resource as well as empowering the student contribution to knowledge. The students acknowledged their increased knowledge surrounding sustainability from engaging in the project.

In terms of the value of a RISE project, from an academic perspective it is interesting to work more closely with students on a smaller project to see how students engage in resources and approach a job search. Reflection on the findings from this project evidences that the development of resources by students for students supports peer learning, this is powerful and really allows the academic to understand the student learning process in the context of sustainability and how to support the development of graduate attributes. It was also clear to see the development of key employability skills of the students from engaging in the project. The application of this extra-curricular project demonstrated the value of participatory research in the development of skills and knowledge (Mintz and Tal, 2016).

At NTU approximately 80 students have engaged in the Fashioning Change workshops. Through peer collaboration they have created a thematic analysis (Braun and Clarke, 2006) of the following insights that underpinned their collective attitudes towards clothing consumption and ownership. The individual wardrobe inventories revealed that many participants had over 30% of garments in their wardrobes that they rarely or never wore. This was often because they had forgotten what they owned or just always reached for the same things as it was convenient. In many cases it was because they felt influenced by trends and having new things was easy and often very affordable.

> I am *definitely* influenced by trends and with high street prices, it is easy just to have things.
>
> (P1A 2020)

The findings showed that the volume of garments owned by many of the participants makes it almost impossible for some things to have frequent wear, because there is often too much choice in an individual's wardrobe.

> In my wardrobe my favorite things are my Vans. I needed to fit into Uni culture and I am on the go quite a lot, so I wear trainers. I bought them before I came here but never wore them until I got here. I bought them because they were on trend, I wasn't a trainer girl. I wear them about four

times a month for me that is a lot because I have loads of clothes and shoes.

(P3D 2020)

Discussions around garments that had been owned a long time were significant in drawing out the deeper meanings attached to these items. Often it was because there was a sentimental attachment.

This sweatshirt belonged to my grandfather and when he died, I was able to keep it. Whenever I wear it, I think of him and I take it everywhere with me.

(P1C 2021)

I got these Doc Martens when I was 15. It took me ages to convince my parents to let me have them. When I did, they represented my move towards adulthood and freedom to make my own choices. I don't wear them anymore but I keep them because they define my teenage years.

(P8W 2021)

Emotional attachment and memories are key to a garment holding value for many of the students (Niinimäki and Armstrong, 2013). While this emotional connection ensures their longevity, it does not always mean that they will be worn with frequency. However, fleshing out what drives value and meaning was key to developing the students' knowledge of the wider issues that impinge upon consumption and clothing use and how that needs to be considered in the context of sustainability. The sharing of their garments with often such emotive stories was valuable as it shed light on the complexities of why things matter to people at an individual level. Through reflective discussions they recognised the importance of understanding the wider meanings of consumer attitudes and behaviours.

It is amazing to realise how diverse and personal our own clothing values are. I can see how it is important to define and understand these as it gives the wider context in which sustainable consumption exists.

(P84B 2021)

Analysis of their insights enabled the students to create a thematic map related to the different motivations and behaviours that they identified. These highlighted the following key themes:

- The quest for individuality.
- The sentimental garment.
- Bargain purchases.

- A wardrobe full of clothes but nothing to wear.
- It is just me.
- Makes me confident.

While many of the insights from Fashioning Change did not directly resonate with what might be considered sustainable behaviours, what they did elicit were reflections from students with actions for change.

> The most surprising thing for me when I did the inventory was how much I rarely wear. I rarely get rid of things. I am the world's worst hoarder. I tell myself it will come back in fashion when it won't. Undertaking the wardrobe inventory made me realise how much stuff I have at university and at home. When I saw what I don't wear in my wardrobe I thought I will try and make an effort to wear them all now. Wear something different every day.
>
> (P6A 2021)

The Fashion Stories activity revealed comparable insights around defining values. Over 200 students have participated in this task. The most frequently stated value was linked to emotional attachment where garments are linked to a memory or have been a gift from someone special. Drawing out these meanings become an intriguing way for our students to learn about what defines individual values in the context of fashion clothing. Both approaches have generated research insights that inform the curriculum with real-time data regarding consumption in the context of sustainability. As these approaches are implemented in future years, the dataset continues to grow and provides an innovative resource for tracking attitudes, behaviours and values as sustainability increases at societal levels.

8.5 Pedagogical Reflections

Reflecting from an MMU perspective, the project while co-curricular was implemented outside a formally assessed unit and involved a small number of students. Post-activity reflections demonstrated that the output was of value to both staff and students. This research-focused, constructivist approach appears to have encouraged a deeper learning experience than the traditionally taught unit, which has tended to apply a more passive approach towards teaching this complex topic. Moving forward a more active pedagogical approach to the subject will be applied to support a deeper learning of this subject area. This approach would enhance the learning experience of all relevant students and should be embedded formally within an assessed unit. The value of peer learning was significant; therefore, a small group approach could be adopted. Findings could be presented to younger cohorts, filtering knowledge further through the wider fashion business curriculum; therefore, it may be impactful for both younger students to hear more experienced peers speaking in this area. For the presenting students it would be valuable in terms of their assertion of knowledge surrounding sustainability, in addition to instilling confidence.

The research was valuable in terms of job specification analysis and enabled students to explore the skills and attributes required to fulfil these roles. This approach exposed the students to real-world issues, forging the links between education and practice, highlighting their responsibility as graduates who could implement a positive change. Moving forward as part of the core taught employability unit (second-year students), students explore a role relevant to their area of study and attend a mock assessment centre event designed to replicate the live environment. It would be useful to highlight roles in responsible fashion and sustainability as part of this unit to highlight career options.

If our students are to be industry ready, it is important to ensure they are aware of job roles which focus on responsible business practice and sustainability; whether this be through the actual role as a Sustainability Assistant or a more traditional role such as Buying, Merchandising or Design, with a business which embodies responsible business approaches and/or sustainable initiatives. This will enable students to engage effectively in experiential learning towards a career in this area. The MMU approach has created a valuable employability resource that can be disseminated widely, ensuring that current and future students are fully aware of career opportunities in this area. The resource is not static as it becomes embedded within fashion-specific employability resources; it continues to grow, enabling future students to add further research in this area.

In contrast to MMU the sessions at NTU were embedded within the formal taught curriculum and directed at both undergraduate and postgraduate students. Drawing from the collected student reflections, the sessions worked well because they were peer led and the subject matter was personal and relatable. Both Fashioning Change and Fashion Stories were interactive and thus facilitated discussion and collaboration between students. Asking the student participants to bring a range of different garment types in the Fashioning Change sessions was, on reflection, more intuitive than the Fashion Stories approach, because it encouraged focus not only on the garments that the students had a positive relationship with, but those that were not worn and sometimes were a regretted purchase. This brought a more holistic understanding of consumer behaviour and attitudes from a range of individual perspectives. Focusing the discussions around students' own clothing and accessories highlighted the value of personalised learning, student collaboration and the co-creation of knowledge, demonstrating the advantage of active learning. While the students were not directed to choose garments to discuss in the context of sustainability, applying an approach that enabled them to draw out their own stories and reflections around their clothing encouraged them to reflect on what this meant in the context of sustainability. This became an intriguing and active way to stimulate debates around sustainable consumption. By applying this student-led, experiential approach to learning, the students were able to co-create knowledge and draw their own conclusions regarding attitudes and behaviours towards sustainable consumption.

While the sessions were successful in facilitating student collaboration and knowledge creation, there was nothing actioned for monitoring the long-term impacts of this learning. As an example, there is clearly an opportunity to reflect at a future date whether the students have changed their attitudes towards sustainable consumption by actioning different behaviours. Moving forward the intention is to embed the sessions in the principles of action research where there are measures in place to track through a survey the longer term impacts of undertaking these cases. Applying this approach will ensure that the longer term impacts of the learning are captured while supporting the educational development of students as sustainable citizens of the future.

Although both authors implemented their approaches independently, through discussion and joint reflections the value of co-collaboration across institutions has become clear. Moving forward there is a need to embed these approaches as examples of cross-institutional models of best practice. For students to succeed in the global fashion industry, they need to consider sustainable practices at all market levels and to have a holistic understanding of the subject from industry through to consumer behaviour. While the approaches were implemented independently, the subsequent collaborative conversations have presented the opportunity for reflection on how these two distinct approaches can benefit student experiences and become a model for student collaboration across institutions.

Capturing the students' reflections of what they gained from undertaking the different approaches across institutions has been hugely valuable in terms of evaluating impact of the approaches for changing mindset and learning experience. Although we acknowledge there is opportunity to evaluate the longer term impacts of learning for students, in particular their attitudes towards sustainable consumption and the tracking of graduate roles in sustainability-focused positions. The evaluations have also been integral to the future development of the approaches. Both approaches are longitudinal in nature and have led to the creation of datasets that can be used through the curriculum, enabling our students to reflect on how industry and consumer attitudes and behaviour have evolved and will continue to change in the future. These student-led approaches have created a dataset of real-time values, attitudes and behaviours which are used within the curriculum to deepen understanding of the inhibitors and drivers of sustainable consumption. For these Fashion Business students to become agents of change, they must be instilled with the knowledge of what drives consumption within the broader context of fashion (Goldberg, 2009).

8.6 Concluding Discussion

Sharing the experiences of the authors' respective approaches has enabled the opportunity as academics to reflect on how best to encourage and empower fashion business students to become sustainability experts (Chitrakorn, 2016). The application of participatory and interactive approaches has fostered a sense of deep learning (Warburton, 2003) that has supported peer collaboration and the co-creation of knowledge that is invaluable to the students' understanding of sustainability from industry as well as consumer perspectives. While the study has recognised that the key to achieving sustainable literacy (Armstrong and LeHew, 2013) is to apply a holistic approach where due consideration is given to both the mechanisms of sustainable practice in business and the wider drivers of consumption. The respective pedagogical approaches have created a unique method for investing these fashion business students with the skills and knowledge that can further embed sustainability within the curriculum.

While the research was initially exploratory, the student reflections from both institutions have been key to highlighting the value of student-led approaches for enhancing learning around the wider issues of sustainability. Key to the participating students' knowledge creation was the integration of peer collaboration and reflection. Asking these students to reflect on what they had each gained from the different activities has been integral for evaluating the impact on the development of their sustainable skills and knowledge. While the authors' individual pedagogical practices were quite different, the application and sharing of these distinct approaches has enabled them to consider how best to share student knowledge across institutions. The pedagogical approaches have created data that presents an important opportunity for cross-institution student-led collaboration through projects and knowledge-sharing activities such as conferences and workshops. Responding to the gap in research that examines how best to integrate sustainability into the curriculum of fashion business courses, this chapter has contributed the potential of student-driven research projects as a model for developing knowledge and skills that will ensure their future as change makers.

Acknowledgements

Both authors would like to thank the students at Manchester Fashion Institute (MMU) and The School of Art and Design (NTU) who participated in these studies. They have made a unique and valuable contribution towards the development of sustainability within the respective fashion business curriculums.

References

Armstrong, C. M. and LeHew, M. L. A. (2013). A Case Study in Sustainability and Fashion Education: Adventures on the Green. *Journal of Sustainability Education*, 4, 1–22.

Barber, N. A., Wison, F., Venkatachalam, V., Cleaves, S. M. and Garnhma, J. (2014). Integrating Sustainability into Business Curricula: University of New Hampshire Case Study. *International Journal of Sustainability in Higher Education*, 15 (4), 473–493. https://doi.org/10.1177%2F2379298119844975

Benn, S. and Dunphy, D. (2009). Action Research as an Approach to Integrating Sustainability into MBA Programs: An Exploratory Study. *Journal of Management Education*, 33 (3), 276–295. https://doi.org/10.1177%2F1052562908323189

Braithwaite, N. and Schlemann, A. (2018). Product Service Systems: A Viable Business Model for Fashion Brands. In C. Becker-Leifhold and M. Heuer (Eds), *Eco Friendly and Fair: Fast Fashion and Consumer Behaviour*. London and New York: Routledge, 132–143.

Braun, V. and Clarke, V. (2006). Using Thematic Analysis in Psychology. *Qualitative Research in Psychology*, 3 (2), 77–101. https://doi.org/10.1191/1478088706qp063oa

Chitrakorn, K. (2016). Six Fashion Careers of the Future. *Business of Fashion*. www.businessoffashion.com/articles/careers/six-fashion-careers-of-the-future. Accessed on 25 September 2021.

Cole, C. (2010). Overconsumption Is Costing Us the Earth and Human Happiness. *The Guardian*, 21 June, www.theguardian.com/environment/2010/jun/21/overconsumption-environment-relationships-annie-leonard. Accessed on 12 April 2021.

Dewey, J. (2011). *Democracy and Education*. New York: Simon and Brown.

Egan, J. (2004). *Skills for Sustainable Development*. London: Office of the Deputy Prime Minister.

Fisher, J. and Bonn, I. (2011). Business Sustainability and Undergraduate Management Education: An Australian Study. *Higher Education*, 62, 563–571.

Forum for the Future (2004). *Learning and Skills for Sustainable Development*. London: Higher Education Partnership for Sustainability.

Goldberg, M. (2009). Social Conscience. In P. Villiers-Stuart and A. Stibbe (Eds), *The Handbook of Sustainable Literacy*. Devon: Green Books.

Haigh, M. (2005). Greening the University Curriculum: Appraising an International Movement. *Journal of Geography*, 29 (1), 31–38. https://doi.org/10.1080/03098260500030355

Helyer, R. (2015). Learning through Reflection: The Critical Role of Reflection in Work-Based Learning. *Journal of Work-Applied Management*, 7 (1), 15–27. https://doi.org/10.1108/JWAM-10-2015-003

Hiller Connell, K. and Kozar, J. (2012). Sustainability Knowledge and Behaviors of Apparel and Textile Undergraduates. *International Journal of Sustainability in Higher Education*, 3 (4), 394–407. http://dx.doi.org/10.1108/14676371211262335

Ianole, R. and Cornescu, V. (2013). Overconsumption Society through the Looking-Glass of Behavioral Economics. *Procedia Economics and Finance*, 6, 66–72. https://doi.org/10.1016/S2212-5671(13)00115-9

Mintz, K. and Tal, T. (2016). The Place of Content and Pedagogy in Shaping Sustainability Learning Outcomes in Higher Education. *Environmental Education Research*, 24 (2), 207–229. https://doi.org/10.1080/13504622.2016.1204986

Murzyn-Kupisz, M. and Holuj, D. (2021). Fashion Design Education and Sustainability: Towards an Equilibrium between Craftsmanship and Artistic and Business Skills? *Education Science*, 11 (9). https://doi.org/10.3390/educsci11090531

Niinimäki, K. and Armstrong, C. (2013). From Pleasure in Use to Preservation of Meaningful Memories: A Closer Look at the Sustainability of Clothing via Longevity and Attachment. *International Journal of Fashion Design, Technology and Education*, 6 (3), 190–199.

QAA. (2021). Education for Sustainable Development. www.qaa.ac.uk/quality-code/education-for-sustainable-development. Accessed on 25 September 2021.

Radclyffe-Thomas, N., Varley, R. and Roncha, A. (2018). Balancing the Books: Creating a Model of Responsible Fashion Business Education. *Art, Design and Communication in Higher Education*, 17 (1), 89–106.

Rhee, J. and Johnson, K. K. P. (2019). The Wardrobe Diet: Teaching Sustainable Consumption through Experience with Undergraduates in the USA. *International Journal of Fashion Design, Technology and Education*, 12 (3), 283–292. https://doi.org/10.1080/17543266.2019.1590864

Sterling, S. (2011). *The Future Fit Framework: An Introductory Guide to Learning and Teaching for Sustainability in HE*. York: The Higher Education Academy.

Stubbs, W. and Cocklin, C. (2008). Teaching Sustainability to Business Students: Shifting Mindsets. *International Journal of Sustainability in Higher Education*, 9 (3), 206–221. http://dx.doi.org/10.1108/14676370810885844

Taber, K. S. (2011). Constructivism as Educational Theory: Contingency in Learning and Optimally Guided Instruction. In J. Hassaskhah (Ed), *Educational Theory*. New York: Nova Publishers.

Turker, D. and Altuntas, C. (2014). Sustainable Supply Chain Management in the Fast Fashion Industry: An Analysis of Corporate Reports. *European Management Journal*, 32 (5), 837–849. https://doi.org/10.1016/j.emj.2014.02.001

Vogue. (2020). Fashion's Circular Economy Could Be Worth $5 Trillion. www.voguebusiness.com/sustainability/fashions-circular-economy-could-be-worth-5-trillion. Accessed on 1 October 2021.

Warburton, K. (2003). Deep Learning and Education for Sustainability. *International Journal of Sustainability in Higher Education*, 4(1), 44–56. https://doi.org/10.1108/14676370310455332

Wong, B., Chui, Y. T., Copsey-Blake, M. and Nikolopoulou, M. (2021). A Mapping of Graduate Attributes: What Can We Expect from UK University Students? *Higher Education Research & Development*. https://doi.org/10.1080/07294360.2021.1882405

Chapter 9

Sustainability and the Fast Fashion Business Model

Rose Marroncelli

9.1 Introduction

This chapter addresses the subtheme, 'Breaking the economic system: How can we change the fashion economic system, one that has been based on fast fashion, hyper consumerism and exploitation into a more circular, and socially more balanced ecosystem?' It can be argued that breaking this economic system will require a collaborative, global effort between both companies and consumers. One factor may involve shifting consumer mindsets around purchasing habits and over-consumption. This research questions the fastness of the trend cycle and perceived style obsolescence. A possible solution which addresses the 'obsolescence of desire' is to manufacture products with classic and timeless designs (Mont, 2008, p. 5). This strategy addresses consumers who tend to develop emotional attachment to their products. However, the implementation of this design strategy depends on changed consumer behaviour and patterns. In the fashion industry, changing consumer behaviour is dependent upon social factors, not just material properties (Fletcher, 2012). The FashionMap archive, housed at Nottingham Trent University (NTU), will be utilised to question the fastness of fast fashion.

FashionMap is a unique collection of high street fashion garments and accessories from 2000 to 2018, which belongs to the School of Art and Design at NTU. Second-year Fashion and Textile Design students created this collection through research projects that explored seasonal high street trends. The Fashion and Textile Design students brief was to research and buy an outfit from the high street in Nottingham, which reflected a current seasonal trend. This activity took place twice a year, for Spring/Summer and Autumn/Winter, and approximately six different trends were identified for each season, by six different groups of students (three womenswear and three menswear trends). This had led to an accumulation of over 1900 garments and accessories, which contribute to the FashionMap archive. In addition to this, there is also a database of accompanying student photoshoots for each trend. Trends were identified through popular culture, fashion magazines and celebrity influences. The introduction of the digital age will have had an

DOI: 10.4324/9781032659053-9

influence on how trends were identified over the duration of the FashionMap project. In the early 2000s, magazines would have been a key resource, but there will have been a gradual shift towards online sources. All garments have been sourced from the central shopping area in Nottingham, including some stores which would be considered fast fashion. A content analysis has been undertaken to select garments from FashionMap, which will in turn be used as discussion points in two focus groups, one with males and one with females. The research aim is to address and question the fastness of fashion by gaining an understanding of gendered attitudes and behaviours towards style obsolescence, and identify opportunities for change. It must be noted that this is a small section of a much larger project (a PhD thesis).

9.2 Literature Review

This section supports the context of the chapter and will flesh out existing debates around the issues of fast fashion and its relationship to trends and sustainability. This will create a knowledge base which can be debated with an in-depth content analysis of trends and individual garments in the FashionMap archive.

9.2.1 Trends

'Fashions are, by definition, temporary cyclical phenomena adapted by consumers for a particular time and situation' (Sproles, 1981, p. 116). A fashion refers to a style (e.g. clothing, shoes, and handbags) that is widely accepted by a group of consumers at a given time (Joung, 2014). Acceptance of a style follows a life cycle comprising of four stages: introduction, growth, maturity and decline. Easey (2009) defines the fashion cycle as a 'bell shaped curve.' The introduction phase is where new fashions emerge and may take time to gain acceptance. During the growth stage competition increases as the trend gains exposure and appeal. At the maturity stage, the trend has reached mass appeal, and finally the trend will decline, falling out of fashion (Easey, 2009), which creates style obsolescence. The fast fashion accelerated business model evolved in the 1980s and involves increased numbers of fashion collections every year. This generally means quick turnarounds and decreasing prices. The life cycle of a fast fashion garment is typically a month or less (Doeringer & Crean, 2006).

FashionMap is an archive which is built upon the study of trends. It is therefore important to establish the context of how trends work. The word 'trend' was first used as a verb in the sixteenth century, meaning, 'the way that something bends' (Goncu-Berk, 2017). The typical twenty-first-century meaning, referring to change, is relatively new. Trends can apply to both fashion and also many different industries in wider society. The word 'trend' was used to describe stylistic and cultural changes in the 1960s, with the term 'trendsetter' appearing in 1962 (Goncu-Berk, 2017).

Georg Simmel is regarded as one of the great influences on the development on the sociological interpretation of fashion, and his approach plays a major role in creating a model for understanding fashion (Rocamora & Smelik, 2016). Simmel believed that fashions could be used as a distinguishing feature between classes. In his 1957 essay 'Fashion,' Simmel discusses fashion as a form of imitation. Fashion has the power to unite certain members of social classes and segregate others. According to Simmel, the elite initiate fashions, which the mass then imitates. 'Fashion does not exist in tribal and classless societies' (Simmel, 1957, p. 541). Carter (2003) comments on the work of Simmel (1904), and the links between class and fashion. Carter notes that the upper class need the lower class, because without their recognition, competition would not exist (Carter, 2003). This is also known as 'trickle-down theory.' When compiling trends and outfits for the FashionMap archive, students were briefed to explore how trends from the catwalk have trickled down to the high street; the archive is therefore based on the trickle-down model. 'Innovation takes place at a higher level and then spreads downwards, because the lower social classes strive to move upwards, which results in them always being one step behind' (Svendsen, 2004, p. 39). Blumer (1969) observes that fashion carries the stamp of approval of the elite.

Trickle-down theory has been criticised for over-simplifying contemporary society (McCracken, 1988). King (1963) argued that trickle-down theory did not help the sophisticated marketeer understand fashion behaviours in the 1960s (Divita, 2019) and he proposed a competing theory, known as 'trickle across theory' (Field, 1970). This is where new styles trickle across horizontally within classes rather than vertically across classes. A further theory proposed in the late 1960s called 'trickle up' theory dictates that 'fashions no longer "trickle down," they usually "bubble up" from various subcultures' (Steele, 2015, p. 285). The influence of street fashion is acknowledged as a key component of trickle up theory. The street has been written about as being pivotal to the evolution of fashion, and street style is still seen as innovative and influential today (Woodward, 2009).

The most recent development in the theory of trend diffusion is known as 'trickle round' theory (Bellezza & Berger, 2019). This theory suggests that fashion trends originate from the elites and move downwards, but that sometimes low status is also mixed with high. The elites can adopt items associated with low status groups as a way to distinguish themselves from middle status individuals. It must be acknowledged that whilst trickle 'down,' 'across,' 'up' and 'round' theories of fashion are useful tools to explain aspects of trends within FashionMap, such as from which groups in society trends may originate, they cannot be used to describe the complete trend cycle. Furthermore, it is difficult to place 'fad' trends into any one of these theories, as they do not detail the timescale or afterlife of a trend. According to Divita (2019), 'trends also may not have clearly defined ending and beginnings.'

9.2.2 Fast Fashion

In the 1990s, price pressures and high levels of competition meant that UK retailers shifted their sourcing of merchandise to the Far East for a low-cost advantage. This led to supply chains becoming more complex as a result of extensive geographical distance. As a result, retailers introduced practices such as JIT (just in time manufacturing) with a focus on shorter supply lines and quicker time to market (Bhardwaj & Fairhurst, 2010). Retailers in the UK started providing increased variety and fashionability, whilst also delivering low-cost products. Mid-season purchasing was added to previous two-season calendars, resulting in the 'throwaway market.' The 'throwaway market' became known as fast fashion, which is now the trend or norm (Bhardwaj & Fairhurst, 2010). Trends are at the centre of the fashion system, but they also evidence the complexities of sustainability in fashion. Veblen (2007) noted how fashion is a typical form of waste. When styles become out of fashion, old clothes are easily discarded, even if they are in perfect condition. The fast fashion business model may seem to question the longevity of style and this chapter examines this further.

Woodward's (2009) study of street style trends has however questioned the fastness of fashion, as some trends appear to be timeless. Woodward notes how the infrastructure of the fashion system moves at a rapid pace, with constantly changing styles and increased capacity, but that this is not matched by the rate at which people replace their clothing. She states, 'There is not a rapid shifting change of styles, rather street styles tend to emerge more slowly at the intersection between new looks and older styles' (Woodward, 2009, p. 95). The subsequent research into trends takes a content analysis of images and garments from the FashionMap archive and will examine how often trends do re-emerge. The question emerges, 'how fast is fast fashion?' This research question has directed the methodology and following discussion.

9.2.3 Methodology

Researching from the FashionMap archive will involve drawing from two methods, a content analysis and focus groups. A content analysis can be defined as a systematic, replicable research technique which draws conclusions objectively by identifying specific characteristics of messages (Stemler, 2000). The content analysis will be used to identify and track significant trends in FashionMap archive. This method was approached by selecting six significant trends in FashionMap, and identifying examples of these trends throughout the archive (the six trends will be discussed in the below section). The items of clothing selected through this process will be used as discussion points in two focus groups. One focus group will be with males and the other with females, in order to facilitate a gendered analysis. Fashion is highly gendered, and much has been written about the relationship between women and clothing (Woodward, 2007) (Guy et al., 2001). There is however a limited understanding of comparable male relationships. This will bring a specific perspective to the question of how fast is fast fashion.

With regard to gender, the sample research participants have been asked to respond to garments from FashionMap archive that were originally sourced according to male/female stereotypes. The intention is to understand how participants respond to these gender stereotyped trends/garments and whether that has implications for the longevity of trends and garment types. Participants were selected through snowball sampling and were asked to define the gender that they identified with. This has fallen under male and female identifications. It must be noted that the study has not set out to exclude other gender identifications. The complexities of gender in 2021/2022 present challenges for both researchers and retailers. In 2017, the retailer John Lewis became the first major UK store to remove boy and girl's labels from children's clothing, with the aim to reduce gender stereotypes (Newbold, 2017). This research aims to question traditional gendered stereotypes. 'Who we become as gendered beings is enmeshed in a social process' (Trier-Bieniek, 2014, p. 5).

Trends have been documented through their frequency of appearance over the lifespan of the archive. The evolution of these trends became a starting point when choosing garments for the content analysis. The following trends have been specifically selected as they frequently reoccur and can also be viewed through the lens of gender. They either apply to female, male or both genders. This is crucial criteria as it facilitates a gendered analysis. The selected trends are as follows: The sexualisation of fashion, unisex, kitsch, subcultural style, denim and vintage. Trends are interconnected and often overlap; they do not exist as isolated entities. It must be noted that although six trends have been identified in the FashionMap archive; many other trends also exist—both within the archive and throughout history. Focusing on six specific trends has allowed for a detailed analysis.

9.2.4 *Final Selection of Garments for Focus Group Use*

The final selection of garments for focus group use is listed below. Depending on archive availability, between two and five garments have been chosen for each trend category. These garments will be located from the physical archive and used to stimulate discussions in the focus groups (Tables 9.1–9.6).

The next stage is to assess which garments retain sustainability through style and emotional durability. Garments selected from FashionMap archive will act as discussion points in the focus groups. Participants were shown images from the above table on a projector screen during the focus groups.

Table 9.1 The Sexualisation of Fashion

Item	Observation/Year/archive location
Image	Capturing information from the artefact.

Black corset
2001/2002

Grey corset
2008

Table 9.1 (Continued)

Item	Observation/Year/archive location
 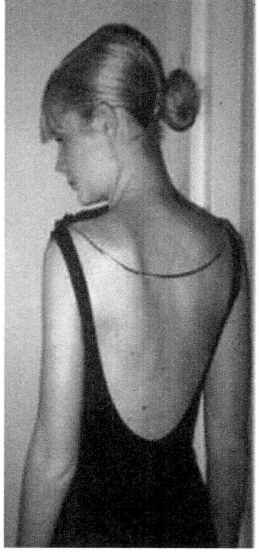	Little black dress 2000/2001
	Sequin pants 2008

(Continued)

Table 9.1 (Continued)

Item	Observation/Year/archive location
	White lace top 2012/2013

Table 9.2 Unisex

	Body doubles (matching) 2012/2013

Table 9.2 (Continued)

Unisex—the future is floral
2012/2013

Unisex—utility
2015/2016

Washed out
2016/2017

Table 9.3 Kitsch

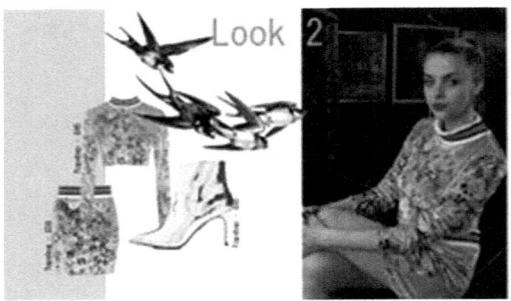 Jasmine garden 2016/2017

 Men's—Mr Brightside
2011/2012

Table 9.4 Subcultural Style

 Bad romance
2010/2011

Table 9.4 (Continued)

Glam punk
2013/2014

Men's – indie rock
2003/2004

Men's rock n roll
2005/2006

(*Continued*)

Table 9.4 (Continued)

White t-shirt
2002/2003

Table 9.5 Denim

DIY Denim
2014/2015

Men's pink
2004/2005

Table 9.5 (Continued)

Space Odyssey
2015/2016

Women's studded
jeans
2000/2001

Table 9.6 Vintage

1920s
2003/2004

(Continued)

Table 9.6 (Continued)

Folklore
2008/2009

Men's 70s
wallpaper
2012/2013

In addition to this, they were also shown the physical garments alongside and were asked two questions for each look: 'What year do you think this style was created?' and 'Would you wear this outfit today?' The aim of these questions was to gauge the enduring style and fashionability of these fast fashion garments, in order to assess which looks retained sustainability through style. A particular focus was placed on gaining participants opinions on items from the FashionMap archive, and also their own wardrobes, thus allowing for an analysis and discussion surrounding the fastness of fashion.

Two focus groups were undertaken: one with male participants and the other with female participants. Snowball sampling was used to identify participants. Both focus groups comprised six participants in Nottingham, a regional UK city. Young adults were the chosen demographic for this research. Also known as 'Millennials,' or 'Generation Y,' this demographic is categorised as individuals born between 1980 and 1995 (Lam et al., 2016). Millennials value environmental and social issues, and are willing to pay extra money for socially responsible products, but still consume fast fashion (Sorensen & Jorgensen, 2019). The affordability and convenience of fast fashion fit in with millennials budget and life stage (Lam et al., 2016).

9.2.5 Findings and Discussion

Findings from the content analysis evidenced that trends do re-emerge frequently within the FashionMap archive, which challenges some of the existing debates surrounding the fastness of fashion. The monochrome trend has been used as an example here to demonstrate how often trends do re-emerge. Monochrome gained notable significance during the 1990s, following on from the excess and opulence of 1980s style. Designers such as Calvin Klein, Yohji Yamamoto and Issey Miyake lead the way for new minimalistic styles (Olivia, 2017). Yamamoto's use of black became a prominent feature within his collections, and the designer 'built a career on proving that black is beautiful' (Menkes, 2000). Table 9.7 shows reoccurrence of the monochrome trend between 2003 and 2015. The repetition of this trend throughout FashionMap questions the fastness of fashion, building upon Woodward's (2009) debate.

It is clear that between 2003 and 2015 there are variances within the monochrome trend, but a core element of using the colours black and white remains consistent throughout each outfit. Fashions are temporal by nature, and although new trends are continuously created, most of them are not greatly different from existing fashions; they are modifications of previous ones (Eundeok, 2011). Fashions are caught up in a recurrent process of innovation and emulation (Blumer, 1969). This is evidenced through the monochrome trend with incremental additions such as floral or colourful accents complementing the style. This section has evidenced that the 'fastness' attributed to fast fashion does not always refer to the speed of new trends emerging, but it could instead allude to the speed at which garments are purchased and discarded by consumers.

Having fleshed out discussions surrounding the fastness of fashion in the above section, attention will now move onto the focus group findings. One of the main conclusions uncovered through analysing and coding transcriptions was that it became apparent how small, incremental changes linked to trends mean that garments become 'uncool' to the consumer and fall out of fashion. A key code identified was that participants would wear 'part or parts' of the

Table 9.7 Monochrome Trend as Evidenced in FashionMap

Year	Monochrome trend as evidenced in FashionMap
2003/2004	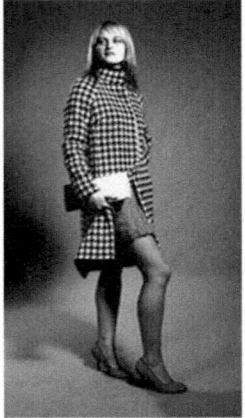
2006/2007	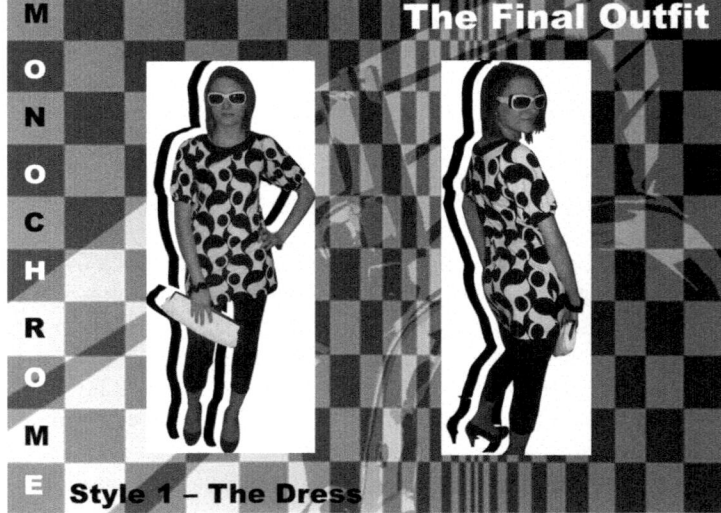

Table 9.7 (Continued)

Year	Monochrome trend as evidenced in FashionMap
2007/2008	  
2011/2012	

(Continued)

Table 9.7 (Continued)

Year	Monochrome trend as evidenced in FashionMap
2012/2013	
2012/2013	
2014/2015	

Table 9.7 (Continued)

Year	Monochrome trend as evidenced in FashionMap
2014/2015	

Figure 9.1 Unisex 2012/13, FashionMap archive NTU©.

outfit, but not the whole outfit today. As example of this is the female trend for unisex, which was from the year 2012/2013. After seeing the image on screen and being shown the matching suit, one participant stated, 'I don't think I'd wear it as an outfit, maybe separately' (see Figure 9.1).

Figure 9.2 Unisex 2016/17, FashionMap archive NTU©.

Similarly, for the next unisex trend, pictured below, a participant stated, 'I like the socks, I have those socks actually.' This identified one specific part of the outfit which the participant would wear today (please refer to Figure 9.2).

The below male trend for kitsch (Figure 9.3) was presented to the male focus group, with one respondent stating, 'I probably would wear the trousers with a black t-shirt, if they were the only bright part of the outfit. If that makes sense.'

It is apparent that for some styles, the whole outfit worn together becomes style obsolescent, but parts of the outfit remain in fashion. This common theme was mentioned six times throughout the duration of both focus groups. This shows how small, stylistic details are incredibly important to the consumer but also questions the speed of design obsolescence and the fastness of fashion. The purchasing and wearing of clothing often conceals the complexities of the term 'fast fashion,' (Woodward, 2009) as evidenced through this research, as not all parts of the outfit follow 'fast' trend cycles.

The second key theme identified is that several participants mentioned that they would wear the given outfit, but only if a part of the outfit were to be different, or altered in some way. Examples of this viewpoint are visible below:

Figure 9.3 Kitsch 2011/12, FashionMap archive NTU©.

I think I would wear it, but I would buy it in a size up.

(Participant A)

I'd probably wear it if it was a bit shorter, if it didn't look a bit more like a trench coat.

(Participant C)

If you cut those things off, then yes.

(Participant D)

The colour of the shirt is fine, the thing which puts me off is the sharpness of the colour of the buttons.

(Participant B)

The trousers are just slightly too bright.

(Participant A)

> I like the pattern. I don't like the cut, those trousers, with a different cut, I would wear.
>
> (Participant F)

> I like the doc martin sort of style definitely, but not with the gold, it's too much.
>
> (Participant D)

> I love these, these are Dolly Parton, and I would wear them all day. I'd have them like several sizes too big, I wouldn't want them cut like they were on her, I'd want them quite different, but I think they're tacky. And I like that.
>
> (Participant K)

This highlights the subtle design features which render certain designs style obsolescent. As evidenced through the literature review analysis of the mono-chrome trend, there were variances within the trend between the years 2003 and 2015, but a core element of using the colours black and white remained consistent throughout each outfit. Fashions are temporal by nature, and although new trends are continuously created, most of them are not greatly different from existing fashions; they are modifications of previous ones (Eundeok, 2011). Fashions are caught up in a recurrent process of innovation and emulation (Blumer, 1969). However, the incremental style differences are important, as although they might only be a small deviance from the desired look, such as the colour of a button as mentioned above, this feature means that the outfit becomes rejected and redundant.

The final key theme identified is that several participants stated how they 'liked but wouldn't wear' garments and outfits from the FashionMap archive. This particular trend was mentioned eight times during both focus groups, and specific examples can be seen below:

> I really like the styling in the shoot, but it's not the same as wanting to wear the outfit.
>
> (Participant D)

> I wouldn't wear it, but I don't know why, I kind of like it.
>
> (Participant B)

> I like the idea of it, but I'd probably look at myself in the mirror, and wouldn't like it.
>
> (Participant F)

> For me, it is almost nice, but I dunno, there is something that puts me off it, I don't know what. But I do quite like it.
>
> (Participant A)

This key theme could be linked to unused clothing in wardrobes. The value of unused clothing in UK wardrobes is estimated to be £30 billion (WRAP, 2015). Petersson McIntyre's (2021) study, which focused on (un)sustainable wardrobes, uncovered that consumers relied on routines and a 'self-perceived inability to explain or motivate actions' (Petersson McIntyre, 2021, p. 737) when describing unused clothing in their wardrobes. It was noted that consumers commonly stated 'I don't know why I do it' when explaining the purchases of unused items, which is similar to my own participants reactions when describing items which they liked but wouldn't wear. This shows that understanding consumer behaviour in relation to consumption and interpretation of trends can be complex.

The three key themes identified above display the importance of incremental style differences on the fashionability and longevity of trends. However, despite this, an overarching theme emerged, which was that none of the garments discussed in the focus groups looked 'out of place.' When asked to reflect on the term 'fast fashion' after learning the correct years which each outfit was bought, one of the female participants stated:

> If you saw anybody wearing any of those things out in the street now, you wouldn't think oh, that's very 2003, 2004. Everybody would still look pretty normal in those things.
>
> (Participant C)

Similarly, a male participant held the same viewpoint:

> For me, I struggled to place any of them really. I'm not particularly fashion conscious myself anyway, but I don't look at these outfits and think that any of them look massively out of place. For me, it does challenge thinking about fast fashion.
>
> (Participant D)

This evidences how the fast fashion business model may seem to question the longevity of style, but when studied in detail, trends do frequently re-emerge. These trends may have fallen out of fashion and come back round the trend cycle, or they have remained timeless pieces, due to being a classic look. This pattern is reflective of the fashion product life cycle, as discussed in the literature review. The two examples below show how participants are aware of this cycle:

> The thing which threw me off a little bit was the one with converse and band shirts, I think the correct year was 2003, but I guessed the timeline was 2012/2013. When I was at uni, there was a lot of people dressing like that, including myself. So obviously, it's come back around, so it made it hard for me to judge where it started.
>
> (Participant G)

Figure 9.4 Subcultural Style 2003/04, FashionMap archive NTU©.

> We have established the chiffon-esk pleated skirt has been in for the past 20 years, and it's not going anywhere.
>
> (Participant A)

Recycling fashion ideas is part of 'historic continuity,' which is 'the steady evolution of clothing including the continual recurrence of symbolism, styles, and elements of decoration' (Divita, 2019, p. 83). Timeless fashion styles may also be known as 'accidental classics' in the FashionMap archive. The 'accidental classic' is identified as a style which has retained longevity, despite the fact that it is intended to be 'fast' fashion. This section has evidenced how the cyclical nature of some trends can contribute to a more circular, socially balanced fashion system.

Figure 9.5 Vintage (1920s) 2003/04, FashionMap archive NTU©.

9.2.6 Gendered Analysis

Fashion is highly gendered, and much has been written about the relationship between women and clothing (Woodward, 2007) (Guy et al., 2001). There is however a limited understanding of comparable male relationships. The relationship between gendered views and the fastness of fashion will be highlighted in this section. Historical studies support the viewpoint that women are more involved in fashion and clothing than men (O'Cass, 2003). Women may thus have greater knowledge about clothing than men (Hansen & Jan, 2009). In this study, men and women were asked the same questions for six identified trends, so that their answers could be compared. This research supports the view that women have greater knowledge about clothing than men. Both genders were shown the same image of a unisex trench coat (Figure 9.6); they were also shown the physical coat in the focus groups.

Figure 9.6 Unisex 2015/16, FashionMap archive NTU©.

When asked, 'would you wear this garment today?' neither gender displayed an affinity for the coat. The male participants made two comments regarding the coat's appearance:

> I'd probably wear it if it was a bit shorter, if it didn't look a bit more like a trench coat.
>
> (Participant B)

> It kind of looks like a suit bag.
>
> (Participant F)

By comparison, female participants made significantly more remarks regarding a wider range of the coat's visual attributes,

> I really like the styling in the shoot, but it's not the same as wanting to wear the outfit.
>
> (Participant G)

You can see from here, that the coat has a kind of nasty shine. It looks to me like a copy of something that Noel Gallagher would wear. It looks like a copy of that, but they've not quite hit the fabrics or maybe they can't make fabrics that well.

(Participant J)

I think the sleeve pockets are an unnecessary detail.

(Participant A)

I feel like it's a bit odd without a hood as well, it's a bit like a parka, but someone has cut the hood off.

(Participant C)

It's also doing that weird exposed zip thing, but the zip doesn't go all the way to the bottom.

(Participant D)

With the flap under the zip, it looks like they've put a bit of effort into that detail.

(Participant A)

I suppose the short, exposed zip situation is so that you can move.

(Participant C)

It is apparent that female participants have identified a greater number of features on the coat signalling as to why they wouldn't want to wear the garment. 'It has been suggested that male and female consumers demonstrate considerably different approaches in their decision-making and purchasing behaviour when shopping for clothing for a variety of different reasons' (Koca & Koc, 2016, p. 234). Despite the fact that females have identified a greater number of features on the coat, both genders are essentially making the same point in that they wouldn't wear the garment today for various reasons. This research does therefore question gender norms traditionally associated with fashion; it is not the case that women 'care more' about fashion, simply because their decision-making and purchasing behaviour is different to that of males. When both genders were asked to guess which year each trend was selected in the focus groups, they scored equally, with both genders guessing the correct year five times. However, the females had 14 trends to guess, whereas the males only had 8. This means that females guessed correctly 36% of the time, and males 63%. This shows that the males had a high awareness of placing fashion trends in recent history, which is contrary to the historical viewpoint that women may have greater knowledge about clothing than men (Hansen & Jan, 2009). However, it is also possible that males may have remembered the trends more accurately than females. In male fashion, there are fewer options of different clothes and styles when compared to female fashion, which could make the male trends easier to remember.

9.3 Conclusion

The aim of this chapter has been to question the fastness of fashion by gaining an understanding of gendered attitudes and behaviours towards style obsolescence and identify opportunities for change. 'Questions about clothing, fashion, and sustainability must relate to matters of gender, affects, and emotions' (Petersson McIntyre, 2021, p. 752). This chapter has addressed the subtheme, 'Breaking the economic system,' to assess the 'fastness' of fast fashion.

The research has shown how trends are at the centre of the fashion system, but they also evidence the complexities of sustainability in fashion. When styles become out of fashion, old clothes are easily discarded, even if they are in perfect condition. It has become apparent that incremental style differences are incredibly important. Although they might only be a small deviance from the desired look, as demonstrated in the findings and discussion section, these features mean that the outfit becomes rejected and redundant. However despite this, certain styles remain timeless, meaning that they have achieved sustainability and longevity through style. The longevity of garments can also be considered through the quality and durability of fabrics used.

Following the world-wide pandemic, as a post covid and lockdown reflection, it may be the case that consumers re-evaluate their wardrobes, and in particular unused clothing in the wardrobe. Breaking the economic system will require a shift in consumer mindsets; the constant need for newness does need to be questioned to order to address over-consumption. You can love fashion and be sustainably conscious, and shopping second hand may be part of the solution here. As demonstrated through the FashionMap archive, the fast fashion business model may seem to question the longevity of style, but when studied in detail, trends do frequently re-emerge.

Bibliography

Bellezza, S., & Berger, J. (2019). Trickle-Round Signals: When Low Status Is Mixed with High. *Journal of Consumer Research*, 47. https://doi.org/10.1093/jcr/ucz049

Bhardwaj, V., & Fairhurst, A. (2010). Fast Fashion: Response to Changes in the Fashion Industry. *The International Review of Retail Distribution and Consumer Research*, 20(1), 165–173. https://doi.org/10.1080/09593960903498300

Blumer, H. (1969). Fashion: From Class Differentiation to Collective Selection. *The Sociological Quarterly*, 10(3), 275–291.

Carter, M. (2003). *Fashion classics from Carlyle to Barthes*. Berg.

Day, C., Beverley, K., & Lee, A. (2015). Fast fashion, quality and longevity: A complex relationship. *PLATE*. www.plateconference.org/fast-fashion-quality-longevity-complex-relationship/

Divita, L. (2019). *Fashion forecasting* (5th ed.). Bloomsbury.

Doeringer, P., & Crean, S. (2006). Can Fast Fashion Save the US Apparel Industry? *Socio-Economic Review, 4*(3), 353–377. https://doi.org/10.1093/ser/mwl014

Easey, M. (2009). *Fashion marketing* (3rd ed.). Blackwell Publishing.

Eundeok, K. (2011). *Fashion trends: analysis and forecasting.* Berg.

Field, G. A. (1970). The Status Float Phenomenon. *Business Horizons, 13*(4), 45–52.

Fletcher, K. (2012). Durability, Fashion, Sustainability: The Processes and Practices of Use. *Fashion Practise, 4*(2), 221–238. https://doi.org/10.2752/175693812X13403765252389

Goncu-Berk, G. (2017). Fashion Trends. In *Bibliographical guides.* Bloomsbury Academic. https://doi.org/10.5040/9781474280655-bibart12001-ed

Guy, A., Green, E., & Banim, M. (2001). *Through the wardrobe: women's relationships with their clothes.* Berg.

Hansen, T., & Jan, J. M. (2009). Shopping Orientation and Online Clothing Purchases: The Role of Gender and Purchase Situation. *European Journal of Marketing, 43*(9), 1154–1170. https://doi.org/10.1108/03090560910976410

Joung, H. M. (2014). Fast-Fashion Consumers' Post-Purchase Behaviours. *International Journal of Retail and Distribution Management, 42*(8), 688–697. https://doi.org/10.1108/IJRDM-03-2013-0055

King, C. W. (1963). Fashion Adoption: A Rebuttal to the "Trickle-Down" Theory. In S. A. Greyser (Ed.), *Towards scientific marketing* (pp. 108–125). Chicago, IL: American Marketing Association.

Koca, E., & Koc, F. (2016). A Study of Clothing Purchasing Behavior by Gender with Respect to Fashion and Brand Awareness. *European Scientific Journal, ESJ, 12*(7), 234. https://doi.org/10.19044/esj.2016.v12n7p234

Lam, H. Y., Yurchisin, Y., & Cook, S. C. (2016). Young Adults' Ethical Reasoning Concerning Fast Fashion Retailers. Paper presented at the International Textile and Apparel Association Annual Conference Proceedings.

McCracken, G. (1988). *Culture and consumption. New approaches to the symbolic character of consumer goods and activities.* Indiana University Press.

Menkes, S. (2000, September 5). Fashion's Poet of Black: YAMAMOTO. The New York Times. /www.nytimes.com/2000/09/05/style/IHT-fashions-poet-of-black-yamamoto.html

Mont, O. (2008). Innovative Approaches to Optimising Design and Use of Durable Consumer Goods. *International Journal of Product Development, 6*(3–4), 227–250. https://doi.org/10.1504/IJPD.2008.020395

Newbold, A. (2017, September 4). Childrenswear Goes Genderless at John Lewis. *British Vogue.* www.vogue.co.uk/article/john-lewis-genderless-childrens-wear

O'Cass, A. (2003). Fashion Clothing Consumption: Antecedents and Consequences of Fashion Clothing Involvement. *European Journal of Marketing, 38*(7), 869–882. https://doi.org/10.1108/03090560410539294

Olivia, S. (2017, March 17). Designers who Shaped 90s Minimalism. Vogue. www.vogue.it/en/fashion/trends/2017/03/17/designers-who-shaped-90s-minimalism/?refresh_ce=

Petersson McIntyre, M. (2021). Shame, Blame, and Passion: Affects of (Un)sustainable Wardrobes. *Fashion Theory – Journal of Dress Body and Culture*, 25(6), 735–755. https://doi.org/10.1080/1362704X.2019.1676506

Rocamora, A., & Smelik, A. (2016). *Thinking through fashion: a guide to key theorists*. I.B. Tauris.

Simmel, G. (1904). Fashion. *International Quarterly*, 10(1), October, 130–155.

Simmel, G. (1957). Fashion. *American Journal of Sociology*, 62(6), 541–558. https://about.jstor.org/terms

Sorensen, K., & Jorgensen, J. J. (2019). Millennial Perceptions of Fast Fashion and Second-Hand Clothing: An Exploration of Clothing Preferences Using Q Methodology. *Social Sciences*, 8(9). https://doi.org/10.3390/socsci8090244

Sproles, G. B. (1981). Analyzing Fashion Life Cycles: Principles and Perspectives. *Journal of Marketing*, 45(4), 116–124. https://doi.org/10.2307/1251479

Steele, V. (2015). Anti-Fashion: The 1970s, Fashion Theory. *Fashion Theory: The Journal of Dress, Body and Culture*, 1(3), 279–295. https://doi.org/10.2752/136270497779640134

Stemler, S. (2000). An Overview of Content Analysis. *Practical Assessment, Research, and Evaluation*, 7(17), 2000–2001.

Svendsen, L. (2004). *Fashion: A philosophy*. Reaktion Books.

Trier-Bieniek, A. (2014). *Gender & pop culture a text-reader*. Sense Publishers.

Veblen, T. (2007). *The theory of the leisure class*. Oxford University Press.

Woodward, S. (2007). *Why women wear what they wear*. Berg.

Woodward, S. (2009). The Myth of Street Style, Fashion Theory. *Fashion Theory: The Journal of Dress, Body and Culture*, 13(1), 83–101. https://doi.org/10.2752/175174109X381355

WRAP. (2015, March 3). Clothing | WRAP. https://wrap.org.uk/resources/guide/textiles/clothing

Chapter 10

Sustainable Consumer Behavior in Fashion

Enabling and Disabling Factors

Silvia Blas Riesgo, Mariangela Lavanga and Mónica Codina

10.1 Introduction

As assessed by Roberts (1996), since the 1990s, the sustainability focus has been on consumer purchase behavior, in contrast to the 1960s and 1970s when the emphasis went mainly to corporate and political solutions. In recent years it has been stated that there is an increasing demand for sustainable fashion (McKinsey, 2022, 2021, 2020); however, it seems that consumers fail to translate that interest into purchasing behavior (Jacobs et al., 2018; McNeill & Moore, 2015). Previous research has highlighted that one of the main barriers (if not the main) for sustainable consumption is the perceived high price associated with sustainable products (Wiederhold & Martinez, 2018; Chan & Wong, 2012; Bray et al., 2011).

It can be argued that consumer interest has increased considerably but with little effect on actual consumer demand (Hassan et al., 2016; Reimers et al., 2016; Ha-Brookshire & Norum, 2011). Due to the rising trend of sustainable fashion, it becomes crucial for the government, businesses and other organizations to understand consumers' driving forces. To this date, consumer attitudes, values, drivers and barriers regarding sustainable fashion remain relatively under-researched.

Therefore, a better understanding of why and how consumers engage in a particular behavior is needed. As a methodology, we have implemented a mix-method approach consisting of three focus groups (n = 23) followed up by a survey with 1,063 respondents to investigate and compare the attitudes, values and perceptions of risks to engage with slow fashion and/or collaborative fashion consumption among non-sustainable fashion consumers (SFC) (i.e., NSFC or average consumers) and SFC in Spain.[1] The focus group data were processed following a means-end chain analysis. The underlying premise of means-end chain is that consumers make decisions based on cognitive links between product attributes, possible consequences and their personal values. The survey questionnaire was designed under the Theory of Reasoned Action principles to identify the most influential factors in consumers' fashion purchasing behavioral intention (BI). In this chapter, we analyze the data through Structural Equation Modeling.

DOI: 10.4324/9781032659053-10

Country of residence can play a role in shaping the decision-making process to buy sustainable products (Bucic et al., 2012). For example, British and German consumers are to be found as concerned about sustainability issues (see Henninger et al., 2016; BoF, 2015); however, Spanish consumer's attitudes toward sustainability remain under-researched. Thus, we have focused on the Spanish consumers and the Spanish fashion market for the present research, which present particular characteristics.

In summary, the aim of this research is (a) to discuss the identified consumer drivers and barriers to participate in collaborative fashion consumption and slow fashion in Spain and (b) to present the main determinants of sustainable fashion purchasing behavior intention.

10.2 Literature review

10.2.1 Low prices and increased consumerism

In many ways, consumerism has become a defining characteristic of modern societies (Stearns, 1997). Shopping is a leisure activity done not out of necessity but rather out of luxury. Such consumerism is in direct conflict with sustainability (Babin et al., 1994; Jansen-Verbeke, 1987). The amount of clothes bought in the EU per person has increased by 40% in just a few decades (1996–2015), driven by a fall in prices and the increased speed with which fashion is delivered to consumers (European Parliamentary Research Service, 2019). It has been estimated that in 2015 EU citizens bought 6.4 million tons of new clothing—12.7 kg per person (European Clothing Action Plan, 2017). And trends are similar globally: Peters et al. (2019) calculate that global per-capita production has increased from 5.9 kg to 13 kg per year over the period 1975–2018, and according to a McKinsey (2016) analysis, an average consumer buys 60% more clothes per year than 15 years ago but keeps them only half the time.

The production efficiency added to the rising consumption has significantly lowered the price of clothing. The prices of garments have risen at a slower pace with respect to the rest of consumer goods (Euromonitor, 2017; McKinsey, 2016). That means garments became less expensive and more affordable. As a consequence, consumers started to buy more items but the overall expenditure on clothing and footwear in the EU on average per person decreased. In particular, the prices of garments in the EU increased by only 3% between 1996 and 2015, while consumer prices, in general, rose by about 60% (European Environmental Agency, 2015).

10.2.2 Sustainable products and sustainable business models

While fast-fashion and overconsumption dominate the fashion regime, several niches are emerging that challenge the dominant structure, such as slow fashion and new business models (see Buchel et al., 2022 for a sustainability transition approach to the fashion industry). Sustainable business models have become increasingly relevant for companies in the fashion industry (Kant Hvass, 2015). The current awareness of fashion and sustainability has led to new business practices and, therefore, new ways of consumption. Furthermore, the practice of slow fashion (see Figure 10.1), a term introduced by Fletcher in 2007, represents a shift in the production and consumption of fashion garments from quantity to quality, from volume to value (see Brydges et al., 2014 for an early analysis of slow fashion businesses).

Sharing economy (Belk, 2014) and collaborative consumption (Botsman & Rogers, 2011) are not new concepts, but they have recently come to enjoy growing popularity across different industries (Becker-Leifhold & Iran, 2018). Reusing fashion items can help reduce the need for brand-new production and thus lead to decreased wastage. It seems a viable opportunity for the industry to close material loops, decrease resource reliance, reduce waste, provide product durability and extend product use time (life span). Iran and Schrader (2017, p.472) defined collaborative fashion consumption as a consumption trend

in which consumers, instead of buying new fashion products, have access to already existing garments either through alternative opportunities to acquire individual ownership (gifting, swapping, or second hand) or through usage options for fashion products owned by others (sharing, lending, renting, or leasing).

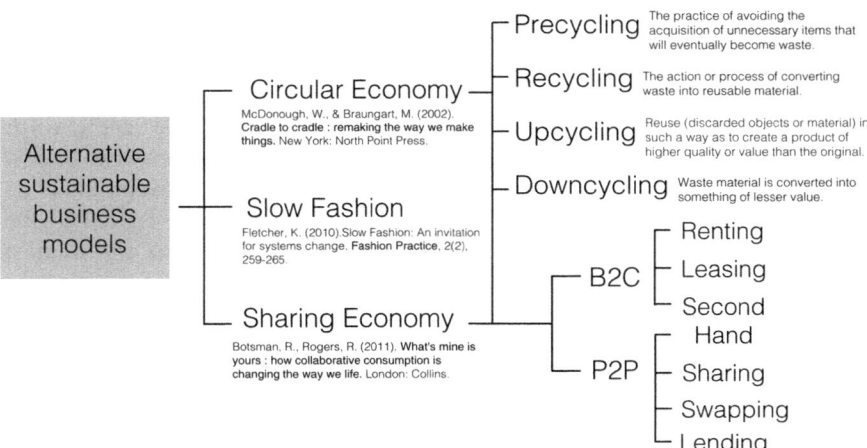

Figure 10.1 Map of alternative sustainable business models.

The different forms of collaborative fashion consumption can be broadly categorized into peer-to-peer and business-to-consumer (Iran & Schrader, 2017; see also Henninger et al., 2021 for a recent review of collaborative fashion consumption).

10.2.3 The consumer side

Consumers are willing to pay higher prices for products and services offered by businesses engaged in socially and environmentally relevant activities (Johnstone & Tan, 2015; Bockman et al., 2009). However, there has not been an evident correlation with sustainable consumption (Kong et al., 2016; Henninger, 2015). The attitude toward sustainable consumption does not translate into action (see Blas Riesgo, 2019; Jacobs et al., 2018; Wiederhold & Martinez, 2018; Chan & Wong, 2012; Bray et al., 2011). Butler and Francis (1997) found that product attributes such as price, quality and appearance would trump ethics in making clothing decisions. Similarly, Goworek et al. (2013) pointed out that consumers' sustainable behavior depends significantly more on their habits than their knowledge of sustainable business practices.

Behavioral models are often used to study the attitude-behavior gap. In particular, Ajzen's Theory of Reasoned Action (Ajzen & Fishbein, 1980) and its later published extension, the Theory of Planned Behavior (Ajzen, 1991), argue that a consumer's behavior can be explained through his/her intentions, formed by attitudes, social and personal norms and his/her perceived behavioral control.

10.2.4 The Spanish case

Our research looks at the case of Spain and its fashion consumers. The Spanish fashion industry accounts for 2.8% of Spain's GDP, 4.1% of the Spanish labor market and 8.7% of its exports (Modaes.es et al., 2020). According to the Eurostat Household Expenditure report (2019b), Spanish consumers allocate 4.1% of their spending to clothing and footwear (0.5% less than the EU27 average). International fast-fashion groups such as Inditex (best known for its leading brand Zara), Mango and Tendam have their headquarters and logistical facilities in Spain, as well as the highest number of stores. According to the Eurostat Index of Prices for Clothing and Footwear (2019a), the Spanish market has one of the lowest prices' indexes in Europe (10% cheaper than the EU27 average and only above Hungary, Romania and Bulgaria). Thus, the predominance of the so-called fast-fashion brands in the Spanish fashion market has contributed to a consumer culture of low prices resulting in the possibility of consumers being highly price-sensitive.

10.3 Methodology

Methodologically, we have followed a mixed-method approach: firstly, we gathered qualitative data from three focus groups, and secondly, we triangulated that data with a survey.

10.3.1 Focus groups

Three focus groups were held in Madrid (Spain) in July 2019 and were structured as follows: group one (N = 8) and group two (N = 9) included fashion consumers who had never bought sustainable fashion. We divided the first and second groups by age: <30 years old and ≥ 30 years old. The third focus group included consumers who usually buy sustainable fashion. Specifically, six participants, ranging from 21 to 38 years old, were recruited via *Fashion Revolution Spain*, *Slow Fashion Next*, *Humana NGO Spain* and the *Spanish Association of Sustainable Fashion* (AMSE).

The data gathered from the focus groups were transcribed and coded using NVivo 12. We conducted a content analysis, identifying themes, categories and subcategories, thus structuring the data. From there, we performed a means-end chain analysis. The means-end chain analysis is a semi-qualitative research method that underpins consumers' cognitive constructions (Gutman, 1982). The underlying premise is that consumers' decision process follows a cognitive path that links product attributes, possible consequences (functional, social or emotional) and personal values.

10.3.2 Survey

10.3.2.1 Questionnaire development

The questionnaire presented four sections: (1) fashion shopping habits; (2) interests and involvement with sustainable fashion; (3) attitude-behavior scales: fashion consciousness (FC), environmental concern (EC), subjective and personal norm (SN and PN), perceived consumer effectiveness (PCE) and BI[2]; (4) sociodemographic data.

With the Theory of Reasoned Action as theoretical background, we developed a model that considers (see Figure 10.2) the following: FC and EC can influence consumer's attitude (AT) toward sustainable fashion. AT, PCE, SNs and PNs determine consumers BI to engage (or not) with sustainable fashion.

1 FASHION CONSCIOUSNESS (FC)

FC can be defined as 'a person's degree of involvement with the styles or fashion of clothing' (Nam et al., 2007, p.103). It does not matter if the person is a fashion journalist or fashion expert, FC is mostly related to the specific

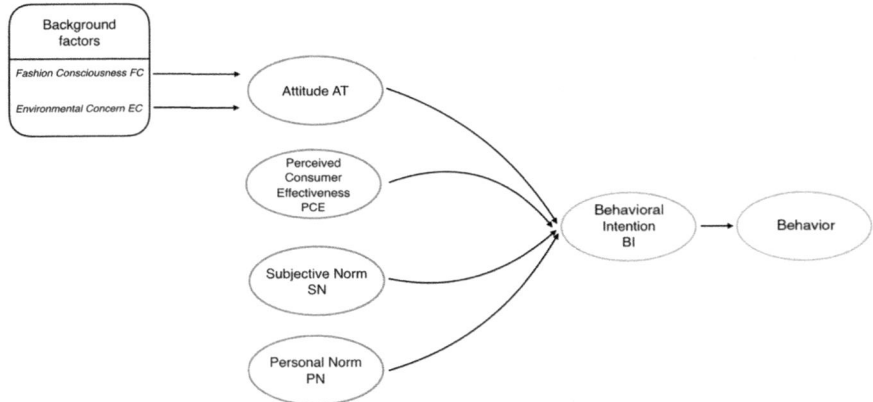

Figure 10.2 Extended theory of reasoned action model (in accordance with Ajzen, 1991).

interest a person has in garments and their appearance (Gutman & Mills, 1982). In our survey, the questions, answered on a five-point Likert scale, relate to fashion's cognitive, conative and behavioral aspects, i.e., whether respondents perceive themselves to be fashionable, whether they are aware of/interested in fashion and whether they are motivated to consume fashion.

2 ENVIRONMENTAL CONCERN (EC)

EC is generally defined as the extent to which a person is to the degree to which an individual is concerned about environmental vulnerability, the ecological effects and the ineffective nature of actions taken to protect the environment (Dunlap & Jones, 2002). EC is assumed to positively impact the attitude toward sustainable fashion since sustainable fashion is considered less damaging to the environment. In our survey, EC was measured using six items on a five-point Likert scale.

3 ATTITUDE (AT)

The first predictor of intention is the attitude toward a behavior. Attitude refers to the degree to which somebody has a favorable (or unfavorable) perception of the given behavior. In our survey, consumers' attitude toward sustainable fashion was measured with a 16-item scale developed by Jung and Jing (2014). The scale comprises five dimensions that affect decision-making in sustainable fashion consumption: functionality, exclusivity, authenticity, localism and equity.

4 SUBJECTIVE AND PERSONAL NORMS (SNS AND PNS)

SN is usually defined as an individual's perception or 'opinion about what important others believe the individual should do' (Finlay et al., 1997, p.2015), i.e., perform or not perform the behavior in a specific situation. Ajzen (1991) further argues that, in certain contexts, along with perceived social pressures from peers, moral obligations and personal feelings could influence the performance of a behavior. PNs represent an individual's own obligations to implement (or not) a given behavior. In our survey, SN and PN were measured using three items on a five-point Likert scale.

5 PERCEIVED CONSUMER EFFECTIVENESS (PCE)

PCE is defined as the consumers' evaluation of the degree to which consumers consider futile 'to do anything about pollution' and the degree to which the way they consume a product 'will affect the environment and other consumers' (Webster, 1975, p.190). According to Balderjahn (1988), the more consumers believe in their power to affect environmental issues, the more they will engage in non-polluting consumer behavior. In our survey, PCE was measured using six items on a five-point Likert scale.

6 BEHAVIORAL INTENTION (BI)

Intention indicates how much a person is willing to try and the extent of the effort she/he is willing to make in order to engage in a particular behavior (Ajzen, 1991). The stronger the intention, the more likely the person will perform the behavior in question (Ajzen, 1991). In our survey, BI was measured through a two-item scale adapted from Hyllegard et al. (2012).

10.3.2.2 Sample

The data collection took place in February 2020 in the form of an online survey in *Google Forms*. The research sample consisted of Spanish consumers from 16 years old, from all Spanish regions in a balanced proportion, to ensure the research sample's relevance and representativeness. The final sample size comprises 92 SFC and 971 NSFC (see Table 10.1).

10.4 Results

The main results of our study are presented in two parts: in part one, we draw an overview of the Spanish sustainable fashion market, highlighting the drivers and barriers for consumers to engage with native sustainable fashion brands, collaborative fashion consumption and slow fashion; in part two, through the premises of the Theory of Reasoned Action and Structural

Table 10.1 Description of the sample: Sustainable fashion consumers (SFC) vs non-sustainable fashion consumers (NSFC)

Characteristics	SFC (sample = 92)	NSFC (sample = 971)
Gender		
Male	16 (17%)	183 (19%)
Female	76 (83%)	788 (81%)
Age		
16–18	7 (7%)	156 (16%)
19–24	18 (20%)	355 (37%)
25–34	23 (25%)	205 (21%)
35–44	19 (21%)	92 (9%)
45–54	18 (20%)	94 (10%)
>54	7 (7%)	69 (7%)
Income (monthly household income)		
<1,000€	14 (15%)	182 (19%)
1,000–1,499€	24 (26%)	228 (23%)
1,500–1,999€	20 (22%)	184 (19%)
2,000–2,999€	19 (21%)	210 (22%)
3,000–4,999€	12 (13%)	121 (12%)
>5,000€	3 (3%)	46 (5%)
Education		
No studies or incomplete primary education	0 (0%)	2 (0%)
I have finished a primary education	5 (6%)	81 (9%)
I have finished high school	11 (12%)	305 (31%)
I have taken a professional education	14 (15%)	143 (15%)
I have finished a bachelor's degree	38 (41%)	303 (31%)
I have finished a master's degree	22 (24%)	118 (12%)
I have completed a Ph.D.	2 (2%)	19 (2%)

Equation Modeling analysis, we discuss the main determinants of sustainable fashion BI.

10.4.1 Awareness of Spanish consumers for sustainable fashion

In our recent article (Blas Riesgo et al., 2022b), we examined the awareness of Spanish consumers for sustainable fashion. We report here our main findings to contextualize the Spanish case.

Overall, 90.0% of our respondents are aware of the existence of sustainable fashion; 73.0% indicated to be able to define sustainable fashion; 74.3% declared interest in sustainable fashion; 39.5% stated they bought a sustainable fashion item at least once. When asked about why they don't buy sustainable fashion or why they don't buy it more often, the majority of respondents mentioned (see Figure 10.3): 'because I cannot discern when a brand is really sustainable or when it just claims to be it in order to improve its image' (47.6%), 'because it is too expensive' (42.6%) and 'because it is not available where I live' (30.6%). While price, unavailability and aesthetics are often recognized as barriers for sustainable fashion, it is mostly the low level of trust and credibility in fashion companies the main barrier for the Spanish consumers to buy sustainable fashion (Blas Riesgo et al., 2022b).

A total of 92 consumers (8.65%) indicated they buy sustainable fashion regularly. These SFC don't buy from sustainable fashion brands because (see Figure 10.4) they prefer to buy second-hand (27.0%), they think it is too expensive (20.9%) and they do not trust companies' sustainability claims (18.8%). Thus, the results suggest that the higher the awareness for sustainability, the less SFC buy brand-new items, i.e., they prefer second-hand (Blas Riesgo et al., 2022b).

When we looked at collaborative fashion consumption, 85.9% of SFC and 63.1% of NSFC indicated they bought second-hand garments; 62.0% of SFC and 43.8% of NSFC declared they sold apparel or accessories. Only 6.5% of respondents have rented garments or accessories at least once. In summary, SFC have a higher preference for collaborative fashion consumption than NSFC; they buy and sell garments; however, they still prefer to own their clothing rather than renting. One reason may be that rental business models are still in their infant stage in Spain (Blas Riesgo et al., 2022b).

10.4.2 Barriers to collaborative fashion consumption

During the focus groups, we dug into the barriers to collaborative fashion consumption (second-hand, renting and leasing). The main barriers identified concern product attributes such as cleanliness, style, fit, convenience and trust, related to personal values of social status, social acceptance, sense of belonging, self-identity and self-representation.

1 **Cleanliness**: As garments are worn close to the skin, Spanish consumers show health concerns about products' hygiene and overall cleanliness of clothes (bacteria from pre-owners, disease transmission, odor and dirtiness). These concerns may have increased due to the Coronavirus crisis, a topic that asks for further research.
2 **Convenience**
   a **Alter Consumption Habits**: Spanish consumers are used to low-price apparel from fast-fashion brands; renting or leasing could dramatically change their consumption habits. In the three focus groups, consumers stated that they dislike returning items, both for time costs (as scheduling appointments with the delivery services) and detachment

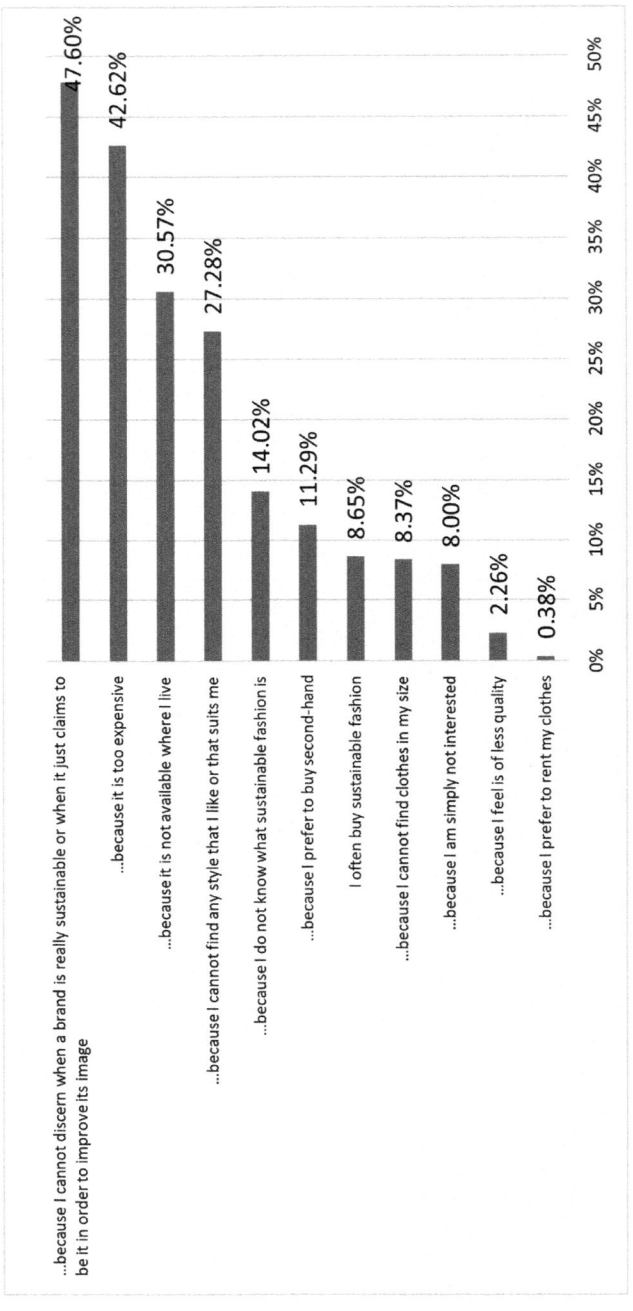

Figure 10.3 Frequency break-down of the answers from the question 'why haven't you bought sustainable fashion, or you do not buy it more often?' for the overall dataset (source: Blas Riesgo et al., 2022a).

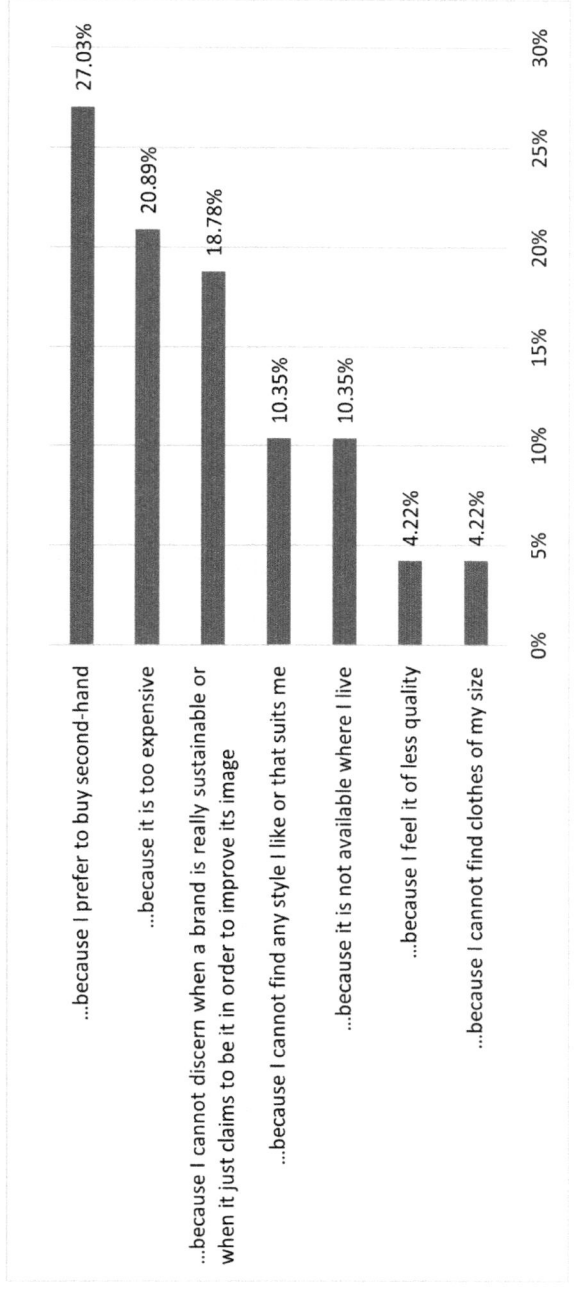

Figure 10.4 Frequency break-down of the answers from the question 'why haven't you bought sustainable fashion, or you do not buy it more often?' for the sustainable fashion consumers (SFC) (source: Blas Riesgo et al., 2022a).

emotional reasons. Therefore, renting or short-term leasing is not well regarded. Renting is only seen as an option for specific events, such as weddings, or for transition periods in life, like maternity or growing up children.

b **Lack of ownership**: Spanish consumers indicated they are not ready to renounce the ownership of their clothes. The sharing economy has flourished in other markets, such as commuting services (BlaBlaCar) or accommodation (Airbnb); however, since clothing is seen as an extension of the self and it is closely related to self-identity and social status and acceptance, garments have an additional emotional component that prevents consumers from sharing them.

c **Time costs**: Fast-fashion stores are ubiquitous, whereas second-hand stores are scarce, requiring additional searching and commuting time. Besides, it usually takes much more time for consumers to find items in their style and size (and right fit) in second-hand stores. In Spain, second-hand stores usually belong to NGOs (such as Humana) and differ considerably from conventional fast-fashion spaces in their ambience and clothes disposition. Consumers find second-hand stores poorly organized, and this leads to frustrating shopping experiences. Searching online for second-hand items or online renting is also perceived as a much more time-consuming task than searching in conventional brands' websites.

d **Lack of availability**: As pointed out before, the number of second-hand stores and renting services is scarce, especially outside big cities, so potential consumers have to make an extra time effort to find what they need.

3 **Lack of knowledge**: Renting is still a fledgling business in Spain, and many consumers are not aware of which companies provide the service, its terms and conditions. They indicated they are not aware of online rental services.

4 **Lack of information and trust**: Perceived price-for-value challenges. Participants were especially skeptical about counterfeits in luxury mid-range goods and that the product they would receive would be the same as they see in the picture while shopping online from both second-hand business-to-consumers and peer-to-peer sites. They complain about the lack of information about the provider's guarantees and how exceptional cases, such as damages and subsequent customer liability, would be treated.

5 **Self-image and social-image**: Consumers stated that they hide deliberately from their friends and family to buy second-hand apparel because they feel that they would be labeled 'poor' or 'cheap.' In Spain, there is still a stigma around buying second-hand clothing, on the one hand, for hygiene reasons; on the other hand, it is associated with lower social status and,

therefore, with a sentiment of lack of social acceptance. This could be explained because most second-hand stores in Spain belong to NGOs. Moreover, younger consumers refuse to buy in the second-hand market because it lacks *trendiness*, jeopardizing their self-identity and perceived social status.

10.4.3 Drivers to collaborative fashion consumption

The main reasons that drive Spanish consumers to participate in collaborative fashion consumption are, in general, utilitarian motivations (primarily financial), whereas for SFC, sustainability concerns the following:

1 **Utilitarian motives**: Second-hand is valued as a good alternative for saving money and, thus, relates to a sense of financial security. In fact, FGs participants stated that they became first in touch with second-hand when amid a personal financial crisis. Initially, they approached the second-hand market with skepticism, but once they passed that initial barrier, they have adopted it as a lifestyle. For SFC, second-hand is their way to go sustainable because, with sustainable fashion brands, they have size limitations (especially plus sizing) and lack of their preferred styles (working styles). For consumers lacking spare time, renting is regarded as a practical option because they can avoid washing and ironing.
2 **Aesthetic motives**: Preference for past styles (nostalgia) or searching for a specific product. Average consumers from the ≥30 years old focus are disengaged with the current trends and in the second-hand market can find garments that adjust better to their taste or style. Others go to the second-hand market searching for a specific product from a past season that they liked but missed the opportunity to buy. Sustainable consumers like the idea of not being uniformed with the 'mass' of consumers; hence, buying second-hand enables them to define their personal style in opposition to the traditional market's mass trends, which is related to a sense of self-identity and self-enhancement.
3 **Hedonic motives**: Consumers are thrilled to hunt for bargains (especially among luxury products) and to search for rare items that otherwise would be unattainable to them. Furthermore, renting might trigger hedonic values because it allows consumers to experiment with new styles without paying total costs, and both the second-hand market and renting allow consumers access to high-fashion goods that would be otherwise unaffordable.
4 **Sustainability motives**: SFC believe that by avoiding the traditional market, they are being resourceful and preventing wasteful disposal of items, which relates to a sense of achievement and happiness for being responsible for the environment. Moreover, they know that once they are done with their items, they can resell them again in the second-hand market,

thus closing the loop. The quote from Orsola de Castro, co-founder of *Fashion Revolution*, 'the most sustainable garment is the one already in your wardrobe,' is their motto. They consistently question personal needs and focus on purchasing clothing only when there is a genuine need.

10.4.4 Slow fashion

Jung and Jin (2014) developed a 16-item scale that explores five fundamental dimensions of slow fashion: equity, authenticity, functionality, localism and exclusivity. We applied the scale to understand Spanish consumers' attitude toward slow fashion and sustainable fashion by extension.

As presented in Figure 10.5 (and Appendix Table 10A.2), SFC scored high on all five dimensions: localism (4.23), authenticity (4.17), equity (4.15), functionality (4.11) and exclusivity (3.38). On the other hand, for the NSFC, functionality comes first (3.78), followed by localism (3.45), authenticity (3.11), exclusivity (2.84) and equity (2.74). 'I tend to keep clothes as long as possible rather than discarding them quickly' was the statement with the highest score for both groups. Overall, it seems that for the NSFC it is more critical to maximize product life span and efficiency, disregarding or paying less attention to the other dimensions of sustainable fashion. Equity is the least evaluated factor. Even though specific advertisement campaigns target the fashion industry's working conditions, such as 'Who made my clothes?' by *Fashion Revolution*, this topic is yet out of the top of the consumers' minds.

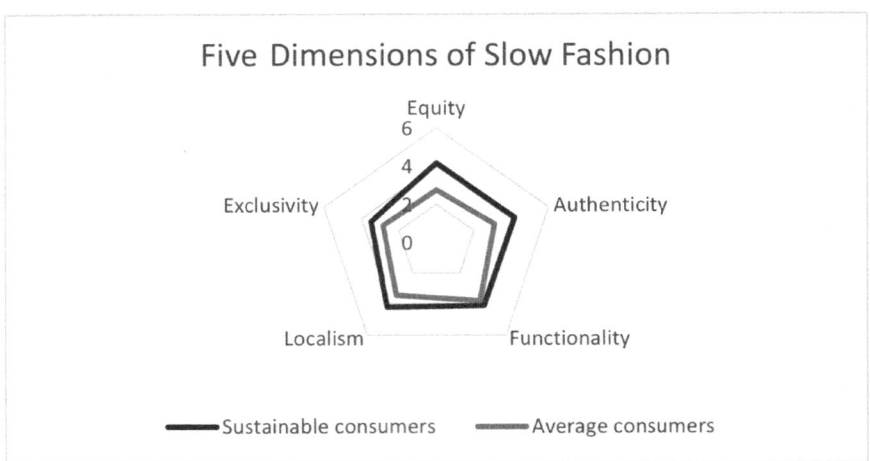

Figure 10.5 Mean of the five dimensions for the sustainable consumers and the average consumers.

10.4.5 Main determinants of sustainable fashion behavioral intention

In this section, we explore the main determinants of BI toward sustainable fashion by presenting the results of Structural Equation Modeling analysis conducted under the premises of the Theory of Reasoned Action. The results will be presented by comparing SFC with NSFC.

We first checked the reliability and the discriminant validity of the model. The measure of the correlation among latent variables was used to assess the discriminant validity. These values should not exceed a threshold of 0.9. As shown in Table 10.2, all the values are below the indicated threshold, suggesting a good validity. To test the reliability Cronbach's alpha was used. As represented in Table 10.3, all the obtained values are above the suggested threshold of 0.7 (Cronbach, 1951).

We followed Hu and Bentler's (1999) Two-Index Presentation Strategy guidelines to establish the goodness of fit. The first parameter was the Normed Fit Index, evaluated to be 0.907, indicative of a very good fit (Lohmöller, 1989). The second parameter was the standardized root mean residual which value was 0.059, well below the threshold of 0.09 (Hu & Bentler, 1999).

Table 10.2 Correlations of latent variables for discriminant validity

	1	2	3	4	5	6	7
AT	1						
BI	0.49	1					
EC	0.36	0.50	1				
FC	0.29	0.11	0.00	1			
PCE	0.30	0.42	0.48	0.05	1		
PN	0.50	0.63	0.48	0.07	0.37	1	
SN	0.28	0.36	0.15	0.12	0.13	0.46	1

Table 10.3 Mean, standard deviation (SD), reliability (Cronbach's alpha) and number of items for the different latent variables

Scale	Mean	SD	Cronbach's alpha	Items
AT	3.324	0.801	0.872	16
EC	4.336	0.785	0.795	6
FC	3.164	1.209	0.923	4
PCE	3.716	0.551	0.756	6
PN	3.148	1.264	–	1
SN	2.469	1.104	0.701	2
BI	3.723	1.142	0.873	2

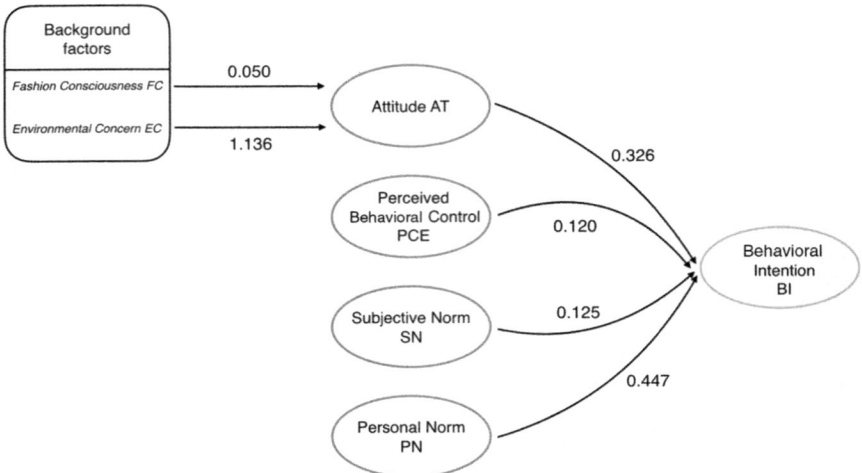

Figure 10.6 Extended theory of reasoned action model with path coefficients from the structural equation modeling for the sustainable fashion consumers (SFC).

Once we assessed the goodness of the model's fit, we analyzed the results of SFC and NSFC independently (Figures 10.6 and 10.7). A few items (PCE 1 and 2) were dropped from the measurement model due to their insignificant weights.

In the case of SFC, the model can explain 67.4% of the variance (R^2) toward BI. Whereas for NSFC, the model explains 57.2% of the variance. In the literature (see Henseler et al., 2009; Chin, 1998), an R^2 value above 67% is considered a substantial contribution; therefore, in the case of the SFC, the explanatory power of the model appears to be very good; while for NSFC, there may be additional latent variables, not considered in our model, that influence BI.

SFC		Estimate	Std.Err.	Std.all
AT				
	EC	0.441	0.146	1.136
	FC	0.012	0.023	0.050
BI				
	PCE	0.208	0.218	0.120
	SN	0.071	0.044	0.125
	AT	1.066	0.588	0.326
	PN	0.333	0.070	0.447

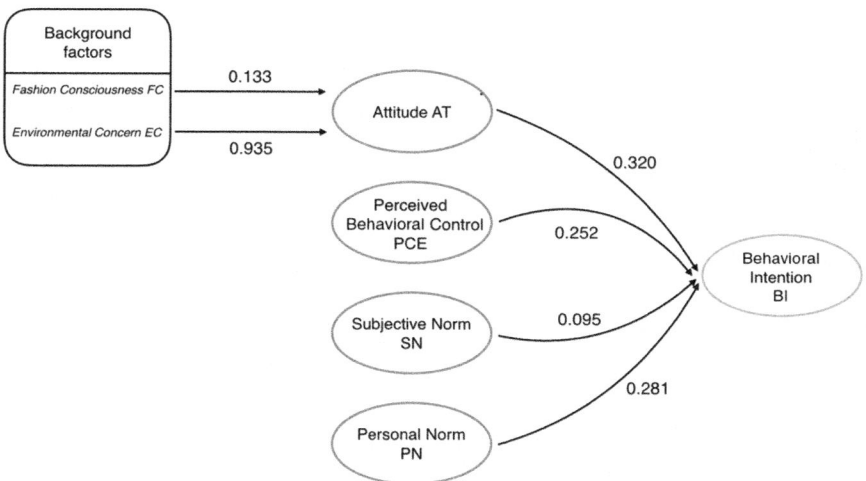

Figure 10.7 Extended theory of reasoned action model with path coefficients from the structural equation modeling for the non-sustainable fashion consumers (NSFC).

Table 10.4 Path coefficients for sustainable fashion consumers (SFC) (above) and non-sustainable fashion consumers (NSFC) (below) expressed in terms of the completely standardized solution (Std.all = both latent and observed variables are standardized)

NSFC		Estimate	Std.Err.	Std.all
AT				
	EC	0.349	0.040	0.935
	FC	0.039	0.011	0.133
BI				
	PCE	0.578	0.093	0.252
	SN	0.123	0.049	0.095
	AT	1.199	0.187	0.320
	PN	0.243	0.032	0.281

Analyzing the path coefficients of the Structural Equation Modeling, we found that for both kinds of consumers, FC did not impact AT, whereas EC was found to have a strong influence on AT (see Table 10.4). Regarding BI, in the case of SFC, the most influential factor was PN, followed by AT, SN, and the less influential was PCE. On the contrary, for NSFC, AT had the strongest impact on BI, while SN had a negligible contribution.

10.5 Conclusions

The persistent unsustainability issues in our society require government, businesses, education and other organizations to better understand consumers' driving forces toward sustainable products. Our study looked at the fashion market in Spain and highlighted that consumer perceptions of sustainable fashion differ considerably among SFC and NSFC.

Participants indicated that the main barrier to buying from sustainable fashion brands (or doing it more often) is linked to the fact that they cannot distinguish when a brand is really sustainable or just greenwashing consumers. While brands are becoming more active in sustainability communication, there is still lots of confusion and lack of trust among consumers. Unfortunately, practices like greenwashing (see Jones, 2019; Miller, 2017) in conjunction with scandals, such as Boohoo's most recent allegations about worker exploitation by a supplier in the English town of Leicester (Cernansky, 2020), might have affected consumers' trust in brands and companies' sustainable claims.

The second most selected barrier for not buying sustainable fashion was its high price. One could argue that the very low prices of fast fashion have contributed to increasing consumers' sensitivity toward prices. Companies are starting to open up their factories and repair atelier to educate consumers on how garment is made but also repaired (i.e., MUD jeans or the recently opened United Repair Center in Amsterdam in collaboration with Patagonia). These processes may result in a higher willingness to pay for sustainable fashion and increased value and appreciation for sustainable fashion by consumers.

Our descriptive statistics, also discussed in our recent article (Blas Riesgo et al., 2022b), show that sustainability matters to a very small part of our respondents (8.65%). Furthermore, not the GEN Z but the Millennials and Baby Boomers are the consumers actually buying sustainable fashion, in contrast with recent studies (see, for example, Vatamanescu et al., 2021 for an overview of consumers' demand for sustainable products pre- and post-Covid). These results align with a recent Deloitte report (2020), which claims that *surprisingly*, Gen Z is the least engaged in environmental issues, in contrast with Millennials, who are the most engaged.

Regarding collaborative fashion consumption, the main barriers concern product attributes such as cleanliness, style, fit, convenience and trust, related to personal values of social status, social acceptance, sense of belonging, self-identity and self-representation. Conversely, the main drivers were, in general, utilitarian motivations (primarily financial), whereas for SFC, sustainability concerns. The results are in line with previous studies that pointed to functional and hedonic needs as enablers of collaborative fashion consumption (Arnould & Bardhi, 2005) and, for some consumers, biospheric values (Becker-Leifhold & Iran, 2018).

Lastly, the results of the Structural Equation Modeling indicate that for SFC, PNs (i.e., their moral values) have the strongest influence on their BI to buy sustainable fashion. Conversely, for NSFC, attitude is the primary indicator of BI, whereas social norms (i.e., perceived pressure from society and peers) exert a negligible influence in their intended behavior. As also indicated in our recent article (Blas Riesgo et al., 2022b), Spain may lack a strong 'sustainability culture.' These findings endorse and significantly add to the literature on SFC choice behavior and may help retailers and marketers to create more tailored retailing and communication strategies.

Our study gives a picture of the Spanish fashion consumer before the Covid-19 pandemic. Therefore, it can provide a reference point for future research into the changes in the sustainable fashion market. Data are drawn from a focus group and a survey done in 2019. Our methodological approach can be replicated in Spain and in other countries. In general focus groups and questionnaires are a good tool to explore complex behavior and experience a consumer's eye view of the world and the topic at hand (Tynan & Drayton, 1988). Even though our sample was relatively large, it was skewed toward women and younger respondents. Future research studies could perform a similar analysis with a less skewed sample and within other countries to determine to what extent culture influences sustainable fashion consumption. Lastly, since this research is solely focused on the consumers' perspective, future research may concentrate on how fashion brands disseminate and communicate their sustainability initiatives and/or the volume and frame of sustainability contents in mass media outlets to help clarify why there is a lack of trust/credibility in this respect.

Appendix

Table 10A.1 Theory of reasoned action measurement scales: Mean (std)

	Sustainable consumers	Average consumers
Fashion Consciousness (FC) (Cronbach α = 0.923)	3.41 (1.17)	3.02 (1.16)
How much do you like fashion?	3.86 (1.20)	3.59 (1.21)
How much do you talk about fashion with friends and family?	3.13 (1.23)	2.70 (1.15)
Do you look for information about fashion and style?	3.42 (1.35)	3.06 (1.44)
How frequently do you look for information about fashion and style?	3.22 (1.33)	2.75 (1.34)
Environmental concern (EC) (Cronbach α = 0.795)	4.57 (0.93)	4.21 (1.00)
I am worried about the environment	4.65 (0.73)	4.13 (0.91)

(*Continued*)

Table 10A.1 (Continued)

	Sustainable consumers	Average consumers
The conditions of the environment influence the quality of my life	4.65 (0.72)	4.05 (1.06)
I am willing to make sacrifices to protect the environment	4.67 (0.70)	4.09 (0.95)
I think it is important to protect and preserve the Earth for future generations	4.80 (0.62)	4.50 (0.85)
I think that the environmental crisis is being exaggerated*	3.88 (1.52)	4.06 (1.22)
I believe sustainability is important	4.74 (0.68)	4.41 (0.86)
Subjective Norm (SN) (Cronbach α = 0.701)	2.87 (1.20)	2.24 (1.04)
My family and friends expect me to buy more sustainable products	2.78 (1.36)	1.89 (1.10)
Society expects me to buy more sustainable products	2.96 (1.28)	2.59 (1.30)
Perceive Consumer Effectiveness (PCE) (Cronbach α = 0.756)	4.45 (1.01)	4.04 (1.13)
Unless everyone starts to change their consumption habits, it does not make sense for me to change mine*	4.35 (1.15)	4.07 (1.07)
The individual consumer can do nothing to reduce pollution*	4.33 (1.16)	3.99 (1.22)
Given that what a simple person does is not going to have any effect on pollution levels or natural resource scarcity problems, what I do will make no difference*	4.29 (1.22)	4.15 (1.10)
Each consumer's behavior can have a positive impact on society	4.62 (0.75)	4.21 (1.05)
I believe that I can have a positive impact on the environment if I consume products that are sustainable	4.58 (0.76)	3.95 (1.12)
I believe that buying sustainable clothing can help combat environmental problems	4.53 (0.90)	3.85 (1.15)
Personal Norm (PN) (Cronbach α = NA)	4.24 (1.03)	3.04 (1.23)
I think I have a moral obligation to buy clothes/accessories made sustainably	4.24 (1.03)	3.04 (1.23)

Table 10A.1 (Continued)

	Sustainable consumers	Average consumers
Behavioral Intention (BI) (Cronbach α = 0.873)	4.43 (0.91)	3.53 (1.21)
In the future, I will try to buy clothes produced sustainably	4.55 (0.78)	3.65 (1.15)
In the future, I will try to convince my family and friends to buy clothes produced sustainably	4.30 (1.01)	3.41 (1.25)

Note: *Reverse-coded items

Table 10A.2 Five dimensions of slow fashion: Mean (std)

	Sustainable consumers	Average consumers
EQUITY (Cronbach α = 0.929)	4.15 (1.06)	2.74 (1.25)
I am concerned about the working conditions of producers when I buy clothes	4.26 (1.04)	2.86 (1.23)
I am concerned about fair trade when I buy clothes	3.95 (1.10)	2.49 (1.21)
Fair compensation for apparel producers is important to me when I buy clothes	4.23 (1.02)	2.86 (1.28)
AUTHENTICITY (Cronbach α = 0.852)	4.17 (1.05)	3.11 (1.39)
Craftsmanship is very important in clothes	4.05 (1.07)	2.85 (1.34)
I value clothes made by traditional techniques	4.23 (1.02)	3.08 (1.42)
Handcrafted clothes are more valuable than mass-produced ones	4.23 (1.06)	3.41 (1.34)
FUNCTIONALITY (Cronbach α = 0.597)	4.11 (1.07)	3.78 (1.11)
I tend to keep clothes as long as possible rather than discarding them quickly	4.52 (0.73)	4.25 (0.91)
I prefer simple and classic designs	3.53 (1.12)	3.45 (1.09)
I prefer to buy less clothes, but of higher quality	4.09 (1.14)	3.39 (1.09)
I often enjoy wearing the same clothes in multiple ways	4.30 (0.97)	4.01 (1.03)
LOCALISM (Cronbach α = 0.867)	4.23 (1.01)	3.45 (1.31)
We need to support Spanish apparel brands	4.38 (0.95)	3.83 (1.36)
I prefer buying clothes made in Spain to clothes manufactured in other countries	4.11 (1.03)	3.19 (1.30)

(Continued)

Table 10A.2 (Continued)

	Sustainable consumers	Average consumers
I believe clothes made of locally produced materials are more valuable	4.19 (1.04)	3.33 (1.18)
EXCLUSIVITY (Cronbach α = 0.873)	3.48 (1.35)	2.84 (1.38)
I am very attracted to rare apparel items	3.71 (1.31)	3.10 (1.31)
Limited editions hold special appeal for me	3.17 (1.39)	2.40 (1.31)
I enjoy having clothes that others do not	3.55 (1.30)	3.02 (1.42)

Cronbach α Overall = 0.872

Notes

1 The data gathered were used by the first author in two other academic publications on sustainable fashion consumption in Spain (see Blas Riesgo et al., 2022a, 2022b).
2 The entire disclosure of the scale items and the respective results are available in Appendix Tables 10A.1 and 10A.2.

References

Ajzen, I. (1991). The theory of planned behavior. *Organizational Behavior and Human Decision Processes 50*, pp.179–211.

Ajzen, I., & Fishbein, M. (1980). *Understanding attitudes and predicting social behavior*. Englewood Cliffs, NJ: Prentice-Hall.

Arnould, E.J., & Bardhi, F. (2005). Thrift shopping: combining utilitarian thrift and hedonic treat benefits. *Journal of Consumer Behavior 4*(4), pp.223–233.

Babin, B.J., Darden, W.R. & Griffin, M. (1994). Work and /or fun: measuring hedonic and utilitarian shopping value. *Journal of Consumer Research 9*, pp.132–140.

Balderjahn, I. (1988). Personality variables and environmental attitudes as predictors of ecologically responsible consumption patterns. *Journal of Business Research 17*(1), pp.51–56.

Becker-Leifhold, C., & Iran, S. (2018). Collaborative fashion consumption—drivers, barriers and future pathways. *Journal of Fashion Marketing and Management 22*(2), pp.189–208. DOI:10.1108/JFMM-10-2017-0109

Belk, R.W. (2014). You are what you can access: sharing and collaborative consumption online. *Journal of Business Research 67*(8), pp.1595–1600.

Blas Riesgo, S. (2019). The consumption side of sustainable fashion: understanding the attitude-behavior gap among the Spanish consumers. In N. Kalbaska, T. Sádaba, F. Cominelli, & L. Cantoni (Eds.), *Fashion communication in the digital age* (pp. 111–117). Springer International Publishing. https://doi.org/10.10007/978-3-030-15436-3_10

Blas Riesgo, S., Codina, M. & Sádaba, T. (2022a). Does sustainability matter to fashion consumers? Clustering fashion consumers and their purchasing behavior in Spain. *Fashion Practice: The Journal of Design, Creative Process & The Fashion Industry*. https://doi.org/10.1080/17569370.2022.2051297

Blas Riesgo, S., Lavanga, M. & Codina, M. (2022b). Drivers and barriers for sustainable fashion consumption in Spain: a comparison between sustainable and non-sustainable consumers, *International Journal of Fashion Design, Technology and Education*. DOI:10.1080/17543266.2022.2089239

Bockman, S., Razzouk, Y., & Sirotnik, B. (2009). Going green—from left to center stage: an empirical perspective. *Journal of the American Academy of Business* 14(2), pp.8–17.

BoF (Business of Fashion) (2015). *How can we safeguard the people who make our clothing?* www.businessoffashion.com/community/voices/discussions/how-can-we-safeguard-the-people-who-make-our-clothing

Botsman, R., & Rogers, R. (2011). *What's mine is yours. How collaborative consumption is changing the way we live*. London: Collins.

Bray, J., Johns, N., & Kilburn, D. (2011). An exploratory study into the factors impeding ethical consumption. *Journal of Business Ethics* 98(4), pp.597–608. DOI:10.1007/s10551-010-0640-9

Brydges, T., Lavanga, M., & von Gunten. L. (2014). Entrepreneurship in the fashion industry: a case study of "slow fashion" businesses. In A. Schramme, G. Hagoort, & R. Kooyman (Eds.), *Beyond frames. Dynamics between the creative industries, knowledge institutions and the urban context* (73–79). Chicago: University of Chicago Press.

Buchel, S., Hebinck, A., Lavanga, M., & Loorbach, D. (2022). Disrupting the status quo: a sustainability transitions analysis of the fashion system. *Sustainability: Science, Practice and Policy* 18(1), pp.231–246. DOI:10.1080/15487733.2022.2040231

Bucic, T., Harris, J., & Arli, D. (2012). Ethical consumers among the Millennials: a cross-national study. *Journal of Business Ethics* 110(1), pp.113–131. https://doi.org/10.1007/s10551-011-1151-z

Butler, S.M., & Francis, S. (1997). The effects of environmental attitudes on apparel purchasing behavior. *Clothing and Textile Research Journal 15*, pp.76–85.

Cernansky, R. (2020). *After Boohoo: tackling fashion's systemic problems*. www.voguebusiness.com/sustainability/after-boohoo-tackling-fashions-systemic-problems

Chan, T., & Wong, C.W.Y. (2012). The consumption side of sustainable fashion supply chain. Understanding fashion consumer eco-fashion consumption decision. *Journal of Fashion Marketing and Management* 16(2), pp.193–215. DOI:10.1108/13612021211222824

Chin, W.W. (1998). Issues and opinion on structural equation modelling. In *MIS quarterly* (pp. 7–16). Minneapolis, MN: Management Information Systems Research Center, University of Minnesota.

Cronbach, L.J. (1951). Coefficient alpha and the internal structure of tests. *Psychometrika 16*(3), pp.297–334.

Deloitte (2020). *Shifting sands: how consumer behavior is embracing sustainability*. www2.deloitte.com/ch/en/pages/consumer-business/articles/shifting-sands-sustainable-consumer.html

Dunlap R.E., & Jones, R.E. (2002). Environmental concern: conceptual and measurement issues. In R.E. Dunlap, & W. Michelson (Eds.), *Handbook of environmental sociology* (pp. 482–524), Westport, UK: Greenwood Press.

Euromonitor International Apparel & Footwear 2016 Edition (volume sales trends 2005–2015); World Bank, *World development indicators—GD* (2017).

European Clothing Action Plan (2017). *Mapping clothing impacts in Europe: the environmental cost.* www.ecap.eu.com/wp-content/uploads/2018/07/Mapping-clothing-impacts-in-Europe.pdf

European Environment Agency (2015). *Environmental indicator report 2014. Environmental impacts of production-consumption systems in Europe.* www.eea.europa.eu/publications/environmental-indicator-report-2014

European Parliamentary Research Service (2019). *Environmental impact of the textile and clothing industry.* www.europarl.europa.eu/RegData/etudes/BRIE/2019/633143/EPRS_BRI(2019)633143_EN.pdf

Eurostat (2019a). *Clothing and footwear price levels in the EU.* https://ec.europa.eu/eurostat/cache/infographs/pricelevels/pricelevels_2019/

Eurostat (2019b). *Household expenditure report.* https://ec.europa.eu/eurostat/cache/infographs/hhexpcofog/hhexpcofog_2019/

Finlay, K.A., Trafimow, D., & Moroi, E. (1997). Predicting health behaviors from attitudes and subjective norms: between-subjects and within-subjects analyses. *Journal of Applied Social Psychology 27*(22), pp.2015–2031.

Fletcher, K. (2007). Slow fashion. *Ecologist 37*(5), p.61.

Goworek, H., Hiller, A., Fisher, T., Cooper, T., & Woodward, S. (2013). Consumers' attitudes toward sustainable fashion: clothing usage and disposal. In *Sustainability in fashion and textiles: values, design, production, and consumption.* Sheffield: Greenleaf Publishing Limited. DOI:10.9774/GLEAF.978-1-909493-61-2_25

Gutman, J. (1982). A means-end chain model based on consumer categorization processes. *Journal of Marketing 46*, pp.60–72. https://doi.org/10.1177/002224298204600207

Gutman, J., & Mills, M.K. (1982), Fashion lifestyle, self-concept, shopping orientation and store patronage: an integrative analysis. *Journal of Retailing 58*(2), pp.64–86.

Ha-Brookshire, J.E., & Norum, P.S. (2011). Willingness to pay for socially responsible products: case of cotton apparel. *Journal of Consumer Marketing 28*, pp.344–353. DOI:10.1108/07363761111149992

Hassan, L.M., Shiu, E., & Shaw, D. (2016). Who says there is an intention-behavior gap? Assessing the empirical evidence of an intention-behavior gap in ethical consumption. *Journal of Business Ethics 136*, pp.219–236. DOI:10.1007/s10551-014-2440-0

Henninger, C.E. (2015). Traceability the new eco-label in the slow fashion industry? *Sustainability 7*(5), pp.6011–6032. DOI:10.3390/su7056011

Henninger, C.E., Alevizou, P.J., & Oates, C.J. (2016). What is sustainable fashion? *Journal of Fashion Marketing and Management 20*(4), pp.400–416. DOI:10.1108/JFMM-07-2015-0052

Henninger, C.E., Brydges, T., Iran, S., & Vladimirova, K. (2021). Collaborative fashion consumption – a synthesis and future research agenda. *Journal of Cleaner Production*, p.319. DOI:10.1016/j.jclepro.2021.128648

Henseler, J., Ringle, C.M., & Sinkovics, R.R. (2009). The use of partial least squares path modeling in international marketing. *Advances in International Marketing 20*, pp.277–319.

Hu, L.T., & Bentler, P.M. (1999). Cutoff criteria for fit indexes in covariance structure analysis: conventional criteria versus new alternatives. *Structural Equation Modelling 6*(1), pp.1–55.

Hyllegard, K.H., Yan, R.N., Ogle, J.P., & Lee, K.H. (2012). Socially responsible labeling: the impact of hang tags on consumers' attitudes and patronage intentions toward an apparel brand. *Clothing and Textiles Research Journal 30*(1), pp.51–66.

Iran, S., & Schrader, U. (2017). Collaborative fashion consumption and its environmental effects. *Journal of Fashion Marketing and Management 21*(4), pp.468–482. DOI:10.1108/JFMM-09-2016-0086

Jacobs, K., Petersen, L., Horisch, J., & Battenfeld, D. (2018). Green thinking but thoughtless buying? An empirical extension of the value-attitude-behavior hierarchy in sustainable clothing. *Journal of Cleaner Production 203*, pp.1155–1169. DOI:10.1016/j.jclepro.2018.07.320

Jansen-Verbeke, M. (1987). Women shopping and leisure. *Leisure Studies 6*, pp.71–86.

Johnstone, M.L., & Tan, L. (2015). Exploring the gap between consumers' green rhetoric and purchasing behavior. *Journal of Business Ethics 132*, 2. DOI:10.1007/s10551-014-2316-3

Jones, E. (2019). Rethinking greenwashing: corporate discourse, unethical practice, and the unmet potential of responsible consumerism. *Sociological Perspectives 62*(5), pp.728–754.

Jung, S., & Jin, B. (2014). A theoretical investigation of slow fashion: sustainable future of apparel industry. *International Journal of Consumer Studies 38*, pp.510–519. https://doi.org/10.1111/ijcs.12127

Kant Hvass, K. (2015). Business model innovation through second-hand retailing—a fashion industry case. *The Journal of Corporate Citizenship 57*, pp.11–32.

Kong, H.M., Ko, E., Chae, H., & Mattila, P. (2016). Understanding fashion consumers' attitude and behavioral intention toward sustainable fashion products: focus on sustainable knowledge sources and knowledge types. *Journal of Global Fashion Marketing 7*(2), pp.103–119. DOI:10.1080/20932685.2015.1131435

Lohmöller, J.B. (1989). *Latent variable oath modelling with partial least squares.* Heidelberg: Physica-Verlag.

McKinsey (2016). *Style that's sustainable: a new fast-fashion formula.* www.mckinsey.com/~/media/McKinsey/Business%20Functions/Sustainability/Our%20Insights/Style%20thats%20sustainable%20A%20new%20fast%20fashion%20formula/Style-thats-sustainable-A-new-fast-fashion-formula-vF.ashx

McKinsey (2020). *The state of fashion 2020.* www.mckinsey.com/~/media/mckinsey/industries/retail/our%20insights/the%20state%20of%20fashion%202020%20navigating%20uncertainty/the-state-of-fashion-2020-final.ashx

McKinsey (2021). *The state of fashion 2021.* www.mckinsey.com/~/media/mckinsey/industries/retail/our%20insights/state%20of%20fashion/2021/the-state-of-fashion-2021-vf.pdf

McKinsey (2022). *The state of fashion 2022.* www.mckinsey.com/~/media/mckinsey/industries/retail/our%20insights/state%20of%20fashion/2022/the-state-of-fashion-2022.pdf

McNeill, L., & Moore, R. (2015). Sustainable fashion consumption and the fast-fashion conundrum: fashionable consumers and attitudes to sustainability in clothing choice. *International Journal of Consumer Studies 39*(3), pp.212–222. DOI:10.1111/ijcs.12169t

Miller, T. (2017). *Greenwashing culture*. London: Routledge.

Modaes.es, Centro de Información Textil y de la Confección, & Moddo (2020). *Informe económico de la moda en España 2019*. www.modaes.es/files/000_2016/0001publicaciones/pdfs/informe_economico_2019.pdf

Nam, J., Hamlin, R., Gam, H.J., Kang, J.H., Kim, J., Kumphai, P., Starr, C., & Richards, L. (2007). The fashion-conscious behaviors of mature female consumers. *International Journal of Consumer Studies 31*(1), pp.102–108.

Peters, G.M., Sandin, G., & Spark, B. (2019). Environmental prospects for mixed textile recycling in Sweden. *ACS Sustainable Chemical Engineering 7*, pp.11682–11690. https://doi.org/10.1021/acssuschemeng.9b01742

Reimers, V., Magnuson, B., & Chao, F. (2016). The academic conceptualization of ethical clothing: could it account for the attitude behavior gap? *Journal of Fashion Marketing and Management 20*, pp.383–399. DOI:10.1108/JFMM-12-2015-0097

Roberts, J.A. (1996). Green consumers in the 1990s: profile and implications for advertising. *Journal of Business Research 36*, pp.217–231. DOI:10.1016/0148-2963(95)00150-6

Stearns, P.N. (1997). Stages of consumerism: recent work on the issues of periodization. *The Journal of Modern History 69*, pp.102–117.

Tynan, C., & Drayton J. (1988). Conducting focus groups—a guide for first-time users. *Marketing Intelligence & Planning 6*(1), pp.5–9. DOI:10.1108/eb045757

Vatamanescu, E.M., Dabija, D.C., Gazzola, P., Cegarro-Navarro, J.G., & Buzzi, T. (2021). Before and after the outbreak of Covid-19: linking fashion companies' corporate social responsibility approach to consumers' demand for sustainable products. *Journal of Cleaner Production 321*. DOI:10.1016/j.jclepro.2021.128945

Webster, F.E. (1975). Determining the characteristics of the socially conscious consumer. *Journal of consumer research 2*(3), pp.188–196.

Wiederhold, M., & Martinez, L.F. (2018). Ethical consumer behavior in Germany: the attitude-behavior gap in the green apparel industry. *International Journal of Consumer Studies 42*(4), pp.419–429. DOI:10.1111/ijcs.12435

Chapter 11

Sustainability and the Secondhand Business Model

Louise Laroque and Andrée-Anne Lemieux

11.1 Introduction

As the secondhand market shows a potential Compound Annual Growth Rate of 15%–20% over the next five years in the apparel, footwear, accessories and luxury items (BCG, 2018), fashion businesses should implement more and more initiatives to enter this attractive market (Kant Hvass, 2015). With the rapid growth of the online resale, driven by a few digitally born actors, a survey conducted by McKinsey (2020) confirms moreover a stronger trend toward online channels and secondhand fashion items since the beginning of the pandemic. Concomitantly, fashion brands and retailers appear to be more and more operative in the secondhand market which participates in the circular economy (Bocken & Co, 2016) by creating a closed-loop system. However, those secondhand initiatives seem to be multifaceted: partnering with existing secondhand digital platforms, launching its own brands' secondhand platform, offering secondhand corners in physical stores, acquiring a stake in a secondhand actor or creating a peer-to-peer platform. In September 2021, the well-established French department store Galeries Lafayette opened the space '(Re)store' almost taking more than 500 m² at their emblematic flagship Galeries Lafayette Haussmann location, dedicated to secondhand and promoting sustainable fashion labels.

In addition, behind these various initiatives, there seem to lie different motivational factors and one of them tends to be focused on the product collection and the analysis of secondhand data.

Moreover, some specific services are emerging, bringing to brands and retailers a data-oriented service, focused on the secondhand market through interfaces between brands and resale marketplaces and data analyses in the process of reselling. As Keunyoung (2020) develops in his research, the role of data in the fashion industry started with the e-commerce boom. This led to a data-driven decision-making approach for some fashion brands and retailers, allowing them to improve sales and margins through three main pillars: sales data, product information and consumer data.

DOI: 10.4324/9781032659053-11

There are both a lack of research on data in the fashion industry (Jain et al., 2017) and on secondhand market business models (Gopalakrishnan and Matthews, 2018). The existing research regarding data in the fashion industry is mainly investigating artificial intelligence (AI) technologies in retail (Thomassey and Xianyi, 2018), customer experience and trendcasting. On the other hand, the existing research studying the fashion secondhand market focuses mainly on secondhand actors as Gopalakrishnan and Matthews (2018) and not on firsthand actors.

However, on a broader scale, research about sustainability in the fashion industry puts forward the key role of circularity, as the last report of Ellen MacArthur Foundation shows (Ellen MacArthur Foundation, 2021). The report showcases testimonies of contemporary designers such as Gabriela Hearst or Marine Serre, insisting on designing clothes that can sustain and thus have many lives through secondhand loops.

In this chapter 50 secondhand initiatives integrated into firsthand retailing are examined through nine key characteristics developed in four main levels: 1. Organization, 2. Secondhand business processes, 3. Product and 4. Data mining.

With this research, our goal is hence to analyze how firsthand actors invest in the secondhand market and how their initiatives can be categorized, leading to the need of new business models and data-oriented services. It aims at identifying trends and specificities that are emerging in this new ecosystem, while integrating in the framework two current subjects in the fashion industry: sustainability on one hand and data mining on the other hand. The use of a qualitative research methodology supported by an extensive literature review on secondhand market evolution and new actors led the researchers to semi-structured interviews and exhaustive study on site and on the web of the sample of 50 initiatives. The analysis of the 50 secondhand initiatives through the framework's key characteristics highlights how these patterns, stakes and perspectives contribute to new collaborative forms in the fashion industry, encouraging circular economy and new sustainable business models through emerging services.

11.2 Methodology

In terms of methodology, a sample of 50 secondhand initiatives was collected using keywords (*second hand*, *resale*, *brands*, *retailers*, *data*) on search engines of two main media of the fashion and luxury industry (Business of Fashion and WGSN). This observation period started on October 15, 2020, and ended on May 15, 2021. Overall, we studied 49 actors of the fashion industry: Abercrombie & Fitch, Adidas, Aigle, Alexander McQueen, Amélie Pichard, American Eagle, Auchan, Audemars Piguet, Ba&sh, Balenciaga, Balzac Paris, Ben Baller, Bocage, Burberry, By Far, C&A, Claudie Pierlot, COS, Cyrillus, Eileen Fisher, Farfetch, Gap, Gucci, H&M, Isabel Marant,

JOSEPH, Kaporal, Kiabi, La Redoute, Levi's, Lululemon, Madewell, Maison Cléo, Maje, Mark Cross, Mulberry, My Theresa, Neiman Marcus, Nordstrom, Okaidi, Patagonia, REI, Richemont, Sandro, Selfridges, Sézane, Sneakerboy, Stella McCartney and Zalando.

This kind of approach proves to be useful in the context of exploratory research while being flexible and allowing in-depth study of complex phenomena (Yin, 2009). In this case, the development process of new secondhand services shows a high level of detail and is moreover influenced by a lot of characteristics. Thus, using a classic quantitative approach for this chapter would lead to a significant simplification and seems inappropriate. In addition, the development processes of new services in the luxury industry are strategic and implemented with confidentiality.

Nevertheless, all the qualitative research methods are not well appropriate to answer this chapter's objectives. To that extent, a case study or a multicase study is qualitative approache of empirical research that allow in-depth study of a complex social phenomenon, a group or a collection of individuals non-randomly selected in order to precisely describe this phenomenon and interpret it while considering the context in which it takes place (Yin, 2009). However, case studies are appropriate when the phenomenon already exists and must be considered and deepened within its daily context (Yin, 2009). In our chapter, only one case study will be presented for the purpose of illustration, but our methodological approach is not based on case studies. Furthermore, case studies do not allow interaction with the observed stakeholders.

To identify some trends and characteristics from our observed phenomenon, we built a database compiling 750 data, by applying our nine key characteristics to each of the 50 initiatives.

11.3 Analysis framework

In order to analyze some trends regarding firsthand actors going to the secondhand retailing market, nine key characteristics were compiled in a framework analysis of four main levels: 1. Organization, 2. Secondhand business processes, 3. Product and 4. Data mining (Figure 11.1a).

The first-level 'Organization' is focused on defining the firsthand actors that take secondhand initiatives, which we call organizations: type of organization, market segment of the organization and possible membership in a sustainable agreement or coalition.

1 **Organization**

   a **Type:** Types of organizations had to be considered regarding the economic activity of the organization and their distribution channels within the fashion industry. As the distribution channels are in a phase

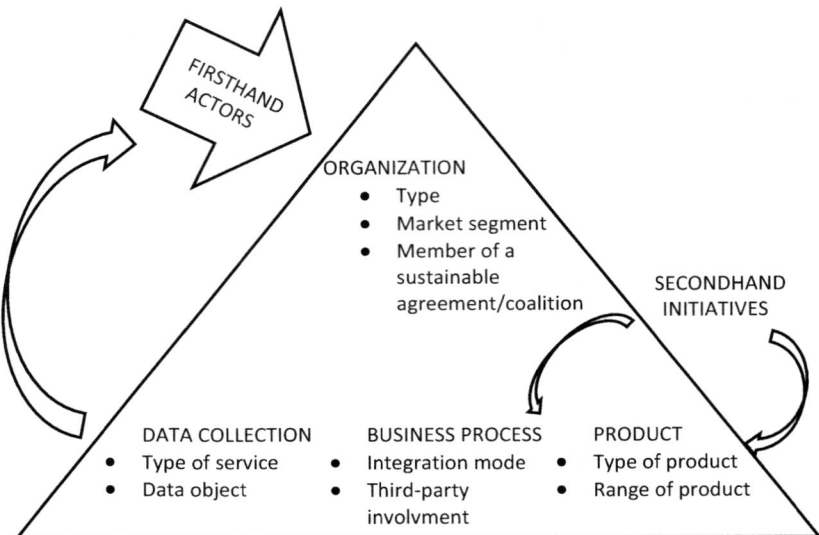

Figure 11.1a Analysis framework of secondhand initiatives' characteristics.

of radical change (Aiolfi & Sabbadin, 2019), we will study both physical stores and e-commerce actors. The physical retailers will be categorized as 'department stores', 'concept stores' or 'retail chains'. The digital retailers will be categorized as 'pure players' and fashion and luxury brands will be part of the same category 'brands'. The last category, 'groups', refers to the 'Luxury Big Business' owning different brands (Donzé, 2018), such as LVMH, Kering and Richemont. The observed organizations of the fashion and luxury industry are categorized in those six different types.

b **Market segment:** Actors of the fashion industry are shaped between fast fashion and luxury: luxury actors are the ones that guarantee the highest level of quality and thus are premium priced (Fuchs et al., 2013; Nieroda et al., 2018), while fast fashion is often characterized by accessible and trendy products and low prices (Amatulli et al., 2016). Moreover, other categories emerged in between those two market segments: industry reports and articles have begun to use the term 'affordable luxury' to highlight the rise in popularity of durable goods, fashion products and food (Mundel et al., 2017). In the research conducted by Mundel et al., participants perceived affordable luxury to be less expensive than luxury goods but maintaining a high quality. Thus, among the firsthand actors studied in this chapter, we split them into four main segments of the fashion market depending on their prices and quality of their products: low-end market that also encompasses fast fashion, mid-range market, affordable luxury and luxury. Some actors are both categorized into affordable luxury and luxury such as department stores like Selfridges or Nordstrom.

c **Member of a sustainable agreement or coalition**: As fashion brands' images are more and more intertwined with sustainability issues (Kumar et al., 2017), consumers pay more attention to the sustainability aspect of the products they buy (Kumar et al., 2017). In this context, we included a sustainable characteristic to examine deeper the sustainable engagement of the firsthand actors while looking at their membership to one or few of the four main sustainable agreements and coalitions of the fashion industry worldwide: the Sustainable Apparel Coalition (SAC), the Fashion Pact, the Global Fashion Agenda and Paris Good Fashion.

The second level of characteristics, 'Second-hand business processes', aims at defining the secondhand business processes that the firsthand actors implemented, by two main characteristics: their integration mode and the involvement of a third party in the process of integrating a secondhand service.

2 Secondhand business processes

a **Integration mode**: As Kerli Kant Hvass develops in her article (2015), the ways of integrating second hand into a business are more and more diversified and form a new phenomenon concerning fashion brands. A survey conducted by the Boston Consulting Group (Bianchi et al., 2020) presents four engagement models for firsthand actors going to the secondhand market: acquisition, partnership, joint venture and newly created offering. However, this typology is applied to the hard luxury segment only. We present a slightly different typology based on the 50 secondhand initiatives we identified: partnership, acquisition, peer-to-peer secondhand platform, integrated secondhand platform and physical secondhand corner. In the peer-to-peer platform, the products transit directly between the secondhand buyer and the secondhand seller, while there is a process of centralization of the products by the brand in the integrated platform. The integrated platform requires a secondhand supply chain.

b **Third-party involvement**: Data mining started in e-commerce with digitally born actors (Keunyoung, 2020). In this context, digital actors specialized in second hand such as Vestiaire Collective or Reflaunt tend to be more efficient regarding data collection and data analysis than traditional players. Among the 50 second hand initiatives, we looked at whether the firsthand actors paired with a digital and specialized actor in order to build their secondhand service.

The third level of characteristics, 'Product', analyzes the fashion and luxury products sold in the frame of those secondhand initiatives and the strategies associated to the products' offer taken by the firsthand actors.

3 **Product**

a **Type:** Fashion is a 'cross sector' that encompasses several industries, such as apparel, footwear, leather or jewelry (Brun et al., 2020). Thus, we divided the products concerned by the secondhand initiatives into five different types: ready-to-wear (RTW), accessories, shoes, hard luxury which includes jewelry and sportswear.

b **Range of product:** As E.S. Rolbina highlights in her article (2016), a retail trade network aims at offering the widest possible range of products so the customers can find all the goods they need in one place. In our research, this applies in particular to the department stores and retail chains that offer diverse types of products from RTW, accessories, shoes, jewelry. On the other side, Rolbina develops the idea that a more specialized product range based on customer value has its own advantages such as the reduction of inventory levels or the increase of the turnover. In our context, the product range strategy does not apply only to physical stores but to all the mentioned actors. In this context, we specified whether the firsthand actors chose a 'generic' product range strategy with a diversification of their products, or a 'specialized' product range strategy focused on one or a very few types of products.

The fourth level of our framework is based on the data collected, analyzed and shared during the implementation of secondhand services by firsthand actors.

4 **Data mining**

a **Type of service:** Coxon distinguishes between data collection and data analysis as two different steps of sorting data (Coxon, 1999). We also used this dichotomy to analyze data mining from the implementation of the secondhand services. We specified whether data were only collected or both collected and analyzed. To obtain those information, we interviewed four actors engaged in secondhand services implementation. As we could not interview all the stakeholders of the 50 initiatives, we used the variable 'nonavailable' if this characteristic remained unknown.

b **Data object:** Data can be split into three main pillars: sales data, product data and consumer data (Keunyoung, 2020). Thus, we questioned which types of data among those three pillars were analyzed through the secondhand initiatives counted. As the previous characteristic, we used the variable 'nonavailable' if we did not have access to this information.

11.4 Case study: Ba&sh RESELL and its characteristics

This case study aims at illustrating the secondhand initiatives' sample by presenting a concrete example and giving the corresponding characteristics from our analysis framework.

In 2021, Ba&sh launched its service RESELL for its clients. The service is accessible from the clients' Ba&sh account and allows to resell in a few steps:

1 As a Ba&sh client, a virtual dressing composed of your previous purchases allows you to put on sale one or few of your items by using the RESELL button. The item is already authenticated and owns a certificate of identity which goes along during the resell process and is available for its next owner.
2 The item is then put on sale on different marketplaces simultaneously.
3 Once the item is bought, the owner receives a packing slip to ship the item to its future owner.
4 Once the secondhand buyer receives the item and confirms its state, the money is transferred to the seller who can choose a bank transfer or a voucher to use on Ba&sh.com.

As there is no interference of the brand during the process of resale, this platform is considered to be peer-to-peer. This service has been constructed by the brand in partnership with Reflaunt, specialized in secondhand services and data mining; and Arianee, specialized in blockchains (Figure 11.1b).

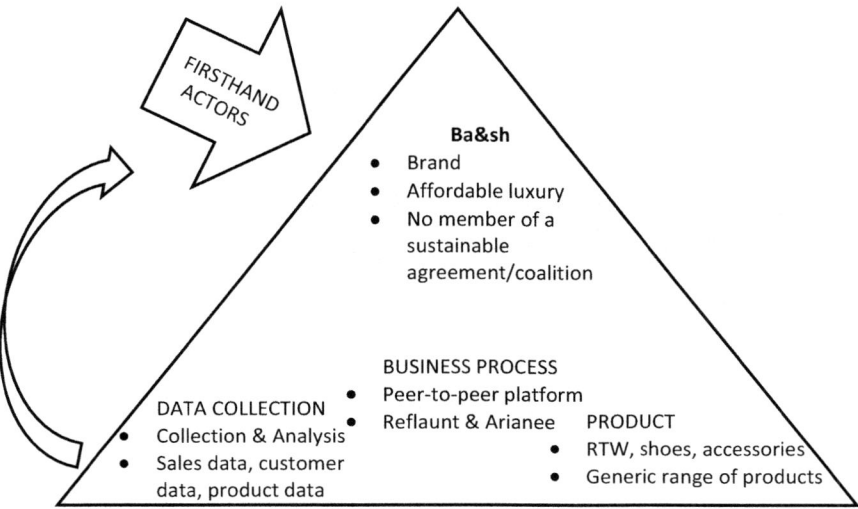

Figure 11.1b Analysis framework applicated to Ba&sh.

In the corresponding analysis framework, here are our nine key characteristics applied to the Ba&sh RESELL platform initiative:

A.1   Organization type: Brand
A.2   Market segment: Affordable luxury
A.3   Member of a sustainable agreement or coalition: No
B.1   Second-hand integration mode: Peer-to-peer platform
B.2   Third-party involvement: Reflaunt and Arianee
C.1   Product type: RTW; shoes; accessories
C.2   Range of products: Generic
D.1   Type of service: Data collection; Data analysis
D.2   Data object: Sales data; product data; customer data

11.5 Results from the application of the analysis framework

Through the nine key characteristics of our analysis framework we applied to each of the 50 secondhand initiatives, here are the major relevant trends. Each trend is illustrated with one or two figures presented in the annex.

The leading firsthand actors implementing secondhand services are fashion and luxury brands (Figure 11.2).

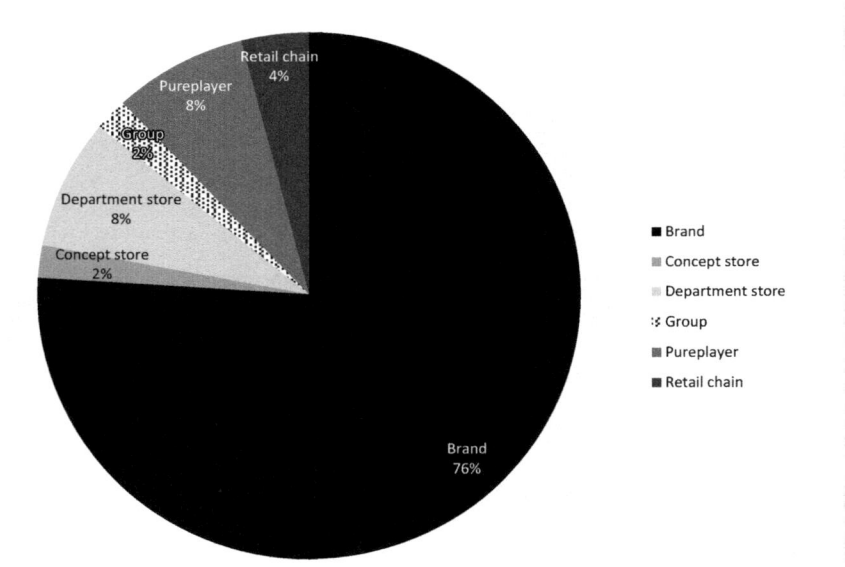

Figure 11.2 Part of organizations' types in the implementation of secondhand business processes.

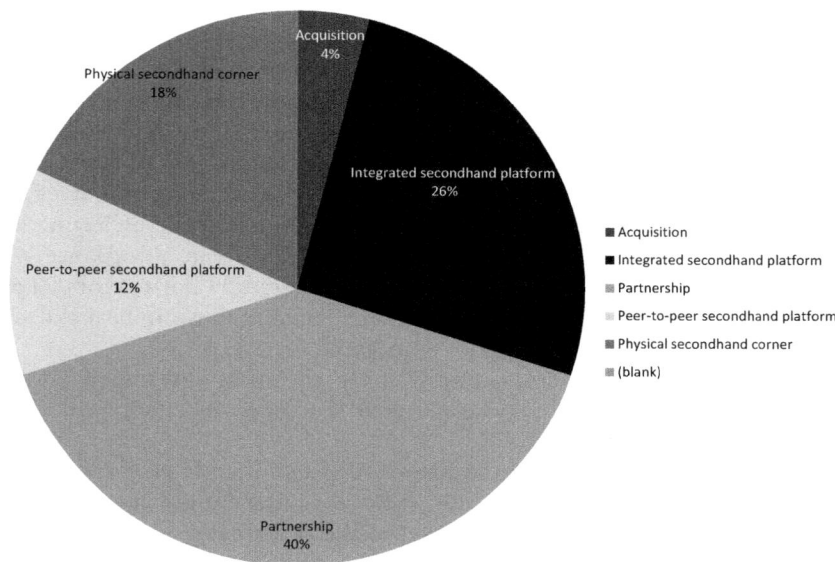

Figure 11.3 Part of secondhand integration modes among the 50 initiatives.

The first observation is that over 50 initiatives counted, 38 are coming from fashion and luxury brands, which are followed by pure players and department stores as the most present categories of firsthand organizations going to the secondhand retailing market. There is a significant presence of brands in the implementation of secondhand initiatives. As Kerli Kant Hvass highlighted, fashion brands going to the secondhand retailing market is a new phenomenon so their preponderance among the traditional players is noticeable.

The preponderant way of integrating secondhand in a business is through partnerships with existing secondhand digital actors (Figure 11.3).

Among the 50 initiatives collected, there is a strong preponderance of partnerships with existing secondhand digital actors. The second preferred integration mode for implementing second hand is the integrated secondhand platform, followed by the peer-to-peer secondhand platform. Those three types of integration modes are all digitized. The only type of physical secondhand initiative is the secondhand corner, which represents only 18% of the initiatives. It highlights the fact that digitalization is ubiquitous in the rise of second hand's initiatives by traditional players.

Firsthand actors mainly rely on a third party in order to build and offer a secondhand service (Figure 11.4).

The other significant observation is that over 50 initiatives, at least 33 involve a third party in the development process of the secondhand initiative. As Figure 11.4 shows, partnerships count for a large part of those initiatives since they are conceived between two parties. However, almost a third of the initiatives involving a third party are integrated secondhand platforms that belong to brands. It highlights the fact that traditional players need a third-party actor to endorse their secondhand service: building and managing the back office and the supply chain of a new service, while collecting and analyzing the data extracted along this process. This is in accordance with what Keunyoung (2020) develops in his article: digitally born actors have a stronger expertise in collecting and analyzing data and thus can be a real support for brands implementing their secondhand service.

Among the firsthand actors, brands have the most diversified integration modes of secondhand services compared to the other firsthand actors (Figure 11.5).

Figure 11.5 crosses the integration modes of secondhand business processes with the different organization types. It appears that brands have the most diversified integration modes compared to the other categories of firsthand actors, with a preponderance of partnerships. In terms of variety of integration modes, brands are followed by pure players and department stores, the same categories of firsthand actors who are the most active in Figure 11.2.

Firsthand actors offering a diverse range of fashion and luxury products implement secondhand services in more diversified ways than the firsthand actors specialized in one type of fashion product (Figure 11.6).

Figure 11.6 shows the proportion of secondhand integration modes per types of range of products: generic range of products or specialized range of products. It appears that actors offering a generic, diverse range of products implement secondhand services in more diversified ways than the actors offering a specialized range of products. Those last ones focus on partnerships with existing secondhand actors, integrated secondhand platforms but also physical secondhand corner, in particular in specialized concept stores.

Among the different market segments of the fashion industry, the mid-range market is the one integrating secondhand in the most diversified ways (Figures 11.7a and 11.7b).

As Figure 11.7a highlights that the part of the different market segments of the fashion industry in our sample is balanced, Figure 11.7b shows how those market segments implement secondhand services in terms of integration modes. It appears clearly that in the segment of affordable luxury, actors mainly develop partnerships with existing secondhand platforms such as Vestiaire Collective or The Real Real and use very few of the other integration modes. In the luxury segment, there is also a preponderance of partnerships,

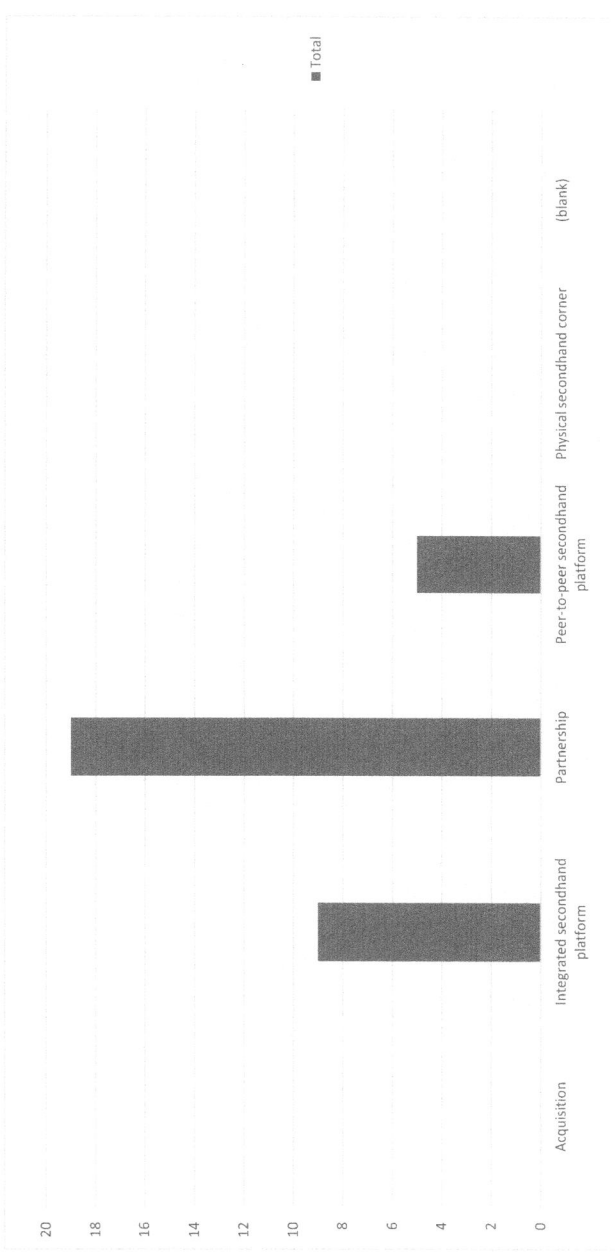

Figure 11.4 Number of initiatives involving a third party depending on the integration modes of the secondhand business processes.

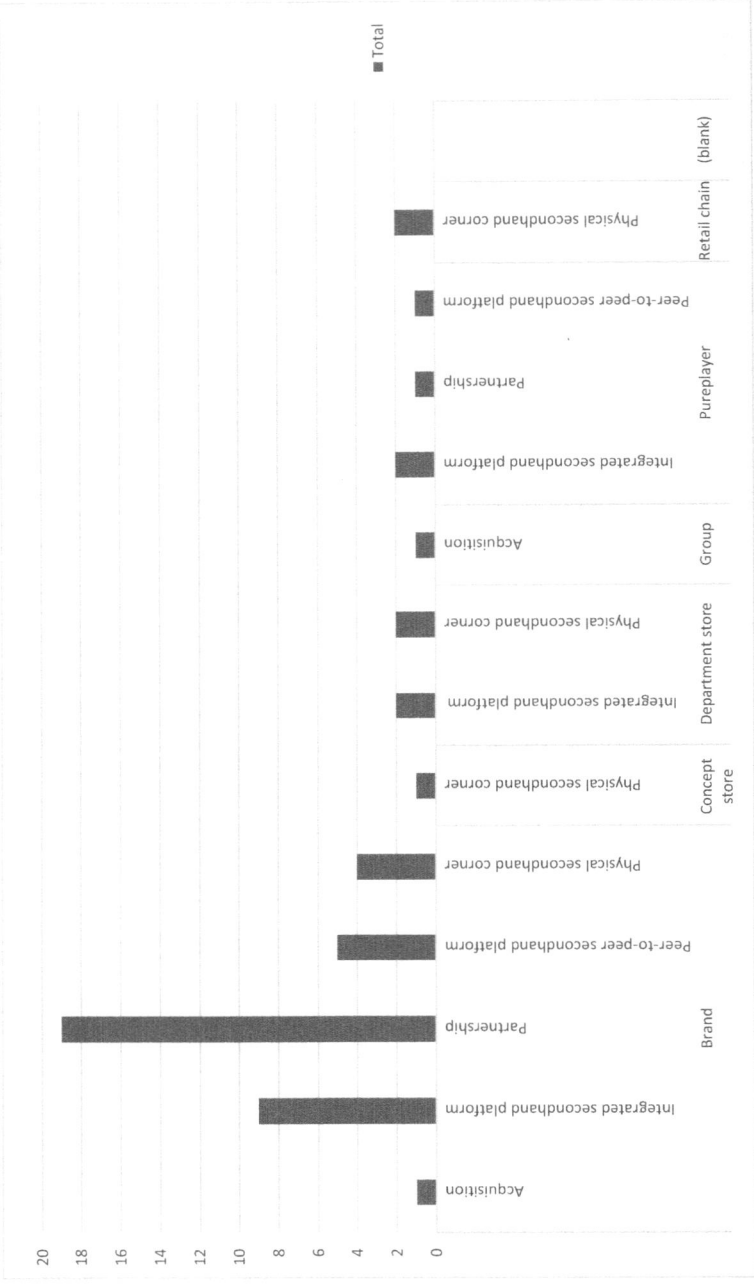

Figure 11.5 Part of secondhand integration modes per type of organization.

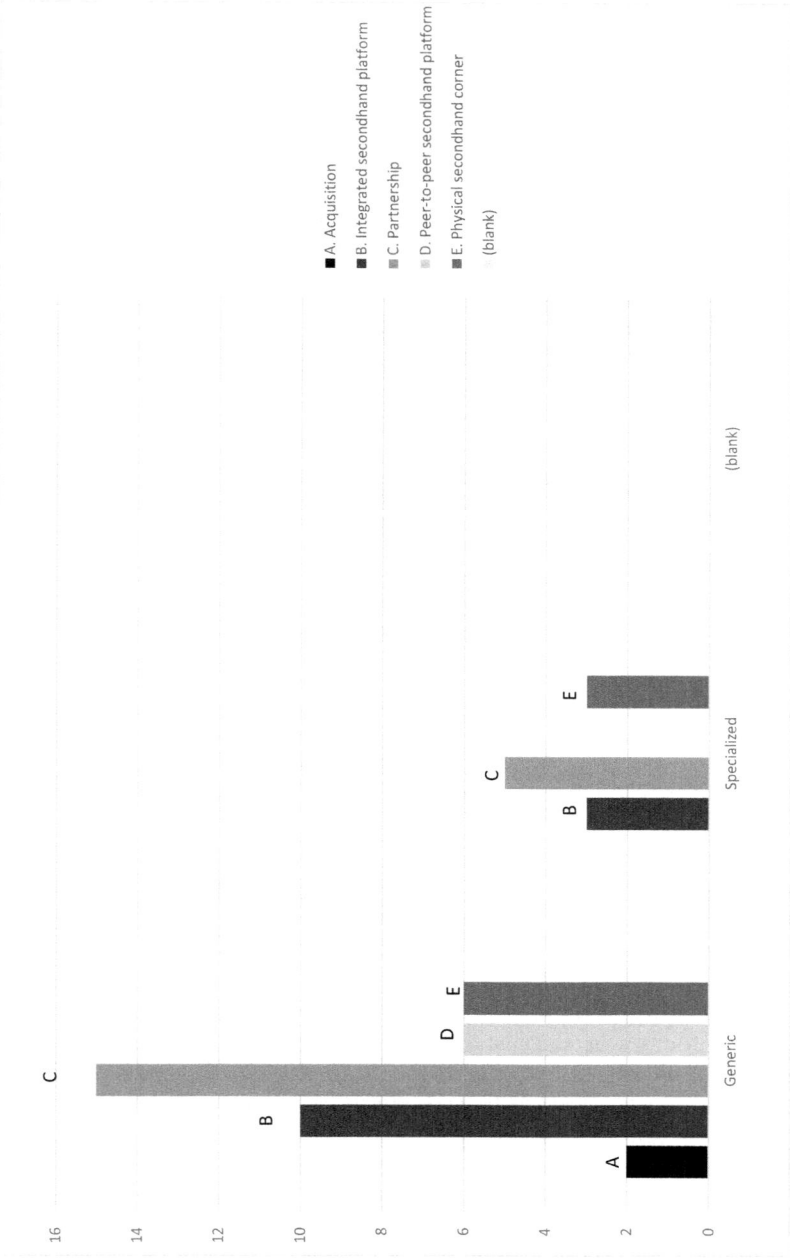

Figure 11.6 Part of secondhand integration modes per ranges of products.

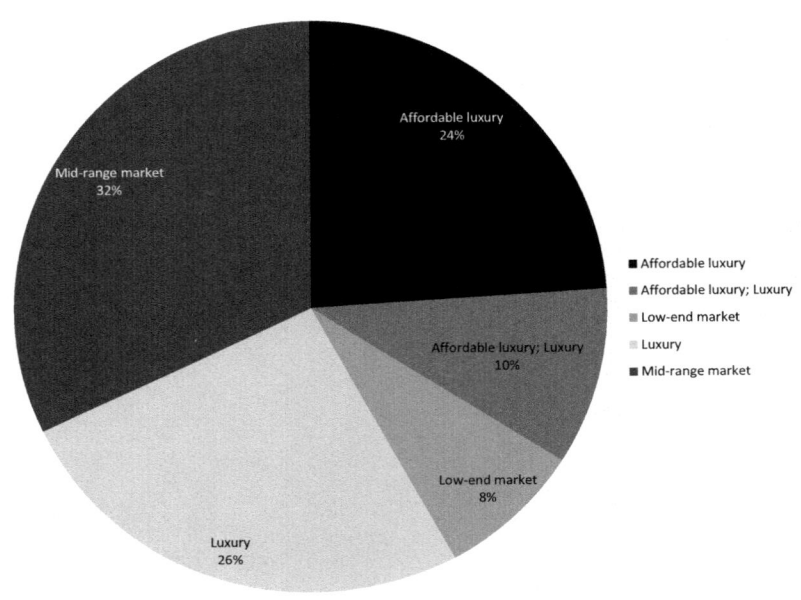

Figure 11.7a Part of the market segments among the 50 initiatives of the sample.

but concomitantly, we observe a noticeable expansion of integrated second-hand platforms.

The mid-range market is the most diversified and balanced in terms of integration modes implementation (using alternatively integrated platforms, peer-to-peer platforms, partnerships and physical secondhand corners), with a slightly higher presence of integrated secondhand platforms.

What can we observe in terms of sustainable engagement of firsthand actors implementing secondhand services (Figures 11.8 and 11.9)?

Figure 11.8 focuses on the sustainable engagement of the organizations by measuring their membership to the main sustainable agreements or coalitions of the fashion industry. Brands have the higher and more diversified sustainable engagement and this can be explained by the fact that on our database, 7 of the 38 studied brands are members of at least two or more sustainable initiatives, simultaneously. Gucci is for example a member of the four sustainable coalitions mentioned, as it belongs to the Kering group.

Figure 11.9 focuses on brands and crosses the secondhand integration modes with sustainable engagement. The first observation is that among

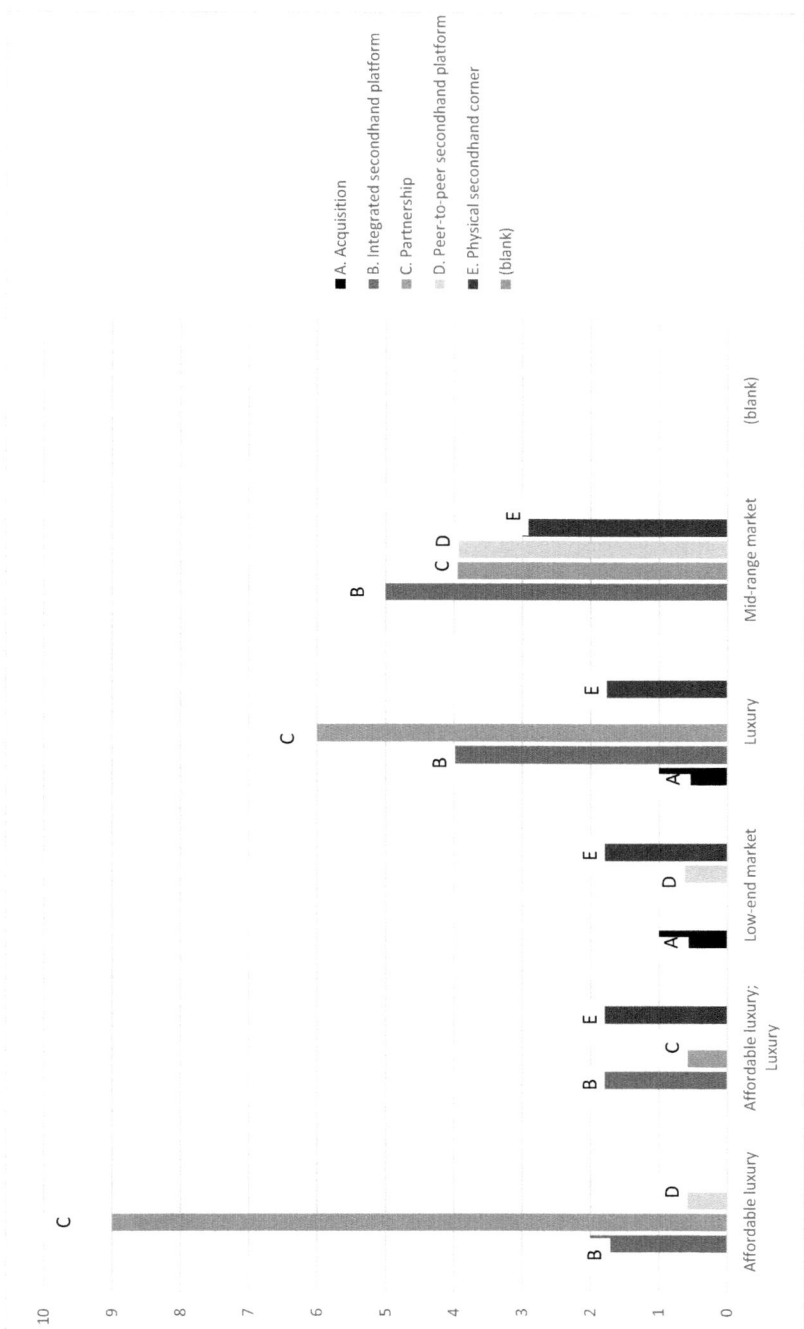

Figure 11.7b Secondhand integration modes per type of market segment.

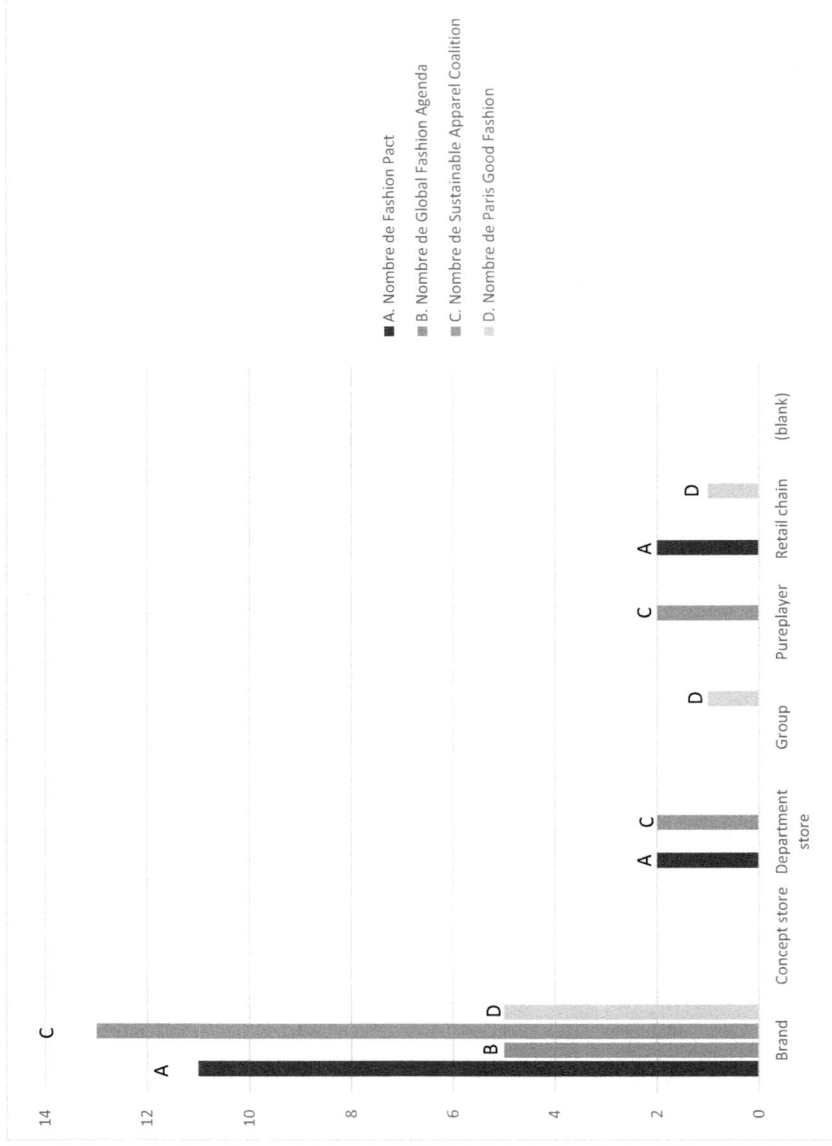

Figure 11.8 Number of sustainable coalitions' memberships per type of organization.

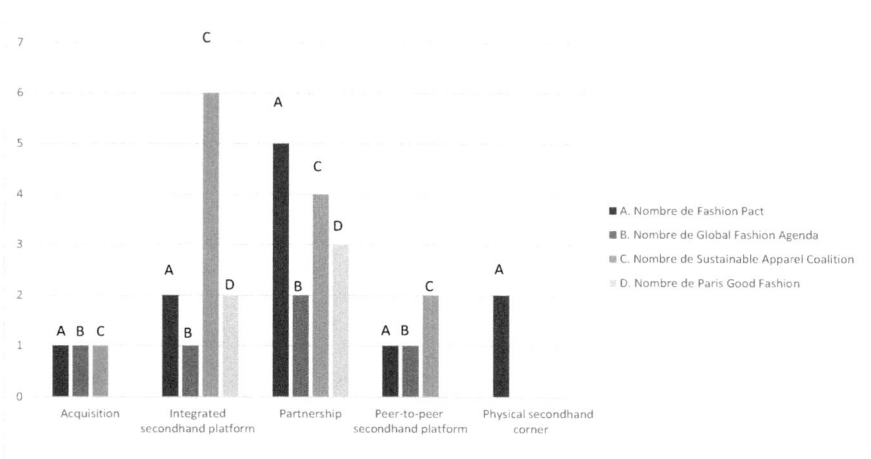

Figure 11.9 Number of sustainable coalitions' memberships per secondhand integration modes among brands' initiatives.

the integrated secondhand platforms, the majority is coming from firsthand actors who are members of the SAC. This coalition has a strong presence in the United States of America, as Walmart and Patagonia are two of its pioneer members (Schwartz, 2011). Concerning partnerships, they are mainly driven by both members of the SAC and members of the Fashion Pact, a younger coalition specially involved in Europe since it was implemented by the Kering group. Moreover, the coalition least represented in the secondhand initiatives is Paris Good Fashion.

What can we observe in terms of data collection and data analysis through the implementation of secondhand services (Figures 11.10 and 11.11)?

It appears that integrated secondhand platforms both collect and analyze data since they are intertwined with the firsthand offer of the actor. In the case of partnerships, data are collected and analyzed by the partner, but they are hardly shared to the traditional player. The only type of data that might be shared to the firsthand actor is sales data during the period of the partnership. Peer-to-peer platforms start collecting data but show a lack of expertise regarding data analysis.

As data mining appears to be a motivational factor behind the implementation of secondhand initiatives, Figure 11.11 shows that yet the information regarding collection and analysis of data is often nonavailable and non-shared. However, the few insights we had through interviews showed that integrated secondhand platforms have the most elaborated expertise regarding data sorting, which is accomplished by the third party building the

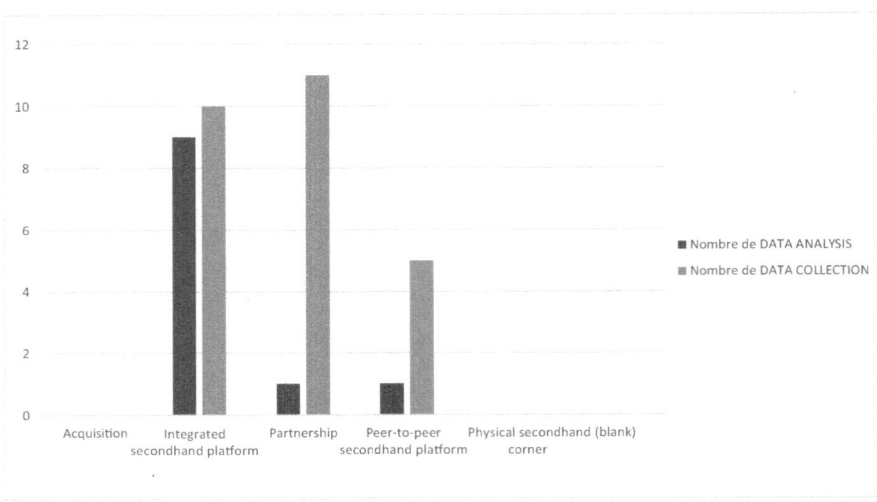

Figure 11.10 Part of data collection and data analysis per secondhand integration mode.

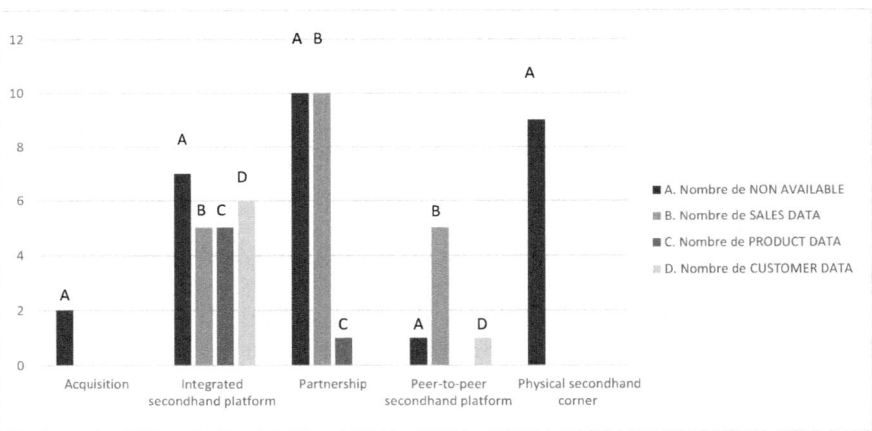

Figure 11.11 Objects of data proceed per secondhand integration modes.

secondhand service. Regarding partnerships, data mining is complex because the secondhand initiative is offered by another entity. Thus, in the secondhand process, data belong to the partner (Vestiaire Collective, The RealReal, Thred Up…). This explains why the type of data that can be shared is mainly data regarding the actual sales of the brands in the frame of a partnership.

More detailed data often remained confidential. Peer-to-peer platforms easily analyze sales data while they are not yet processing data about customers and products.

11.6 Conclusion

Overall, it appears that fashion and luxury brands are the actors most undertaking toward the secondhand market among the traditional players. However, fashion and luxury brands need the involvement of a third party specialized in second hand or digital in order to build their secondhand service. This leads to the development of new actors offering a new business model based on implementing secondhand services for traditional players and analyzing data along the resale process. In the initiatives collected, those third parties are in particular Reflaunt, Trove, Disruptual, Faume. Regarding the market segments, the middle-range segment of the fashion industry appears to be the most diversified in terms of secondhand integration modes. The luxury and affordable luxury segments prefer partnering with second-hand established actors having a luxury expertise such as Vestiaire Collective or The Real Real. Moreover, the large majority of the actors studied are members of one or few of the main sustainable coalitions in the fashion and luxury industry: the Fashion Pact, the SAC, Paris Good Fashion and the Global Fashion Agenda. This highlights the fact that implementing second-hand initiatives takes place in a broader context of evolving toward more sustainability by participating in the circular economy.

Concerning the data mining aspect of the secondhand implementation, the process of collecting and analyzing data remains nebulous; as Figure 11.11 shows, there is a preponderance of 'nonavailable' information regarding the analysis of data during the resale process. Nevertheless, when the resale data are collected and analyzed, different purposes lie behind the data analysis process. As the different objects of data we presented: customer data, product data, sales data; data can serve those three pillars. Keunyoung (2020) shows how the analysis of data can boost a brand's sales. As it was highlighted in the interviews, the main purpose behind customer data collection and analysis is both strengthening the loyalty of the existing customers but at the same time recruiting new customers. Implementing a secondhand service for a brand can drive their secondhand customers to a firsthand purchase (BCG, 2019). During the interviews, the stakeholders mentioned that the data related to the product could help improve the product quality and sustainability by observing the product lifecycle in the secondhand channel. Data analyzed through the secondhand processes could thus also participate in increasing the sustainable engagement or offer of the firsthand actors.

Moreover, it appears that the ways of implementing second hand are mostly digital, as Figure 11.4 shows. Digitalization seems to be a key in the development of secondhand's initiatives. In that sense, the future of data collection and data analysis along the resale process could rely on new technological tools such as AI. This could extend opportunities for new business models such as the third parties presented in our research that position themselves between digital technologies, data analysis and second hand.

11.7 Limitations

Eventually, this research contains some limits that are worth highlighting: the initiatives studied were collected in the two main fashion media of the industry, both English speaking. It was not possible to study the fashion press in all geographic areas. It would have been interesting to include more foreign fashion papers such as TextilWirtschaft in Germany or other sources in other geographic areas and other languages, for example in the Asian fashion press. Moreover, the stakeholders interviewed were mainly from the third parties mentioned or existing secondhand actors. It would have been a great insight to interview more stakeholders directly from firsthand actors such as fashion and luxury brands or retailers. It would have also been interesting to interview stakeholders from well-integrated and the forerunner secondhand platforms such as Patagonia's Worn Wear or Eileen Fisher's Renew. In addition, collecting information about strategic initiatives of fashion and luxury actors, such as the implementation of a secondhand offer or service, remains difficult as it includes confidential information.

11.8 Perspectives

However, the significant multiplication of secondhand initiatives implies new opportunities for the research field. Few subjects of research could be introduced and developed around the implementation of secondhand initiatives by firsthand actors: how to implement and optimize those initiatives according to the characteristics of the firsthand actors or what are the consumer perceptions following those initiatives. There could also be research studies about the new business models created in the frame of those initiatives.

This chapter aimed at studying objectively the dynamics between the firsthand actors and the secondhand market in fashion. However, regarding the multiplication of those initiatives, there could be an important subject around the motivational factors of those initiatives perhaps leading in some cases to greenwashing. Some further qualitative and quantitative research could be relevant to investigate motivational and success key factors in implementing this pillar of circular economy where products should circulate as long as possible.

References

Aiolfi S., Sabbadin E. (2019). Fashion and new luxury digital disruption: the new challenges of fashion between omnichannel and traditional retailing. *International Journal of Business and Management*, vol. 14, no. 8, p. 41.

Amatulli C., Mileti A., Speciale V., Guido G. (2016). The relationship between fast fashion and luxury brands: an exploratory study in the UK market. In: *Global Marketing Strategies for the Promotion of Luxury Goods*. Hershey, PA: IGI Global, pp.244–265.

BCG (2019, April 17). *True-Luxury Global Consumer Insight* (6th Edition). Milano: BCG.

BCG Survey of Vestiaire Collective customers, October 2018. www.prnewswire.com/news-releases/vestiaire-collective--bcg-survey-reveals-why-luxury-brands-should-celebrate-the-pre-owned-boom-300938686.html

Bianchi F., et al. (2020). *The Secondhand Opportunity in Hard Luxury*. Milano: BCG. www.bcg.com/publications/2020/secondhand-opportunity-hard-luxury

Bocken N., de Pauw I., Bakker C., van der Grinten B. (2016). Product design and business model strategies for a circular economy. *Journal of Industrial and Production Engineering*, vol. 33, no. 5, pp.308–320. DOI: 10.1080/21681015.2016.1172124

Brun A., Karaosman H., Barresi T. (2020). Supply chain collaboration for transparency. *Sustainability*, vol. 12, no.11, pp.4429–4450.

Coxon A.P.M. (1999). Sorting data: collection and analysis. *Numéro*, vol. 127.

Donzé P.Y. (2018). The birth of luxury big business: LVMH, Richemont and Kering. In: Donzé P.Y., Fujioka R. (eds), *Global Luxury*. Singapore: Palgrave.

ECLAC (Economic Commission for Latin America and the Caribbean). (2014). *Big Data and Open Data as Sustainability Tool*. A working paper prepared by the Economic Commission for Latin America and the Caribbean, October 2014.

Ellen MacArthur Foundation (2021). *Circular Design for Fashion*.

Fuchs C., Prandelli E., Schreier M., Dahl D.W. (2013). All that is users might not be gold: how labeling products as user designed backfires in the context of luxury fashion brands. *Journal of Marketing*, vol. 77, no. 5, pp.75–91.

Gopalakrishnan S. and Matthews D. (2018). Collaborative consumption: a business model analysis of second-hand fashion. *Journal of Fashion Marketing and Management*, vol. 22, no. 3, pp.354–368.

Granskog A, Lee L, Magnus K-H, Sawers C. (2020, July). *Survey: Consumer Sentiment on Sustainability in Fashion*. New York: McKinsey & Company.

Jain S., et al. (2017). Big data in fashion industry. *IOP Conference Series: Materials Science and Engineering*, vol. 254, p.152005.

Kant Hvass K. (2015). Business model innovation through second hand retailing. *The Journal of Corporate Citizenship*, no. 57. DOI: 10.9774/GLEAF.5001.2015.ma.00005

Keunyoung O. (2020). The roles of data analytics in the fashion industry. *Journal of Textile Engineering & Fashion Technology*, vol. 6, no. 3, pp.102-104. DOI: 10.15406/jteft.2020.06.00237

Kumar V., Agrawal T.K., Wang L., Chen Y. (2017). Contribution of traceability towards attaining sustainability in the textile sector. *Textiles and Clothing Sustainability*, vol. 3, no. 5, pp.8–18.

McKinsey and Company. (2020). The State of Fashion 2020. Online research report. www.mckinsey.com/~/media/mckinsey/industries/retail/our%20insights/the%20st ate%20of%20fashion%202020%20navigating%20uncertainty/the-state-of-fash ion-2020-final.pdf

Mundel J., Huddleston P., Vodermeier M. (2017). An exploratory of study of consumers' perceptions: what are affordable luxuries? *Journal of Retailing and Consumer Services*, vol. 35, pp.68–75.

Nieroda M.E., Mrad M., Solomon M.R. (2018). How do consumers think about hybrid products? Computer wearables have an identity problem. *Journal of Business Research*, vol. 89, pp.159–170.

Rolbina E.S. (2016). Trade network's product range management. *Academy of Strategic Management Journal*, vol. 15, no. Special Issue 1, pp.83–91.

Schwartz A. (2011) Patagonia, Adidas, Walmart team up on sustainable apparel coalition. *Fast Company*, January 2012.

Silva E.S., Hassani H., Madsen D.Ø. (2019). Big Data in fashion: transforming the retail sector. *Journal of Business Strategy*, vol. 41, no. 4, pp.21–27. https://doi.org/ 10.1108/JBS-04-2019-0062

Thomassey S., Zeng X. (2018). Introduction. In *Artificial Intelligence for Fashion Industry in the Big Data Era*. Springer Series in Fashion Business. Singapore: Springer. https://doi.org/10.1007/978-981-13-0080-6_1

ThredUp. (2020). 2020 Resale Report. www.thredup.com/resale/2020/#resale-growth

WGSN. (S.d.). *Re-Commerce: The Resale Market Boom.*

WGSN. (S.d.). *Selling Resale: Key Strategies*

Yin R. (2009). *Case Study Research: Design and Methods.* London: Sage Publications.

Chapter 12

Pricing and Sustainable Fashion

Saartje Boutsen and Charlotte Vandierendonck

12.1 The true cost

Based on existing studies, researchers at ABN AMRO have calculated what the 'true' price should be for indigo blue, unbleached, 600 gram pair of jeans. That is the most popular type of jeans in the world. The trousers are made of cotton and denim from India and assembled in Bangladesh.

The purchase price of such pants—the price that the retailer pays—should actually be almost €33 higher than it is now, the researchers conclude. Textile workers are often paid poorly. The cultivation of cotton and the production of denim cause a lot of environmental pollution. Jeans would be significantly more expensive if textile workers were paid a living wage and if the cost of environmental pollution was included in the price of a pair of jeans.

Of those €33 in hidden costs, €8.40 is accounted for by cotton cultivation, which is water-intensive and uses a lot of fertilizers and pesticides, polluting rivers, lakes and seas. Cotton farmers and workers often receive too little wages, and child labor and forced labor also occur. Most hidden costs—€21.15 per pair of jeans—are in the production of denim textiles: de-stoning, spinning, weaving, wet processing and finishing. In the Indian state of Tamil Nadu, India's largest raw cotton processor, 200,000–400,000 people, often young women, work long days in spinning mills for low wages over three to five years. They often only receive that wage when they have completed their entire employment contract. If they were not forced to work and would work for a living wage, jeans would be €10.85 more expensive. If the environmental damage caused by denim production is included in the price of the pants, it would be an additional €5.85 more expensive (Impact Institute & ABN AMRO, 2019).

So far, this gives only an insight into the extra costs of pre-consumer externalities. In the post-consumer phase, there's also a hidden ecological cost. Overall, it is estimated that the amount of garments produced annually has doubled since the early 2000s, reaching more than 100 billion pieces per year. Today, only 1% of all textile waste is recycled, 73% end up in landfill (Grammen and Vanbaelen, 2021). Additionally, there's a

DOI: 10.4324/9781032659053-12

major microplastic problem. According to the International Union for Conservation of Nature, 35% of microplastics that enter the ocean come from synthetic fibers, like polyester, acrylic and nylon. Every time we wash clothing made of these fibers, they shred. Up to 728,000 fibers can come off at once, spilling into waterways and contributing to the pollution of our ocean and environment. This ecological cost is also not included in the price of a garment.

12.2 'Sustainable' means 'expensive' means 'not affordable'?

The actual cost of a pair of jeans, or the cost of a 'sustainable' pair of jeans that does take into account the environmental and social aspects, is therefore significantly higher. The same logic can be followed for other types of garments in the fashion industry as well as shoes. Nevertheless, fashion discount retailers state that sustainable clothing is possible at equally competitive prices.

Even though it seems like a contradictio in terminis, for example the Irish retailer Primark is convinced that the combination is possible. 'We believe that sustainability shouldn't be priced at a premium that only a minority can afford. Because of who we are, we believe we have the opportunity to make more sustainable fashion choices affordable to all', Primark says. The retailer has the ambition to halve carbon emissions across its value chain by 2030 and to create financial resilience by pursuing a living wage for workers in the supply chain and supporting them with financial literacy training and access to social protection by 2030. On the other hand, they want to continue to offer the same sharpest competitive prices.[1]

The Dutch discount retailer Zeeman, for example, is also ambitiously going for more sustainability: they are fully committed to more sustainable materials, the reduction of plastic packaging, the circular economy and the impact of clothing production on the environment and on the living of local factory workers. It is also the intention that the employees of Zeeman manufacturers earn a living wage. Their suppliers sign for this in their code of conduct. A living wage is a wage that is sufficient to meet all basic needs, such as housing, transport, food and care. After all, the statutory minimum wages set by the government in countries such as India, Pakistan and Bangladesh are often not sufficient to meet these basic needs.[2]

Retailer Lidl, that calls itself a 'smart' discounter, is also committed to sustainability, and they recently launched a campaign named 'able' to connect a sustainable product with a low price. The intention is to make consumers aware that a sustainable product does not necessarily have to be expensive. The supermarket chain indicates that it will continue to raise the bar and that it wants to increase the sale of sustainable products by 10% every year.

All these claims make it seem plausible that sustainability doesn't have to be expensive nor out of reach, but how far do these retailers live up to their claims, and are we sure it's not about greenwashing?

Let's go back to our three examples: Primark, Zeeman and Lidl have published far-reaching annual sustainability reports, in which they document their sustainability policy, strategy, roadmap, actions and results. When we have a look for example to the social aspect of fair working conditions and living wages for textile workers, Primark is giving the most transparent information: they have a code of conduct for suppliers, which is the backbone of their Ethical Trade and Environmental Sustainability Programme. It is a robust set of requirements that forms a key part of the terms and conditions of a supplier's contract. Suppliers are regularly audited and, thereafter, rated by the internal Ethical Trade team. If they meet Primark's minimum standards, they get approved for production. In 2019, more than 3,000 factory audits were conducted. According to a rating categorization with three groups, it turns out that only 3% of the audited factories have good systems in place to ensure ethical compliance. For those only a limited number of minor issues are recorded by the auditor. Overall, 67% have evidence of some good systems in place; however, they did not achieve full ethical compliance, whereas 30% did not meet ethical compliance, with significant and numerous issues. Primark also reports that living wages and working hours, including excessive overtime, remain a challenge.[3] With this data, Primark itself indicates how serious this problem is. It seems impossible to tackle such problems on an international scale without also adjusting something to the pricing scheme. The price that a brand pays to their suppliers should absorb all the elements that fall under International Labour Organization (ILO) conventions and as such respecting the workers' rights. Only with giant leaps and a real commitment to pay its share for workers' living wages, Primark can reach the ambition set forward in its recent press release.

Also Zeeman reports on its efforts on living wages. On the basis of their roadmap, they give concrete substance to this theme, which concretely means that they currently want to gain more insight into the situation at their manufacturers with regard to a living wage. In this way they can better determine what a living wage is and whether the workers in the factory actually receive a living wage, because that is a catalyst, preventing other risks in the supply chain, such as excessive overtime and child labor. In recent years, during social audits they have gained insight into the difference between the legal minimum wage, the actual wage and the living wage.[4] No information is given on the percentage of factories in which a living wage is already paid. A pilot project on living wages will be set up in a factory in India in 2021. Obviously a step in the right direction, but Zeeman has clothing produced in 17 countries and 348 factories, so there is clearly still a long way to go to make living wages the norm in their supply chains.

In Lidl Belgium's sustainability report, you can very clearly find the objectives, associated measurement indicators and information about their progress. It is for example a strong point that they work through the Science Based Targets Initiative. However, if we look at the sustainability targets for textiles, this is a disappointing ambition. At the social level, the goal of having 100% of frontline suppliers audited by BSCI (Business Social Compliance Initiative) by 2018 was achieved, but no clear ambition is mentioned regarding specific human rights such as contributing to a living wage.[5] The sustainability strategy of the German Schwarz Group, to which Lidl belongs, considers

> it is our duty, together with our business partners in the countries concerned, to make decent employment possible through good working conditions and fair wages. As a result, the business activities of the Schwarz Group will positively impact the people who work in its supply chain as well as their families and local communities.[6]

However, no explanation follows on implementation or measures. It remains a statement without evidence.

So it is difficult to hold to the claim that cheap clothing can be really sustainable. There will always be a hidden true cost, ranging from the loss of quality of the fabric to the inferior quality of finishing, the lack of living wages throughout the supply chain and the large environmental impact of the pre- and post-consumer life cycle.

On the other hand, the industry is looking to keep sustainable products accessible to consumers with a lower family budget to be spent on clothing. Today, an average Belgian family spends €900 per year on clothing and shoes. More than 30% of the current Belgian population has an average income that is less than 60–80% lower than the median net equivalent household income. So, if discount retailers want their audiences to continue to buy clothes in the same volumes, they need to continue to work at an extremely low price point. This statement is reinforced by the knowledge that over the past few years, the share of the family budget that went to clothing and shoes has always decreased (Coene et al., 2021).

The responsibility to act against the negative impact of the fast fashion treadmill is threefold. Firstly, there is a particularly large role for the fashion companies themselves. Secondly, governments and the international community have to play an important role in setting rules and standards and assuring compliance with these. Thirdly, it is also the consumer who can make better choices even with a limited budget.

12.3 Responsibility of fashion companies

A large part of our clothing remains *made in misery*. Modern slavery, child labor, serious environmental damage, they remain major challenges in the fashion industry today. A good thing is that—compared to ten to five years ago—more and more fashion brands are recognizing these challenges and are actually working on it, step by step. The notion is growing that this will also mean adjustments to their current business model.

12.3.1 From quantity to quality, from linear to circular

The ecological cost of a garment in the true pricing model can be lowered by producing more environmentally friendly. This does not only mean the switch from conventional cotton to organic cotton, from conventional polyester to recycled polyester, or from viscose to lyocell. This switch to more environmentally friendly materials is absolutely necessary, but still insufficient. Organic cotton remains water-intensive during production, and recycled polyester continues to release microplastics during the washing process. The problem also lies in the enormous amount of waste that the sector generates: while the production volume has doubled over the last 15 years, more than 50% of fast fashion becomes waste within a year. So the challenge is to limit the use of new raw materials and to reduce the enormous volumes of waste, both in the pre- and post-consumer phases. The sector needs a transformation from a linear to a circular system.

To keep fibers longer in the loop, you have to give clothes a longer life, and that you can do in the first place by focusing on quality. A garment made of a high-quality fabric will last longer, it can possibly be reused by a next owner, and even if it will be recycled at the end of its life, it will yield higher quality new yarns. Today, a lot of fast fashion clothes are made of low-quality fabrics and do not survive ten washes. Quality has a price, but isn't it cheaper and more sustainable to buy one shirt of a better quality than three shirts of a low quality? A switch from quantity to quality. Toward customers it is an important message to convey: cherish your clothes, buy only what you really like to wear, so that it lasts longer, and so that no more clothes with price hang tags end up in the trash.

Preventing waste and overproduction is clearly the responsibility of a fashion company and can be an important key performance indicator (KPI) as a sustainability strategy. Also production on demand, good collection planning and efficient stock management can play a significant key role in this. It prevents large quantities of new items from ending up on the waste mountain. Moreover, such an efficiency exercise can also save a company significant costs.

Furthermore, fashion brands can also focus on more circular design. After all, 80% of the impact of a product is determined in the design phase. In addition to the use of more sustainable and quality materials, the environmental cost of a garment can be reduced in the design phase by creating a design that is timeless, that minimizes fabric waste and that is made of mono-material—the more different sorts of fibers a clothing contains, the more difficult it is to recycle.

12.3.2 Real commitment to living wages in the supply chain

A fair living wage is an income earned during normal working hours that meets the basic needs of workers and their families, with some left over for extra expenses or savings. Making sure garment workers are paid fairly is a big challenge for fashion companies. Most fashion companies don't own any factories and don't make their own clothes—they outsource production to independent manufacturers. This means they don't pay garment workers' salaries, nor do they decide how much they are paid.

But there are many things that fashion brands can do to have a positive impact on wages and wage development to give workers and their families better livelihoods, good working conditions and more power in the workplace. They can take responsibility and be actors of change by setting clear standards and expectations for every supplier—mostly done by a code of conduct—and, moreover, also taking action if the standards are not met. They can help suppliers to improve working conditions and implement effective wage management systems. They can provide worker education programs that empower workers to negotiate their own wages and conditions. They can ensure that purchasing practices—the way orders are placed and prices are paid—enables the payment of correct wages. They can engage in dialogues with partners, peers, experts and governments to improve wages at both industry and country levels. They can constantly monitor the level of wages paid in the factories. The Covid-19 pandemic highlighted the relevance of doing this, as a lot of garment workers lost income while social security safety nets were absent in several production countries.

12.3.3 Transparency, honest communication and measurement

Companies should set clear objectives in this regard, measure the progress and report on this. In that way they will become really transparent about the true cost of labor.

H&M Group is one of the fashion retailers who is taking steps in the right direction. As their production contributes to the employment of 1.56 million people, they have a responsibility to uphold the rights and wages of workers in their supply chain. According to H&M, they drive fair wage increases through a global approach that feeds into country-specific strategies while considering national contexts and legal settings. In the past year, they engaged with experts to identify what had worked well in driving wage increases between 2013 and 2019. They learned from the evidence and have refocused efforts. H&M monitors the level of wages paid in their factories constantly, and this data is a key dimension in the group's sustainability index. For each production country, H&M refers on its website to the average wage paid by their suppliers and the percentage above legal minimum wage. In most countries the average wages in H&M manufacturer's factories are around 5–35% higher than the legal minimum wage. But in a country like Bangladesh, living wages are three times or 300% higher than the legal minimum wage, which are too low to have a decent income. Given the significant difference between legal minimum wages and living wages in production countries such as Indonesia, Bangladesh, Cambodia, Myanmar or India, the H&M case shows that there remains a huge challenge to obtain a living wage for all garment workers.

Nevertheless, H&M clearly indicates that consumers do not have to fear price increases. After all, a single factory often produces clothing for several brands, and workers are paid the same amount to make a €200 garment as they are paid to make a €20 garment. That's why increased prices in stores don't lead to increased wages for factory workers, according to H&M. The group is confident that they can offer sustainable fashion at affordable prices because they are a large company, that buys large volumes, that has efficient logistics, their own designers, their own stores, strong market knowledge, long-term relationships with their suppliers and no middlemen. 'Wages are just one of many factors when it comes to pricing products', H&M says. One could indeed assume that the group can compensate for the margin loss caused by a certain sustainability choice by the margin profit on another focus (e.g. higher quality vs wage of the worker). However, it cannot be deduced from the reporting which volumes represent the different price structure models of the clothing. Such information could provide even more understanding of whether the claim of cheap sustainable fashion is correct for those who claim it to be.

Also other retailers seem convinced that ecologically and socially sustainable clothing is possible at the current low-threshold prices. They are taking steps, but there is still a long way to go. Launching a collection made from more sustainable fabrics is not enough to claim sustainability. Transparent evidence is necessary. Some retailers are doing this better than others. However, completely relying on the voluntary approach of companies does not work, according to a study by the European Commission, which showed that only 37% of companies engage in chain care (EC, 2020). Governments will also have to play a role in encouraging companies to focus on sustainable, affordable fashion.

12.4 Responsibility of policy makers

At local, national or within the European or international playfield, governments can use various levers to both accelerate the impact that focuses on respecting workers' rights and focus on environment-enhancing initiatives. The simultaneous use of these levers could have a reinforcing effect. Reference may be made to the following instruments.

12.4.1 Supply chain due diligence

At Flemish, national and European level, legislation for supply chain due diligence is under research and in phase of proposal development. But this is far from an easy exercise. To what extent does the responsibility of European-based companies go if they are responsible for a substantial share of the orders placed with a factory in the Far East and what is the responsibility of local policy makers and suppliers themselves? Today, it is clear that only voluntary initiatives of multinationals to improve working conditions are not sufficient. It is certain that a legal framework for supply chain due diligence can reduce the negative impact in the sector, but the framework must be clear. The different decision-making levels must prepare the proposals and their implementation in a well-streamlined and tailor-made manner for the targeted companies.

Our neighbors have already set a good example. France adopted a 'loi relative au devoir de vigilance' in 2017. In 2019, the Netherlands introduced a Child Labour Duty of Care Act, and a few months ago, the German parliament passed legislation on mandatory chain care. We are also seeing progress at the European level. In 2020, Didier Reynders (MR), European Commissioner for Justice, promised to work on legislation on mandatory chain care.

12.4.2 Extended producer responsibility (EPR)

Extended producer responsibility (EPR) is a policy approach under which producers are given a significant responsibility—financial and/or physical—for the treatment or disposal of post-consumer products. Assigning such responsibility could in principle provide incentives to prevent wastes at the source, promote product design for the environment and support the achievement of public recycling and materials management goals.[7]

When applying this to the fashion sector, this imposes several practical challenges. How should these principles be implemented for the European fashion industry, how to streamline these principles among countries and how to assure that the implementation of the processes and new industry practices are managed in the short term as part of the European Green Deal? Still a lot of research and financial support but moreover a cross-over of innovation and specific industry knowledge is needed to make this possible and to avoid negative spill-over effects. Whether it be tax regulations on fabrics or the obligation for take back systems, or any other measure, in the widely spread Belgian small and medium-sized enterprise (SME) sector where the pressure on margins is already very challenging, a correct and realistic solution must be sought.

12.4.3 Reporting

Today, large listed companies are subject to the obligation to report on their sustainability efforts. From 2024, a larger group of companies will also fall under this obligation. As a result, more retail groups will also fall under the reporting obligation and will have to apply a fixed reporting standard, in which both the impact on climate-related topics will have to be highlighted as well as the efforts to mitigate them. But human rights-related issues will also have to be included. As a result, the European Commission hopes to achieve more transparency and comparability. The call is on companies to take the associated double materiality obligation at heart in all seriousness and depth and to strive for maximum transparency. It is only with clear facts, analysis and actions, supported by strong data and clear objectives, that more and more stakeholders will pull on the same sail. It will become harder not to be transparent if a large group communicates about their practices. In the current regulations in preparation, most SMEs are not subject to a reporting obligation but are encouraged to do so anyway. Given the many SMEs in the fashion sector, having a major impact on employment in East and Central Asia and the Mediterranean regions, it is also called upon to push for a reporting obligation, based on a clear and limited set of standards and KPIs such as supply chain transparency, the use of sustainable materials and waste and end-of-life initiatives.

Regardless of whether regulations are initiated at the European, national or regional level, one cannot ignore the macroeconomic trends that play on world level either. If Europe is going to impose stricter rules on companies based in Europe and impose sanctions on them, one must also look at the actors who also trade on European soil but who escape from taking up any responsibility. The influence of digital sales in the European market is gigantic, but the transparency of some major fashion-oriented e-commerce providers, their sourcing practices and their carbon footprint is often lacking. The knowledge of the consumer about this is often very limited, not being aware of where their parcels are actually being sent from and which true cost is actually behind the story of the parcel and garments inside. Therefore, Europe has and will have an important role in balancing its trade policies and not drop the topic of respect for human rights in economic and political negotiations. No matter how challenging this may be in the current economic and political circumstances, it remains one of the pillars that forms a common ground for us people within the fashion industry to strive for.

12.5 Consumer responsibility

In circles where there is a high awareness of sustainability, there is a strong voice that consumers should take up their responsibility. It is believed that the community has the knowledge and budgets to buy the clothing sold at a true price. This assumption is wrongful and is patronizing lower income consumer groups. It's not that the intention to buy sustainably isn't there. A consumer who buys a T-shirt at €2 on which the label says it's made of organic cotton will be confident that this is a good choice based on the given label info. However, also consumers have to take up part of the responsibility.

12.5.1 Less is more

Buying less is a very simple rule if you are a brick-and-mortar shopper. Do you need a big bag of clothes, or will you focus on buying a selection of high-quality items of which you are sure you'll be able to wear them? However, a parent of two young children may be forced to buy new shoes or pants just because worn clothes simply become unwearable after a season of use. This has nothing to do with the quality of the items, but simply with the intense use of the garments. The offer of high-quality second-hand shoes and trousers for young children is rather low. This challenge illustrates that it is very important to combine the 'buy less' strategy with a strong 'take back and recycle' strategy. Although less could be consumed, the need for new clothing remains a reality. However, the better the quality of the clothing offered, the longer the lifecycle of a garment and the better the end-of-life possibilities.

However, there is an extra challenge to this. E-commerce sales continue to rise, and as a consumer it becomes much more difficult to check the fabric quality and finishing of an item. This leads to bad buys and high return rates anyway. An item may be made of organic cotton; it says nothing about the firmness and thickness of the fabric, and you do not see this on a packshot photo of an item. The 'buy less' rule therefore applies in particular to e-commerce items. One should combine the choice for an item with a good reading of the additional product information and a research of the sustainability commitments of the brand you're buying from.

12.5.2 Understanding labels and product descriptions

Brands use multiple ways to communicate about the sustainability aspects of a garment. Hang tags are used to emphasize specific sustainability features (mostly about climate-related topics, seldomly about respect for human rights), to add certificate logos, to clarify washing instructions or to ask for certain customer engagements. In addition, in Europe, brands are forced to add the product compositions in the labels. However, the sustainable levels of a certain substance are not mandatory, and there is no European regulation for this yet. If a more sustainable fiber is being used, brands often add this information nearby the official product composition. However, as there is only limited regulation on this today, it remains very hard for a customer to interpret the labels.

12.5.3 Asking questions makes the ball roll

It remains a major challenge for a consumer to build up knowledge about sustainable clothing and shoes. Numerous claims and information are communicated to customers, without a coherent frame, and consumers are pointed the finger at for not making sustainable choices. Who's to blame and how to deal with it? Here you can especially advise to keep asking questions, using the chat tools of the online players, and by approaching sales advisors in physical stores. It is obvious that clear and complete answers will not always be available, but it is precisely the continuing questioning of current practices that is part of the process of change that has been set in motion in the long term. Be it on the shop floor or from an institutional angle, the more voices are raised and questions asked, the more players will further move.

12.6 Conclusion

It is not an easy exercise to determine the true cost of a garment—but for sure someone pays the cost if it is not produced in a sustainable way. A garment can be called 'sustainable' if it is produced with respect for human rights and for the environment. But technology and scalability of innovations are today not yet where they need to be, and the current status of respect for good working conditions and decent living wages remains too low, based on data shared in the reports of some well-known retailers.

Supported by responsible choices of consumers and supporting measures of political leaders, fashion retailers can play an important role in making sustainable fashion more mainstream and affordable. It is crucial that they take up their responsibility in the transition from fast fashion to accessible and affordable circular and sustainable fashion. They are part of the solution, given their strong commitments in researching, supporting and financing innovations and their commitment to improve the working conditions in low-wage countries. But these efforts need to be strengthened and sustained, made more measurable and transparent so that a better and clearer distinction can be made between those for whom the commitments are authentic and those who, despite the claims, continue to lag behind. They need to set an example for the rest of the industry, to pick up the lessons of it and help realize the standard of the future.

Notes

1 Primark pledges to make more sustainable choices affordable for all as it unveils extensive program of new commitments, https://corporate.primark.com/en/newsr oom/primark-cares/primark-pledges-to-make-more-sustainable-choices-afforda ble-for-all-as-it-unveils-extensive-programme-of-new-commitments/n/a6a53c03-d486-4ce1-ae55-5795e2b8fa6c, Sept 2021.
2 Zeeman, CSR Report for 2020, www.zeeman.com/media/wysiwyg/pdf/csr_2020. pdf, 2021.
3 Primark, Our performance 2019, https://primark.a.bigcontent.io/v1/static/Our-Performance-2019
4 Zeeman, CSR Report for 2020, www.zeeman.com/media/wysiwyg/pdf/csr_2020. pdf, 2021.
5 Lidl, Sustainability Report 2019, p.34.
6 Schwarz Group, https://gruppe.schwarz/en/responsibility/people
7 OECD, Extended Producer Responsibility, www.oecd.org/env/tools-evaluation/ extendedproducerresponsibility.htm

References

Coene J., P. Raeymaeckers, B. Hubeau, S. Marchal, R. Remmen & A. Van Haarlem (2021) *Armoede en sociale uitsluiting*, Acco Leuven/Den Haag, pp.92–93.
EC (Feb, 2020) Study on due diligence requirements through the supply chain, Part I, Synthesis report.
Grammen C. & Y. Vanbaelen, e.a. (2021) (UCLL—Expertisecentrum Sustainable Ressources), Circulaire economie in de textielsector, Wanderful. Stream, p.19.
Impact Institute & ABN AMRO (2019) True Price of Jeans, https://trueprice.org/wp-content/uploads/2019/06/Impact-Institute-Report-True-Price-of-Jeans.pdf

Index

Note: Endnotes are indicated by the page number followed by "n" and the note number e.g., 15n4 refers to note 4 on page 15. Page locators in **bold** and *italics* represents tables and figures, respectively.